CONTENTS

Acknowledgements vi

INTRODUCTION 1
A Note of Caution 1
The Copyright Act 1

HOW THE COPYRIGHT ACT WORKS 2
Copyright in Canada 3
Copyright in Foreign Works 3
International Copyright 4

WHAT IS PROTECTED? 6
Works Protected by Copyright 7
Databases 8
Multimedia Works 9
Sound Recordings 9
Illustrations and Photographs in Print Materials 10

WHO OWNS COPYRIGHT? 11
Ownership 12
Owning a Copy Does Not Include Owning Copyright 13

HOW LONG DOES COPYRIGHT LAST? 14
Term of Protection 14
Public Domain 15
Works in the Public Domain 16
     Government of Canada and Government of Ontario Materials 17

LEGAL RIGHTS PROVIDED BY COPYRIGHT 18
Moral Rights 18
Economic Rights 19
1. Reproduction 19
2. Performance in Public 20
3. Publication 21
4. Adaptation 21
5. Broadcasting 21

iii

6. Presentation of an Artistic Work 21
7. Rental of Computer Programs and Sound Recordings 22
8. Authorization 22

EXCEPTIONS FOR NON-PROFIT LIBRARIES 23
Definition of a "Library" 23
1. Maintenance and Management of Collections 24
   (a) Copying Rare or Unpublished Originals 24
   (b) Copying Fragile Originals 24
   (c) Copying into an Alternative Format 24
   (d) Copying for Record Keeping and Cataloguing 25
   (e) Copying for Insurance and Police Investigations 25
   (f) Copying for Restoration 25
       What Does "Commercially Available" Mean? 25
       Intermediate Copies 26
2. Fair Dealing 27
3. Copying Periodical Articles for Research and Private Study 28
       Library Record-Keeping Responsibilities 28
       Stamping of Copied Works 29
       Intermediate Copies 29
       Acts Undertaken without Motive of Gain 30
       Contracting Copying Services Outside the Library 30
4. Incidental Inclusion 30
5. Importing Books from Abroad 30
6. Alternate Format Materials for Persons with Perceptual Disabilities 34

EXCEPTION FOR LIBRARIES WITH A LICENCE FROM A COLLECTIVE 36

LICENCES WITH COLLECTIVES 38
CANCOPY and COPIBEC 38
Collective Licences in Canadian Libraries 39
What Can Be Copied under a Collective's Licence? 40
What Cannot Be Copied under a Collective's Licence? 40
Combining the Copyright Act with a Collective Licence 41
Copying Works of Non-Members 42
Exclusions List 42
Indemnity 43
Copying Beyond What a Collective Licence Allows 43

WHAT IS INFRINGEMENT? 45
What Are the Consequences of Infringing? 45

COPYRIGHT ON THE INTERNET 47
Creating a Web Site for Your Library 47
Public Domain Material on the Web 48
Linking to Other Web Sites 49
Copying Link Lists 49
Copying from the Internet 50
Trade-marks 51

FREQUENTLY ASKED QUESTIONS 52

GLOSSARY 65

CONTACTS 68

APPENDICES
Copyright Act
Book Importation Regulations
Exception for Educational Institutions, Libraries, Archives and Museums
    Regulations

v

ACKNOWLEDGEMENTS

The *Copyright Guide for Canadian Libraries* is an initiative of the CLA Copyright Committee, chaired by John Tooth (Manitoba Education and Training). ASTED liaison was provided by Jules Larivière (University of Ottawa).

The guide was prepared with the assistance of an advisory committee, and I would like to thank the members of the committee for their time, energy and assistance. Individual members of the advisory committee supervised focus groups, coordinated responses to questionnaires (which provided the many practical examples found throughout the guide), and reviewed various drafts.

I would also like to extend special thanks to Elizabeth Morton, Editor, *Feliciter/ Monographs*, for her excellent editorial and design work in preparing the guide for publication.

Last, but certainly not least, I would like to thank the Department of Canadian Heritage for the generous funding provided through the Book Publishing Development Program.

INTRODUCTION

Many items in a library collection are protected by copyright. Copyright does not control reading, but it does control many other library activities. Photocopying, digitizing, downloading, printing from the Internet, forwarding e-mail, and the performance of music, sound and video recordings are all activities subject to copyright.

In Canada, recent changes to the copyright law set out new rules for what can, and cannot, be done in a library without infringing copyright. There will be more changes coming as the federal government addresses copyright issues in the electronic world.

This guide provides library staff with basic copyright information. It sets out who is protected by copyright, what is protected, and for how long. It describes the rights copyright provides to creators and the limitations placed on those rights for the benefit of libraries and library patrons.

Knowing these rules will permit libraries to provide maximum service to their patrons while remaining within the confines of the copyright law.

A Note of Caution

This guide has been carefully written to provide an accurate statement of the law and to do so in such a way that library staff can understand how the copyright law applies to staff activities in a library. Readers are cautioned not to alter, summarize, or change the text, because changes may result in inaccurate or incomplete interpretations of the law.

In this guide, a very complex subject has been generalized. The guide is not a substitute for legal advice, which should be sought in cases where the application of general principles is unclear.

The Copyright Act

This guide refers to the provisions of the Copyright Act as amended to September 1, 1999, and to regulations to the Copyright Act of the same date. A copy of the Copyright Act and the regulations in force as of September 1, 1999, may be found at the end of this guide.

HOW THE COPYRIGHT ACT WORKS

Copyright protects things referred to as "works" and "other subject matter"; these are divided into seven categories. Neither "works" nor "other subject matter" is defined in the law. These terms refer to intellectual creations such as books, photographs, and sound and video recordings. Copyright protection is provided to "authors," a term best understood as a synonym for creators. Creators are provided with legal rights over their works.

There are generally recognized uses of these works that are permitted without the consent of the owner of the rights or the payment of royalties. These uses are called "exceptions." The rules provide protection for a limited period of time. This is often referred to as the "term of protection." After the term of copyright protection expires, protection ends. This event is referred to as a work falling into the "public domain."

There are penalties for not following the rules set out in the Copyright Act. Breaking any of the rules is referred to as an "infringement."

Copyright comes into existence automatically when a work is created. In Canada there is no requirement to mark your work with a © or the word "copyright," or to register it, although you may do so under a voluntary system of registration.

How the Copyright Act works is illustrated by the example of an author who writes a book. The Copyright Act provides legal protection to the book under the category of literary works. The law provides the author of the manuscript with a number of legal rights, which include, among other things, the right to publish the manuscript, the right to make photocopies of all or a part of the book once it is published, and the right to make a movie from the book.

Subject to any applicable exceptions, the author sells these legal rights to publishers, movie producers, collectives and others in return for royalties. This is how an author earns revenue from writing.

The legal rights of the author are subject to exceptions that permit certain users, such as libraries and their patrons, to do certain things with the book that would otherwise infringe upon the legal rights of the author.

If anyone other than the copyright owner does something that only the copyright owner has the legal right to do, an infringement occurs. An infringement is subject to various kinds of civil and criminal consequences, which are set out in the Copyright Act.

Copyright in Canada

An important characteristic of copyright law in Canada is that copyright is a matter of federal jurisdiction. This is set out in the constitution. The legal result is that the same copyright rules apply all across Canada. What is permitted or prohibited is the same in every province and territory. Thus, the rules set out in this guide apply to all libraries in Canada.

Copyright in Foreign Works

Although copyright rules are the same in every province and territory, copyright laws differ from one country to another. The law that governs copyright activities is the law of the country *in which the copyright activity takes place*. Therefore, in Canada, Canadian law applies. In the United States, the United States copyright law applies, and so on.

This issue arises in libraries in the context of a question, usually from a patron, whether copyright applies to foreign materials and, if so, what copyright rules apply. The answer to this question is always the same: *Canadian copyright law applies in Canada*.

The rule to be followed is that Canadian law, and only Canadian law, applies in Canada. This means that library staff must determine whether a particular use of a specific work is permitted under the copyright law by applying the rules in the Canadian Copyright Act.

This issue often comes up in connection with American copyright law. The United States Copyright Act permits certain copying that the Canadian Act prohibits, and vice versa. The following two examples illustrate this important concept.

Most United States government publications are in the public domain. But those of the Canadian government are protected by Crown copyright. The law that applies is the law of the country in which the copyright activity takes place. The copyright activities being discussed in this guide take place in Canadian libraries. Therefore, the Canadian copyright law applies.

Under Canadian copyright law a work falling within a protected category, including works created or produced by foreign governments, are protected. The legal result is that United States government publications may not have copyright protection in their own country, but they do in Canada.

Another example is copying magazines published in the United States. Whether copying a photograph from *National Geographic* magazine is copyright infringement in Canada is determined by the rules in the Canadian copyright law. Copyright in a photograph from *National Geographic* may be owned by an

American magazine company or by an American photographer, but a library patron or staff member who wants to reproduce that photograph is governed by the rules in the Canadian copyright law.

The Copyright Act contains many rules. The ones that are important for libraries are outlined in this guide. To look ahead a little bit, the answer to the *National Geographic* question is that the photograph is an artistic "work" that is protected under the Canadian Copyright Act. One of the "rights" of the owner is the right to reproduce the work. Permission of the copyright owner or a licence from a collective representing the copyright owner would be required before making a copy of the photograph.

These examples illustrate how important it is to know the source of information about copyright. Remember, the copyright law that applies in Canada is the Canadian copyright law. Any action you take or views you express about copyright must be based on the *Canadian* copyright law. If a copyright activity, such as photocopying, is taking place in Canada, then you apply Canadian law.

International Copyright

The Canadian Copyright Act protects Canadian works. It also protects most foreign works. Canada has agreed to provide the protection of the Canadian Copyright Act to most foreign works in return for other countries' agreeing to protect Canadian works in their countries.

This international system of copyright protection is established by countries joining various international treaties, conventions and organizations. These include the Berne Convention for the Protection of Literary and Artistic Works under the auspices of the World Intellectual Property Organization, the Universal Copyright Convention, and the World Trade Organization.

This international copyright system is based on a rule called "national treatment." This rule obliges countries participating in the international copyright system to protect the nationals of all the countries that are members of the system in exactly the way each country protects its own nationals.

For example, Canada and the United Kingdom are members of the Berne Convention. Under the rule of national treatment, Canada is obliged to protect the nationals of the United Kingdom in exactly the same way it protects Canadians. The United Kingdom is obliged to do the same for Canadians. The result is that Canadian authors like Rohinton Mistry or Margaret Atwood have the protection of the United Kingdom Copyright Act in the United Kingdom and the Canadian Copyright Act in Canada.

The same pattern repeats itself in the 140 countries that are members of the Berne Convention (as of August 13, 1999). The United States is a member of the Berne Convention. A list of all members is available at <www.wipo.org/>.

WHAT IS PROTECTED?

The Copyright Act protects seven categories of material. To be protected by the copyright law, a work must fall within one of these seven categories. Copyright applies to all original literary, dramatic, musical, and artistic "works." In addition, it protects sound recordings, performances by performing artists, and communication signals, which are collectively referred to as "other subject matter."

Some items in a library collection will have more than one copyright. An example is a sound recording. A recording of Anne Murray singing "Snow Bird" on a CD will have three copyrights. One copyright subsists in the musical composition "Snow Bird," a second in the sound recording, and a third in the performance by Anne Murray.

Some of the categories of protected material are defined, while others are explained by giving examples of material falling within that category. This approach has permitted the Copyright Act to evolve as technology has created new forms of creative expression.

Computer programs are an example. In which of the seven categories do you think computer programs should fall? This question was first answered by the courts, which put computer programs in the category of literary works on the basis that programs are written in a language, albeit a computer language consisting of 1s and 0s. Since 1988 computer programs have been explicitly protected as literary works under Canadian law.

The seven categories of material protected by copyright encompass most of the items in a library collection. The following chart gives examples of works in library collections that fall into each of the seven categories. The list has been created from examples supplied by library staff.

Notice that the same example can appear in two different categories. A CD is an example. In the chart a CD is an example of a musical work and also an example of a sound recording. This is because the original musical work is protected in its own right within the category of musical works. The sound recording of the same musical work is separately protected within the category of sound recordings.

Works Protected by Copyright

Category	Examples from Library Collections
literary work (covers both electronic and non-electronic works)	magazines, books, math and other textbooks, talking books (the underlying work, not the recorded voice), periodicals, journals, monographs, government records and reports, pamphlets, newspapers, poetry, genealogical materials, letters, statistics, computer software, statutes, law reports, judicial decisions, forms, court records, databases, published and unpublished research papers, broker's reports, stock reports, annual reports, manuscripts, microforms (print on plastic), theses, conference proceedings, industry standards, e-mail messages, braille, postings to Internet newsgroups, large print materials, compilations of literary works on a CD-ROM and on a database.
dramatic work	video recordings, documentaries, feature films, National Film Board films, instructional films, radio, television and cable programs, plays, choreography, CD-ROMs containing compilations of dramatic works.
artistic work	patterns, art slides, maps, atlases, architectural drawings, plans, stage and costume designs, digital images, drawings, photographs, charts, mosaics, art prints, compilations of artistic works on CD-ROMs and on web sites.
musical work	sheet music, songs with or without words, audio cassettes, audio CDs.

cont.

Works Protected by Copyright *cont.*

Category	Examples from Library Collections
sound recording	CDs, talking books, oral history tapes, vinyl albums, phonographs, audio books, audio cassettes, papers recorded at seminars, audio tapes of speeches and lectures, sound effects, spoken word recordings, language cassettes for ESL, compilations of sound recordings on CDs.
performer's performance	recorded performances of actors, authors, singers, musicians and dancers on tapes, cassettes, CDs, CD-ROMs, video recordings and films, compilations of performances by performers on records, CDs and in audiovisual formats.
communication signal	These are not found in library collections.

Databases

It is easy to classify most works. For example, a book is an easy fit in the literary category, and a painting is an easy fit in the artistic category. Some works, like databases, are more difficult to classify. A database is a compilation of information that has been arranged in such a way that a user can retrieve particular items of information. Old-fashioned examples of databases are dictionaries and encyclopedias. Computerized databases are the same thing, only in electronic form.

Databases are protected by copyright in a round-about way. Each category of protected work includes compilations of works in that category. For example, the category of literary work includes "compilations of literary works." The Copyright Act defines "compilation" as including "any work resulting from selection or arrangement." Thus, a database of literary works is protected under the category of literary works. A database of artistic works is protected under the category of artistic works, and so on.

A compilation that contains two or more categories of works is protected under the category making up the most substantial part of the compilation. In addition to the database being protected, there is usually protection for the individual works in the database. For example, a full-text database of literary works will have copyright in the database as well as copyright in the individual literary works in the database.

There are many databases in libraries. Databases of scientific, bibliographic and statistical information, indexes, cartographic collections, library catalogues, and full-text databases are examples. These databases will be protected under the category making up the most substantial part of the compilation.

A compilation of data will be protected by copyright provided it is sufficiently original. A 1997 decision by the Federal Court of Appeal in *Tele-Direct (Publications) Inc.* v. *American Business Information Inc.* held that there was no copyright in the plaintiff's yellow pages because there was insufficient skill, judgement and labour involved in the overall arrangement of the compiled information and its arrangement according to headings. However, a compilation of data might be protected by copyright if it were sufficiently original. Whether a particular compilation of data is sufficiently original to be protected by copyright will depend on the degree of skill, judgement and labour involved in arranging and selecting the information.

Multimedia Works

A multimedia work, by definition, contains works from several different media. Text, voice, still images and audiovisual works are combined in a multimedia work. In copyright terms, clips from films, dialogue, music, text, art, photographs and performances can all be included in the same multimedia work.

Each work is protected in its own category. For example, the audiovisual portion of a multimedia work is protected as a dramatic work, the textual portion as a literary work, and the sound portion as a musical work, a sound recording or both.

The multimedia work itself will be protected under the category making up the most substantial part of the compilation.

Sound Recordings

A sound recording does not have to be a recording of a work protected by copyright in order to qualify as a protected sound recording under the Copyright Act. For example, a sound recording of bird songs or whale sounds would be protected even though the material on the sound recording (the animal sounds) is not a musical work protected by copyright.

A second point to note is that a sound track that accompanies a film is protected as part of the *film*. The definition of a sound recording in the copyright law excludes "any sound track of a cinematographic work where it accompanies the cinematographic work." Where the sound track does not accompany the film, it is protected as a sound recording. An example is sound tracks sold as music CDs.

Third, sound recordings often involve more than one copyright. Anne Murray performing "Snow Bird" on a CD will have three copyrights. One copyright subsists in the musical composition, "Snow Bird," a second in the sound recording, and a third in the performance by Anne Murray.

Illustrations and Photographs in Print Materials

Magazines often contain photographs. Children's books often contain drawings or illustrations. Often these works will involve more than one copyright work. The magazine or book is a literary work, and the photograph, illustration or drawing is an artistic work. The copyright in the artistic work may still be owned by the artist or photographer and its use licensed solely for publication in the literary work. The copyright owner can reserve the right to license the work in other venues.

WHO OWNS COPYRIGHT?

The Copyright Act provides copyright protection to what it calls "authors." The word "author" is not defined in the law. An author is usually someone who writes something. However, in the copyright law the word author has a different meaning.

The word author is best explained as a synonym for a creator. An "author" under the copyright law is not only someone who writes something, but also someone who takes a photograph, designs computer software, produces audiovisual materials, composes music, makes maps, or draws plans or illustrations for books. All of these creators are "authors" under the Copyright Act.

As a general rule, the author is the first owner of the copyright. It can be important to know who owns copyright. Where permission to use copyright material is needed, it is the author (or an assignee or licensee of the author) who can give it. Only an author can sell, license or give away copyright. This is done in a contractual agreement, by assignment, by licence, or by gift.

The copyright can be transferred in its entirety or in parts. Ownership of copyright is like a chain, with the author, as the first owner, being the first link in the chain. Links are added each time the author sells, licenses or gives away part of the copyright. One copyright may have many different owners, but it all begins with the author who created the work being the first owner of the copyright.

The rules governing who owns copyright consist of a general rule and eight special rules that apply to particular works. Any of the rules can be modified if both parties agree to do so. For example, a library could hire an independent contractor to create training materials. Applying the general rule, we find that the contractor would be the "first" owner of the copyright. However, a contract between the library and the contractor can specify that the copyright will belong to the library instead. (The contractor has transferred the copyright to the library in return for valuable consideration, i.e., money).

The rules in the Copyright Act will fill the void if the parties say nothing about who will own the copyright. The parties to a contract, however, remain free to modify those rules however they see fit.

Any agreement transferring copyright must be in writing. Licences granting permission to use copyright works should also be in writing or be documented by e-mail. The general rule and the eight special rules are set out in the following chart.

Ownership

Category of Work	Rule
all works unless one of the special rules below applies	The "author" of a work is the first owner of copyright in a work.
photographs	Instead of the "author" being the first owner, the person who owns the initial negative, or the actual photograph if there is no negative, is the first owner of the copyright in a photograph.
commissioned photographs, engravings and portraits	Where the original photograph, engraving or portrait was ordered by someone for valuable consideration (usually money), and the consideration is actually paid, the person placing the order and not the "author" will be the first owner of the copyright.
works created by employees	Where an author is employed, and the work is made as part of that employment, the "employer" instead of the "author" is the first owner of the copyright.
government or Crown works	Copyright in works prepared by or under the direction or control of federal, provincial or territorial governments (Crown works) is owned by the Crown. Municipal governments are not usually Crown entities. The copyright in works created by employees of a municipality usually belongs to the municipality.
sound recordings	Copyright in a sound recording belongs to whoever makes the recording, instead of the "author." A "maker" is the person by whom the arrangements necessary for the first fixation of the sounds are undertaken.

Category of Work	Rule
performances by performers	Copyright in the performances of actors, singers, dancers and musicians belongs to the "performer."
communication signals	Copyright in a signal emitted by a broadcaster belongs to the "broadcaster" of the signal.

Owning a Copy Does Not Include Owning Copyright

There is a difference between ownership of a physical object and ownership of copyright. Ownership of a physical object does not automatically include ownership of the copyright. For example, ownership of a magazine, book, photograph, map, film, or sound recording does not mean that a library also owns the copyright in these objects. All of these works can be in a library's collection and can be "used," but unless the copyright has also been acquired (in whole or in part), the activities restricted by the copyright law (such as making copies or performing in public) continue to apply.

HOW LONG DOES COPYRIGHT LAST?

Ownership of physical property, such as a coat, car or piece of land, is perpetual. Ownership continues until the physical property is sold, consumed, destroyed or given away. Copyright is different because it ends after a period of time.

The time periods are set out in the Copyright Act. As with the rules concerning ownership, there is a general rule and eight special rules that apply in particular cases. The special rules override the general rule. The rules library staff needs to know are set out in the chart below.

Term of Protection

Category of Work	Rule
general rule	Copyright subsists for the life of the author of the work and the remainder of the calendar year in which the author dies, plus an additional 50 years.
works of joint authors	Copyright subsists for the life of the author who dies last, for the remainder of the calendar year of that author's death, plus an additional 50 years.
photographs	*Rule 1* Where the initial owner of the photograph is a natural person, or a corporation in which the majority of voting shares are owned by a natural person who is the "author" of the photograph, copyright subsists for the life of the author of the work, the remainder of the calendar year in which the author dies, plus an additional 50 years.
photographs	*Rule 2* Where the initial owner of the photograph is a corporation in which the majority of voting shares are not owned by a natural person who is the "author" of the photograph, copyright subsists for the remainder of the year in which the photograph is taken, plus an additional 50 years.

sound recordings	Copyright subsists for the remainder of the calendar year in which the first fixation of the sound recording occurred, plus an additional 50 years.
performances by performers	Copyright subsists for the remainder of the calendar year in which the performance is first fixed, plus an additional 50 years. If the performance is not fixed, copyright subsists for the remainder of the calendar year in which the performance is performed, plus an additional 50 years.
government works	Copyright subsists in works prepared by or under the direction or control of the federal, provincial or territorial government (Crown works) until they are published and for 50 additional years.
anonymous and pseudonymous works	Where the identity of the author is unknown, copyright subsists for the shorter of the following two periods: 1. the remainder of the calendar year of *publication* of the work plus an additional 50 years, or 2. the remainder of the calendar year of the *making* of the work and an additional 75 years.

Public Domain

A work in the public domain is free for everyone to use without permission or paying royalties. The phrase "public domain" is a copyright term referring to works that belong to the public.

Works can be in the public domain for a variety of reasons: because the term of copyright protection has expired; because the work was not eligible for copyright protection in the first place; or because the copyright owner has given the copyright in the work to the public.

Any work that is protected by copyright can in a figurative sense be placed in the public domain. The owner must specifically give the work, or certain uses of it, to the public. This is done by stating on the work what uses are donated to the public: for example, that the work may be reproduced, communicated or performed for educational purposes without permission or payment.

The rules relating to works in the public domain are set out in the chart below.

Works in the Public Domain

Type of Work	Reason
titles, names, slogans, short word combinations	To be protected, a "work" must be something more substantial. Sometimes, but not often, a title, if it is original and distinctive, is protected as part of the whole work.
Ideas	Copyright protects the *expression* of an idea but does not extend to the idea itself. Until an idea is expressed in some form, there is no copyright protection. An idea for a plot is an example. Copyright does not protect the idea for the plot. It is only the expression of that idea, as a novel, script or play, that receives the protection of the copyright law.
Facts	It is the expression of facts which is protected by copyright, not the facts themselves. For example, the facts in a magazine article are in the public domain. Anyone can use those facts as long as he or she does not copy the way the author of the article has expressed them. As long as you use your own words you will not infringe copyright.
Expired copyright	When the term of copyright protection ends or expires, works fall into the public domain. A work in the public domain is free for everyone to use without permission or paying royalties. In Canada, you can even modify the work without permission.

Examples of works in the public domain because copyright has expired are plays by Shakespeare or music by Mozart. These examples illustrate two ways in which the concept of "public domain" is qualified. The first qualification concerns a work containing more than one copyright.

An example is a sound recording that reproduces a public domain musical work. The sound recording is protected by copyright, even though the musical work is in the public domain. A sound recording of a Handel concerto is protected by copyright for 50 years from the end of the calendar year in which it was first fixed, even though the music is in the public domain.

The second qualification involves the rearrangement of a public domain work in some way to create a new copyright. An example is a new edition of the works of Shakespeare (which are in the public domain) with enough new footnotes and editorial content to create copyright protection in the edition as though it were a new work. Another common example of this qualification is new arrangements of public domain music.

Another example is a translation of a public domain work. The translation is protected by copyright even though the work that has been translated is in the public domain. Consider the Shakespeare example again. A person who translates a public domain work by Shakespeare into Greek or German would have copyright in the translation. The copyright in the translation would protect the translation against things like unauthorized publication or reproduction.

Government of Canada and Government of Ontario Materials
An example of a copyright owner giving a work to the public is the decision of the federal government to permit copying of its respective laws and judicial decisions without prior permission or payment of royalties.

Anyone can copy federal laws and judicial decisions without charge or asking for permission, provided one is careful to ensure the accuracy of the material copied and to ensure that the copy is not represented as an official version. This permission is granted by an Order-In-Council of the federal government dated January 8, 1997.

The province of Ontario also permits any person to reproduce the text and images contained in its statutes, regulations and judicial decisions without seeking permission and without charge. The materials must be reproduced accurately and must not be represented as an official version.

At the time of writing this guide, copying other provincial or territorial laws or judicial decisions requires permission from the province or territory involved.

LEGAL RIGHTS PROVIDED BY COPYRIGHT

The copyright law provides creators with a number of legal rights that control when, where, and by whom their creations can be used. Creators are provided with two different kinds of rights: (i) moral rights and (ii) economic rights.

Moral Rights

Moral rights protect the integrity of a work and the reputation of its creator. Moral rights come into existence automatically when a work is created and are attached to all categories of works. The "author" of a work owns the moral rights. Because moral rights are personal, the copyright law prohibits a creator from assigning or giving them away.

However, in Canada a creator may "waive" moral rights by agreeing, in a contract, not to exercise the rights. For example, an author of a best-selling novel may agree to waive the right to approve changes made in the film version of the novel.

Moral rights exist for the same term as copyright in the work. The chart below describes the moral rights provided under the Copyright Act.

Moral Rights

Moral Right	Examples in Libraries
Right of association: An author has the right to prevent the use of a work in association with a product, service, cause, or institution in ways which are prejudicial to the creator's honour or reputation.	Some examples of ways this right could apply in a library: using illustrations from book jackets or cartoons to promote the library; an advertising or promotional video using library materials to illustrate the collection; using a poem on a poster to promote library week. The question to ask when creating a display is whether the "association" is prejudicial to the creator's honour or reputation.
Right to remain anonymous	An example of the exercise of this right is an individual anonymously publishing political views that, if published under the author's name, would be prejudicial to that person's reputation.

Moral Right	Examples in Libraries
Right to use a pseudonym	This moral right protects the right of a person to keep his or her identity unknown by using a pen name or *nom de plume*. There are books that list pseudonyms. If an author is identified in one of these books, library staff would not infringe moral rights by using information which is publicly available.
Right to be identified with a work as its author	An example of the exercise of this right is someone claiming to be the author of a work who is not. Students sometimes submit another's work as their own. This is a moral rights infringement provided the author can prove that the action was prejudicial to his or her honour or reputation. By exercising this right, the real author can claim the work as his or her own.
Right to prevent distortions, mutilations, or other modifications to a work that are prejudicial to its creator's honour or reputation	An example of the exercise of this right is the case of Michael Snow, a famous Canadian artist who created the sculpture *Geese in Flight* for the Eaton Centre in Toronto. At Christmas time, the shopping centre put red ribbons around the necks of the geese. The artist argued that the ribbons were akin to putting earrings on Michaelangelo's *David*. The court agreed and, on the basis of this moral right, ordered the Eaton Centre to remove the ribbons.

Economic Rights

Creators have economic rights as well as moral rights. The sections of the Copyright Act describing the economic rights of creators are complicated. In non-legal language, there are eight economic rights.

1 Reproduction

This right provides copyright owners with the right to make copies. The Copyright Act provides copyright owners with the exclusive right to copy the work or a "substantial part" of the work "in any material form." Owners also have the exclusive legal right to authorize others to copy the work or a "substantial part" of the work "in any material form."

The words "substantial part" are important. A copyright owner can control copying a "substantial part" of a work. However, "insubstantial" copying does not fall within the legal authority of the copyright owner to control.

There is considerable debate about what is "substantial" as opposed to "insubstantial" copying. Two things are important in determining substantiality: the quantity copied and the value of what is copied. With respect to the first factor — the amount copied — I suggest as a rule of thumb that 1 or 2 per cent of a work is usually an "insubstantial" part of a work. However, this amount is neither in the Copyright Act nor specifically mentioned in any legal cases, and in fact it may not be allowed should a court have to determine this.

The second factor to consider is the value of what is copied. An example often cited to illustrate this concept is an eight-word sentence taken from a four-hour movie: very small in terms of quantity, but very large in terms of value. The line is "Frankly, my dear, I don't give a damn" from *Gone with the Wind*.

Both quantity and value must be considered when deciding whether copying is "substantial" or "insubstantial." In a library this usually means that copying a few pages from a directory, a single map from an atlas, a section or page from a provincial statute, a song from a book of songs, a brief extract from an instruction manual, or a short clip from a film or video often is not within the authority of a copyright owner to control, because the amount copied is "insubstantial." The application of these legal concepts to real situations arising in a library is explored in the answers to questions 21 and 22 in the "Frequently Asked Questions" section of this guide.

The words "in any material form" are also significant. These words have been broadly interpreted to cover *all* methods of reproduction. Copies made by hand or by machine are both reproductions in "material form." It does not matter whether the copy is paper, electronic, or a plastic transparency.

2 Performance in Public

This right applies to works that are seen or heard. Music, a play, or a video are examples. Some common examples of performances in public in a library are children's story hours, readings, playing music in the library as background or in the staff area, and screening movies or films.

For this right to apply, the "performance" must take place in "public." The right refers to performing a work protected by copyright in "public," not just to performing the work.

An example of this distinction is a rented video. The permission of the copyright owner would be required to show the video at a movie theatre because that is a public place. But the permission of the copyright owner would not be required to show the same video in someone's living room because that is not a public place.

Judicial decisions interpreting the distinction between public and private state that a performance that takes place in a home or in a domestic setting is not a performance in public. Generally, schools and libraries are not domestic or home settings. Therefore, any performances that take place in schools or libraries are usually performances in public.

3 Publication
This right provides a creator with the exclusive right to authorize making copies of a work available to the public. It is for the creator to decide when a work is ready for presentation to the public. "Publication" means making copies of a work available to the public in a quantity that satisfies the reasonable demands of the public.

4 Adaptation
This right provides creators with the exclusive legal right to adapt their works from one form to another. Examples are making a film from a novel, converting a dramatic work such as a play into a non-dramatic work such as a novel or vice versa, making abridgements, preparing captions of films and television programs for the hearing impaired, and adapting a print work for posting to a web site.

5 Broadcasting
Copyright owners have the exclusive right to communicate a work to the public by telecommunication. This right applies in television and radio broadcasting. Television and radio exploitation are examples of communication of a work to the public by telecommunication.

6 Presentation of an Artistic Work
The owner of the copyright in paintings, sculptures, drawings, photographs, and engravings has the exclusive right to present those works at a public exhibition for a purpose other than sale or hire. The right applies only to artistic works created after June 7, 1988. The right does not apply to a map, chart, or plan. This right enables an artist to collect a royalty payment each time a work is exhibited.

The right applies to presentations that take place at public exhibitions. Although "exhibitions" is not defined, it is generally not considered enough for the artistic work simply to be available for viewing. A special step is required, such as a deliberate placement of the artistic work so as to draw attention to it. It is not just any exhibition that attracts the right. Only an exhibition that is "public" qualifies.

The right does not apply if the exhibition is held to sell or lease the artistic works in the exhibition.

7 Rental of Computer Programs and Sound Recordings

The owner of the copyright in a sound recording or a computer program has the exclusive right to control renting. For the right to apply, the rental must be entered into with the intention of making money.

The rental right would not normally apply in a library because libraries that do rent do not make money from doing so.

Copyright protection for computer programs is subject to an exception that permits the making of a single copy for "backup purposes."

8 Authorization

Not only does the copyright owner have the exclusive legal right to exercise the rights provided under the Copyright Act, but he or she is the only one who has the legal right to authorize others to do so. For example, an author has the legal right to publish a work. But authors usually do not publish their own works. Instead, authors "authorize" producers, collectives, or publishers to exercise these rights under contractually negotiated terms and conditions.

EXCEPTIONS FOR NON-PROFIT LIBRARIES

As noted earlier, creators are provided with economic and moral rights over their creations. These legal rights are restricted or limited by "exceptions," which permit the use of a work without permission and without paying royalties.

To benefit from the exceptions under the Copyright Act, a library must be non-profit. If your library is in a for-profit setting (e.g., a law firm, bank or oil company), it does not benefit from the exceptions. If your library does not make a profit but is part of a company that does, then the exceptions do not apply.

Exceptions available to libraries are grouped under the following categories, depending upon your library's situation.

1) All non-profit libraries benefit from the exceptions in the Copyright Act related to the maintenance and management of collections, fair dealing, copying periodical articles for research and private study, incidental inclusion, and importing books from abroad.

2) In addition to the above exceptions, if your library has signed an agreement with a copyright collective, your library qualifies for the exception in the Copyright Act related to self-service copy machines.

3) Furthermore, if your library has an agreement with a collective, your library also enjoys the rights negotiated as part of that specific agreement (for the fee paid to the collective that is distributed to the appropriate rights holders). These rights are separate from, and in addition to, the exceptions granted under the Copyright Act.

Definition of a "Library"

To benefit from the library exceptions in the Copyright Act, a library must fall within the four-part definition of "library" in section 2 of the Act:

1 *The library must be "an institution."*
Dictionaries refer to an institution as an association of persons or a formal organization that constitutes a technical or professional authority in a particular field of work or study.

2 *The library cannot be "established or conducted for profit."*
This excludes libraries operated by "for-profit" corporations, such as law firms, banks and oil companies.

3 *The library must hold or maintain a collection of documents and other materials.*

4 *The library must be open to the public or to researchers.*

Libraries falling within this definition are the beneficiaries of six specific library exceptions in the copyright law. These exceptions permit libraries to do things that would otherwise infringe copyright. These exceptions permit libraries to:

1. make a copy in order to maintain and manage their collections;
2. make a copy to enable a user to "deal fairly" with a work;
3. copy periodical articles for their patrons for purposes of research or private study;
4. make incidental copies;
5. import books from abroad; and
6. supply alternate format materials to persons with perceptual disabilities.

Each of these exceptions is described below.

1 Maintenance and Management of Collections

An exception in section 30.1 of the Copyright Act permits a non-profit library or a staff person acting under its authority to make a copy of a published or unpublished work in its permanent collection, for itself or for another library, in order to perform any one of the following six maintenance or management activities:

(a) Copying Rare or Unpublished Originals

Making a copy "if the original is rare or unpublished and is deteriorating, damaged or lost" or is at risk of becoming so is permitted as a maintenance or management activity.

If a copy is commercially available in a medium and of a quality that is appropriate, the copy cannot be made. The definition of "commercially available" appears below.

(b) Copying Fragile Originals

Making a copy "for the purposes of on-site consultation if the original cannot be viewed, handled or listened to because of its condition or because of the atmospheric conditions in which it must be kept" is permitted as a maintenance or management activity.

If a copy is commercially available in a medium and of a quality that is appropriate, the copy cannot be made. The definition of "commercially available" appears below.

(c) Copying into an Alternative Format

Making a copy "in an alternative format if the original is currently in an obsolete format or the technology required to use the original is unavailable" is permitted as a maintenance or management activity.

If a copy is commercially available in a medium and of a quality that is appropriate, the copy cannot be made. The definition of "commercially available" appears below.

(d) Copying for Record Keeping and Cataloguing
Making a copy "for the purpose of internal record-keeping and cataloguing" is permitted as a maintenance or management activity. It does not matter whether the work is commercially available.

(d) Copying for Insurance and Police Investigations
Making a copy "for insurance purposes or police investigations" is permitted as a maintenance or management activity. It does not matter whether the work is commercially available.

(f) Copying for Restoration
Making a copy "if necessary for restoration" is permitted as a maintenance or management activity. It does not matter whether the work is commercially available.

What Does "Commercially Available" Mean?
It was noted above that making a copy of rare and unpublished originals in (a), fragile originals in (b), and alternative format copying in (c) is not permitted if the work is "commercially available in a medium and of a quality that is appropriate for the purpose."

The term "commercially available" is defined in section 2 of the Copyright Act. The definition provides for two ways in which a work can be "commercially available":

1. on the Canadian market or
2. under licence from a collective society.

In both cases, the work must be available within a reasonable time and for a reasonable price and must be located with reasonable effort.

A library has an obligation to ascertain whether or not a work is commercially available before it makes a copy for one of the purposes set out in (a), (b) or (c). To meet this obligation, staff will need to make reasonable inquiries to determine whether a particular work is or is not commercially available.

If the copy you need to make is a photocopy of a published print work, it is possible that CANCOPY or COPIBEC will have the authority to license the making of the copy. COPIBEC licenses users in Quebec. CANCOPY licenses users everywhere else in Canada. Through reciprocal agreements with each other and with collectives in other countries, the two Canadian collectives license published works throughout Canada and from around the world. This means that all the published, print material licensed by these two collectives is commercially available. When material is commercially available, the exceptions in (a), (b) and (c) are not available.

Here is a suggested procedure to follow:
Check to see if your library has a licence with CANCOPY or COPIBEC. If it does, check to see if the copying is authorized by the licence. If it is, then go ahead and make the copy.

If the copying is not authorized under your library's licence or if your library does not have a licence, then contact the appropriate collective to see if it can provide a licence. Both CANCOPY and COPIBEC are equipped to issue individual licences. If a licence can be provided, the work is commercially available. The library must obtain a licence and cannot make the copy under the exception.

If the collective cannot provide the licence, then the library must take whatever other steps are reasonable to determine whether the work is commercially available. Try to contact the author or the publisher. Library staff members will have to decide for themselves what is reasonable in the circumstances.

If you can reasonably conclude that the work is not commercially available, then you may go ahead and make the copy under the maintenance and management exception. Staff should keep a record of any steps taken to determine whether a work is commercially available to demonstrate that the statutory obligation has been met, should the need to do so arise.

If the work to be performed in public is a feature-length film, then the copyright owner could be represented by either Audio Ciné Films Inc. or the Visual Education Centre. Public performance licences for television programs and other audiovisual works are available from the distributors of these works. If the work is an artistic work, the organizations to contact are VIS-ART or CARFAC. See the "Contacts" section of this guide for information on how to reach these organizations.

Intermediate Copies
If you make an intermediate copy in order to make a copy under the management and maintenance exception, then you must destroy the intermediate copy when it is no longer needed. An example of a situation where an intermediate copy would be made is making a copy of a fragile original under (b) from which copies are made for patron use. This provision requires that the intermediate copy be destroyed when it is no longer needed.

2 Fair Dealing

Another exception available to libraries is "fair dealing." Sections 29, 29.1 and 29.2 of the Copyright Act provide that it is not an infringement of copyright to deal "fairly" with a work for the purposes of research, private study, criticism, review, or news reporting. For the latter three purposes, the law also requires that the source and the author's name, if it is given in the source, be mentioned.

Fair dealing applies to all works. "Fair dealing" is not defined in the Copyright Act, but the courts and legal commentators have tried to interpret what it means.

Fair dealing is also available to an agent acting on behalf of another. Library staff can make copies on behalf of their patrons or the patron of another library for four of the five purposes set out in the fair dealing provision: research, private study, criticism, or review.

Library staff cannot make copies on behalf of their patrons or the patron of another library for news reporting, which is the fifth purpose set out in the fair dealing provision.

The copy given to the patron must not be in digital form.

Any court, in deciding whether a particular activity is "fair," will consider a number of factors:

• **How much of the work has been copied.** Fair dealing almost always involves a short extract. The quantity of copying is therefore important. One Canadian case decided that the quotation of a work in its entirety is not fair dealing: *Zamacois* v. *Douville et al.*, 3 Fox Pat. C. 44; (1943) D.L.R. 257. Another case left open the possibility that, in limited circumstances, copying a whole work could be fair dealing: *Hubbard* v. *Vopser* [1972] 1 All E. R. (C.A.) 1027 at 1031.

• **The nature of the work copied.** Copying factual works is more likely to be considered "fair" than copying works of fiction.

• **The possibility of competition between the extract or quotation and the original work.** If people don't need to buy the original work because of fair dealing, then the extract probably is competing with the original. Fair dealing should not harm the market for the original work.

• **How the copy has been used.** Use for academic or non-commercial research purposes is more likely to be considered "fair" than use for commercial research purposes for financial gain.

• **The value of what is copied.** If what is copied is an important part of the work, it can be "unfair" to copy it, even if it is only a small part of the work. An example often cited to illustrate this is an eight-word sentence taken from a four-hour movie: very small in terms of quantity, but very large in terms of quality. The line is "Frankly, my dear, I don't give a damn" from *Gone with the Wind*.

- **Whether the work has been published.** One judge has said that fair dealing does not apply to unpublished works: *British Oxygen Co.* v. *Liquid Air Co.*, (1925) 1 Ch. 383 and *Beloff* v. *Preston* [1973] R.P.C. 765 (Ch. D.).

Finally, library staff should remember that fair dealing should not be confused with the much broader American concept of fair use.

3 Copying Periodical Articles for Research and Private Study

Another exception permits a library to copy periodical articles. The exception is long and has numerous conditions. Breaking the exception out into its component parts results in the following set of rules to be followed by library staff when they copy periodical articles for a patron's research or private study.

Section 30.2 of the Copyright Act permits a non-profit library to make a single copy of an article from a scientific, technical or scholarly journal, provided the copy is to be used only for research or private study. The library is also able to make a single copy of an entire article in a newspaper or other periodical if the issue is at least 12 months old at the time of copying and the copy is used for research or private study. Works of fiction, poetry, and dramatic and musical works are specifically *excluded*. The exception is limited to "reprographic reproduction," i.e., photocopying.

A library may make the specified copy for its own patron or for the patron of another library. The person receiving the copy must be given a paper, not a digital, copy. Any intermediate copy must be destroyed once the copy is given to the patron.

The copy must not be made with motive of gain. A library will have a "motive of gain" if it recovers more than the costs, including overhead costs, associated with making the copy.

Library Record-Keeping Responsibilities

Regulations provide that between September 1, 1999, and December 31, 2003, a library, or a person acting under the authority of one, must record the following information when a copy is made under the exception permitting the making of a single copy of a periodical article for research or private study and when making a copy for a patron under fair dealing:

- record the name of the library making the copy
- record the name of the requesting library (if an interlibrary loan)
- record the date of the request

- record sufficient information to identify the item being copied, such as
  (1) the title
  (2) the ISSN or the ISBN
  (3) the name of the newspaper, the periodical or the scholarly, scientific or technical periodical in which the work is found, if the work was published in a newspaper, a periodical or a scholarly or technical periodical
  (4) the date or volume and number of the newspaper or periodical, if the work was published in a newspaper or periodical
  (5) the date or volume and number of the scholarly, scientific or technical periodical, if the work was published in a scholarly, scientific or technical periodical, and
  (6) the number of pages copied
- record the information either by retaining the copy request form or in any other manner that is capable of reproducing the information in intelligible written form within a reasonable time
- keep the records for at least three years from the date of making the copy
- make available once a year to the copyright owner, the owner's representative, or a collective society authorized by the owner of copyright in the work to grant licences, upon request, the information with respect to copies made of a work
- make the information available to the person making the request within 28 days after the receipt of the request or any longer period that is agreed to both by the library and the requester.

The request must be in writing, must indicate the name of the author of the work and the title of the work, and must be signed by the person making the request. It must include a statement by that person that the request is made under regulation 4 (5)(a) as the owner of the copyright, or 4(5)(b) as the representative of the owner, or 4(5)(c) as a collective society authorized by the owner to grant licences on behalf of the owner.

Stamping of Copied Works
The library is required to give the patron requesting the copy notice that, "Any copies made or provided must be used only for the purposes of research and private study, and that any use of the copy for a purpose, other than research or private study, may require the authorization of the copyright owner of the work in question".

This can be done by stamping the copy where the copy is provided in a printed format, or as appropriate, where the copy is provided in another format.

Intermediate Copies
An intermediate copy made in order to copy a periodical article must be destroyed once the copy is given to the patron, e.g., where a photocopy is made

in order to fax a copy to a patron. This subsection requires the photocopy to be destroyed because it is an intermediate copy.

Acts Undertaken without Motive of Gain
Library staff cannot make a copy under fair dealing or copy a periodical article for research or private study *if the activity is carried out with motive of gain.* A library will not have a "motive of gain" if the library making the copy or a person acting under its authority recovers no more than the costs, including overhead costs, associated with the making of the copy.

Contracting Copying Services Outside the Library
The condition prohibiting motive of gain may present a problem for libraries in relation to the contracting out of photocopying services to private firms. The section prohibits a library, as well as "any person acting under its authority," from making a copy under the exception dealing with copying periodical articles for private study or research where a motive of gain is involved.

A private firm providing copying services on behalf of a library would be "a person acting under the authority of the library." Even though the motive of the library in contracting these services outside of the institution is not to make a gain, the firm which provides these services on the library's behalf will do so only if *it* can make a "gain."

4 Incidental Inclusion
Sometimes a work can be quite innocently reproduced or performed. Videotaping a public event at the library and incidentally capturing the background music on the tape or taking a photograph that unintentionally reproduces a painting on the wall behind the subject of the photograph are two examples of incidental copying.

These incidental copies are not infringements, even though they reproduce the music and the painting, because of an exception permitting the making of incidental copies. Section 30.7 of the Copyright Act provides that it is not an infringement of copyright to incidentally and not deliberately
(a) include a work or other subject matter in another work or other subject matter or
(b) do any act in relation to a work or other subject matter that is incidentally and not deliberately included in another work or other subject matter.

5 Importing Books from Abroad
The Copyright Act provides copyright owners and exclusive Canadian distributors with rights to control the importation of books into Canada. However, there are exceptions to these rights.

Two copies of a book may be imported for personal use. *A library or an educational institution may import no more than one copy of a book.* Used textbooks for use within an educational institution in a course of instruction, except textbooks of a scientific, technical or scholarly nature, may also be imported.

Under section 45 of the Copyright Act, copies made with the consent of the copyright owner in the country where the copy was made can be imported.

For example, if a copyright owner licenses the publication of a book in the United States, copies published under that licence are "copies made with the consent of the copyright owner in the country where the copy was made" and may be imported. However, if the copies made in the United States were made without a licence from the copyright owner, they cannot be imported.

It is lawful for a person to import:

(a) not more than two copies for his or her own use;
(b) copies for use by a department of the Government of Canada or a province;
(c) at any time before copies of a work or other subject matter are made in Canada, copies, except copies of a book, which is required for the use of a library, archive, museum or educational institution;
(d) not more than one copy of a book for the use of a library, archive, museum or educational institution;
(e) copies of any used books, except textbooks of a scientific, technical or scholarly nature for use within an educational institution in a course of instruction.

Libraries that are part of a department of the federal or a provincial government may import as many copies of a work as they wish under the exception in section 45(1)(b) of the Copyright Act.

Libraries that are not part of a department of the federal or a provincial government, such as most school libraries, may not import as many copies of a work as they wish. These other libraries must bring themselves within one of the other sub-paragraphs in section 45(1) if they wish to import under an exception.

Section 27.1 of the Copyright Act provides copyright protection to exclusive distributors. An "exclusive book distributor" is defined in section 2 as a person who has been appointed as the only distributor of the book in Canada.
The copyright protection is available provided certain performance standards are met. These standards require that an efficient distribution system be created and maintained in Canada and that the costs of acquiring books in Canada not be prohibitively high. The performance standards are set out in regulations to the Copyright Act. They came into force on September 1, 1999.

When ordering books for a library after September 1, 1999, it is necessary to order the book from an exclusive Canadian distributor if there is one. Buying from a foreign distributor includes buying online from a foreign-based distributor such as Amazon.com. The procedure to follow is set out below.

Step 1
Determine how many copies of the book the library will be ordering. If only one copy is being ordered, the library may order the book from any supplier it chooses. If more than one copy is being ordered, proceed to step 2.

Step 2
If more than one copy is being ordered, consult the latest edition of one of the following to determine whether the book is available from an exclusive Canadian distributor:

(i) *Canadian Telebook Agency Microfiche* or *Books in Print Plus — Canadian Edition*, published by R. R. Bowker (if the book is an English-language book), or *Banque de titres de langue francaise* (if the book is a French-language book), or
(ii) a catalogue supplied by the exclusive distributor, copyright owner, or exclusive licensee to the library, at the request of, and in the form requested by, the library.

If the edition of the book being ordered is available from an exclusive Canadian distributor listed in (i) or (ii), buy the book from the listed distributor.

Step 3
If, when placing the order, you consider the prices charged by the exclusive Canadian distributor to be too high, it may be possible for the library to buy the book from a foreign supplier.

The regulations set out how much more an exclusive Canadian distributor may charge than a foreign supplier. If the price differentials set out in the regulations are not respected, the distributor loses the legal right to require the library to buy the book from the distributor. The library can then buy from a foreign supplier. The allowable price differentials are set out below.

Price differentials
If the book is an import from the United States, the price differential cannot exceed the list price in the United States, plus the current exchange rate, plus 10 per cent of the price after conversion, minus any applicable discounts. To put it another way, the difference in the cost of buying a book from an exclusive Canadian distributor rather than from a distributor in the United States (after calculating the exchange) can be no more than 10 per cent.

If the book is imported from Europe or any other country, the price differential cannot exceed the list price in the country from which the book is imported, plus the current exchange rate, plus 15 per cent of the price after the conversion. In other words, for books from other countries, there can be no more than a 15 per cent difference in the cost of the book from an exclusive Canadian distributor rather than from a foreign distributor.

Step 4
If, after the order has been placed, you decide that fulfillment is taking too long, it may still be possible for the library to buy the book from a foreign supplier.

The regulations specify the times within which exclusive distributors are required to fill orders. (The regulations do not extend to the time spent in transit after material has been shipped, however.) If the shipping times set out in the regulations are not met by a distributor, the distributor loses the legal right to require the library to buy the book from the distributor. The library can then buy from a foreign supplier. The minimum shipping times are set out below.

Minimum shipping times
For books in stock in Canada, during the first year of the new system, the book must be shipped to the purchaser within five days of placing the order. The first year commences on September 1, 1999, and ends on August 31, 2000. After the first year, the book must be shipped to the purchaser within three days for English-language books and within five days for French-language books.

For books imported from the United States and not in stock in Canada, the book must be shipped within 15 days in the first year and within 12 days after the first year.

For books imported from Europe and not in stock in Canada, the book must be shipped to the purchaser within 35 days in the first year. After the first year, the book must be shipped within 30 days for English-language books and within 60 days for French-language books.

For books imported from any other country and not in stock in Canada, the book must be shipped to the purchaser within 60 days in the first year and 50 days after the first year.

Step 5
If problems with a particular distributor occur, consult the delivery times and price differentials set out in the regulations. If the distributor is not meeting the performance standards set out in the regulations, advise the exclusive Canadian distributor that, if improvements are not made, the library will exercise its right to purchase books from a foreign supplier until the problem has been corrected. If

the distributor's performance does not improve after a warning, proceed to buy from the foreign supplier.

Keep a precise record of the manner in which the offending exclusive Canadian distributor has failed to meet the performance standards set out in the regulations.

6 Alternate Format Materials for Persons with Perceptual Disabilities

Creating, producing or using material in a format specifically designed for persons with a perceptual disability often requires doing things that would infringe copyright. For example, creating a braille version of a book involves a translation from one language to another. Creating a talking book involves a reproduction. Creating captions for the hearing impaired requires an adaptation of the original work. Using sign language to perform a play or to present a literary work in a classroom or library is a public performance. Creating an electronic copy of a work involves a reproduction.

Reproduction, translation, adaptation and public performance are all exclusive rights of a copyright owner. An exception, in section 32 of the Copyright Act, permits the making of multiple copies of works in alternate formats. Translation, adaptation and performance in public in sign language are also covered by this exception.

There are two conditions. First, the exception does not authorize the making of a large print book. Second, the exception does not apply where the original work is already commercially available in a format specifically designed for persons with a perceptual disability.

Under this exception, reproduction, translation, adaptation or public performance are not an infringement of the copyright if they have been carried out for the benefit of a person with a perceptual disability. Therefore, it is necessary for a person or organization acting for the benefit of a person with a perceptual disability to ensure that the person's disability is of a type covered in the definition. The definition of perceptual disability is as follows:

> "Perceptual disability" means a disability that prevents or inhibits a person from reading or hearing a literary, musical, dramatic or artistic work in its original format, and includes such a disability resulting from
> (1) severe or total impairment of sight or hearing or the inability to focus or move one's eyes,
> (2) the inability to hold or manipulate a book, or
> (3) an impairment relating to comprehension.

It is recommended that libraries seeking to use this exception designate a central authority to ensure that the definition of perceptual disability is consistently and correctly applied.

The development of a written policy for staff use is also recommended for libraries engaged in the preparation of alternate format materials.

EXCEPTION FOR LIBRARIES WITH A LICENCE FROM A COLLECTIVE

In addition to the above exceptions, if your library has signed an agreement with a collective, your library qualifies for the exception in the Copyright Act related to the use of self-service copy machines by library patrons.

It is difficult for a library to control what is copied on self-serve copying machines. Because of this fact, section 30.3 of the Copyright Act provides that a library is not legally responsible for what its patrons do on self-service photocopying machines on the library's premises, subject to two conditions. Both conditions must be met.

1 A copyright notice, containing at least the following information, is affixed to, or within the immediate vicinity of, every photocopier, in a place and in a manner that is readily visible and legible to persons using the photocopier. Additional information can be added to the sign if deemed necessary in the circumstances of a particular library.

WARNING!

Works protected by copyright may be copied on this photocopier only if authorized by:

1. the *Copyright Act* for the purpose of fair dealing or under specific exceptions set out in that Act;
2. the copyright owner; or
3. a licence agreement between this institution and a collective society or a tariff, if any.

For details of authorized copying, please consult the licence agreement or the applicable tariff, if any, and other relevant information available from a staff member.

The Copyright Act provides for civil and criminal penalties for infringement of copyright.

It is recommended that libraries have a copy of this guide and a copy of any licence with CANCOPY or COPIBEC at the reference desk.

2 The library is participating in a licensing system available for reprographic reproduction. A library will meet this condition if:

- it has a licence for reprographic reproduction with a collective society;
- it is in the process of negotiating such a licence with a collective society;
- a tariff, or the terms and conditions of a licence, for reprographic reproduction have been established by the Copyright Board; or
- the responsible collective has filed a proposed tariff with the Copyright Board.

Many libraries meet the second condition because they have a licence with CANCOPY or COPIBEC.

If this condition is not met, a library could be held responsible if a patron makes an unauthorized "reprographic reproduction" (photocopy) of a work protected by copyright using a machine installed on the library's premises.

Even if your library does not have a licence with CANCOPY or COPIBEC, it is still a good idea to post a copyright warning near photocopying machines. It is also a good idea for all libraries to post a copyright warning like the one above near computers that provide access to the Internet or CD-ROMs.

In some circumstances, a library might enter into a photocopying agreement directly with an author. For example, an author could directly license the local library to photocopy up to 15 per cent of a work by that author. If a patron of the local library ignores this limit and copies, say, 25 per cent of a book by that author, the local library could rely on the exception for self-service copying machines to eliminate its liability for the infringement committed by the patron because the library has a licence with the author. In this case, because the library has a licence with the author, the exception applies even if the library does not have a licence with a collective.

LICENCES WITH COLLECTIVES

A collective is an organization that administers the legal rights provided under the Copyright Act on behalf of the copyright owners and rights holders that are members of that collective.

Collectives can license only what copyright owners and rights holders authorize them to license. For example, if a collective is authorized by its member publishers and authors to allow copying of only up to 10 per cent of a work, then the collective can authorize a library to copy only up to 10 per cent of a work.

There are different kinds of collectives. COPIBEC and CANCOPY license photocopying. The Visual Education Centre (VEC) and Audio Ciné Films Inc. license the public performance of feature-length films. SOCAN licenses the public performance of music.

CANCOPY and COPIBEC

The most important collectives for libraries are COPIBEC and CANCOPY (Canadian Copyright Licensing Agency). Both collectives license photocopying and other forms of "reproduction."

These collectives came into existence in response to the increasing use of photocopiers everywhere, including libraries. Convenient and practical as photocopiers may be, they nevertheless facilitate infringement of the rights of many authors and publishers.

CANCOPY and COPIBEC now license this and other kinds of photocopying. They do not wish to stop photocopying. Their purpose is to earn revenue from copying for the authors and publishers who are the owners and operators of the collectives that represent them.

CANCOPY licenses users throughout Canada except Quebec. COPIBEC licences users in Quebec.

Through reciprocal agreements with each other and with collectives in other countries, the two Canadian collectives license published works throughout Canada and from around the world.

These two collectives represent authors and publishers of printed, published works such as textbooks, magazines, newspapers, and scholarly journals. They license schools, libraries, governments, and businesses to photocopy the material represented by the collective; for practical purposes, this covers most of the published material in Canadian libraries.

The licences permit the making of copies without infringing copyright, as long as the copying remains within the negotiated limits of the licence. These limits are discussed in the next section.

Collective Licences in Canadian Libraries

CANCOPY and COPIBEC have negotiated licences with many different kinds of Canadian libraries.

Licences with provincial and territorial ministries/departments of education and school boards in every province and territory cover not only schools but also the libraries in those schools.

There is a model agreement at the post-secondary level negotiated between the Association of Universities and Colleges of Canada and CANCOPY; this agreement covers university libraries.

There is another agreement with the federal government; it covers the National Library as well as the libraries located within the federal government.

There is a model agreement for signing by public libraries negotiated by the Council of Administrators of Large Urban Public Libraries, the Provincial and Territorial Libraries Directors' Council, and CANCOPY.

All of these library licences allow staff and patrons in all kinds of Canadian libraries to copy portions of works from periodicals, journals, newspapers and books without infringing copyright.

It is important to remember always that these licences apply to *published* material only. Unpublished material is not covered by either collective. However, since library collections consist mainly of published material, the fact that only published material is covered by collective licensing is not highly significant.

Libraries carrying out archival functions in relation to unpublished works have special exceptions that apply to archival activities.

All library licences are not the same. The licences were negotiated at different times and with different kinds of libraries. For example, licences with provincial or territorial governments applying to schools or school boards include making as many copies as are necessary for communication to parents, making class sets for one or more classes that a teacher may have, plus two copies for the teacher. The public library licence, in comparison, mentions none of these kinds of copying, but does refer to "reproduction by fax transmission" to accommodate interlibrary loan.

It is therefore important to know the terms of the licence that applies in your library. Your library organization and the collectives themselves provide explanatory material. Telephone advice is also available from a variety of sources. Please refer to the "Contacts" section at the end of this guide.

What Can Be Copied under a Collective's Licence?

In general terms, under the CANCOPY and COPIBEC licences, a library may copy up to 10 per cent of a publication or more than 10 per cent if it is
- an entire chapter from a book;
- an entire short story, play, essay, article, or poem (from a publication containing other works);
- an entire periodical or newspaper article or page;
- an entire entry from an encyclopedia, dictionary, annotated bibliography, or similar reference work;
- an entire artistic work (drawings, paintings, prints, photographs, and works of sculpture or architecture) reproduced in a book or periodical;
- copies to replace damaged or missing pages in a publication belonging to the library;
- a single copy of a rare or fragile publication in a library, in order to prevent deterioration (if reasonable efforts have been made to purchase a replacement copy and if the collective has been notified); and
- a single copy to replace a missing or damaged out-of-print work in a library collection (if reasonable efforts have been made to purchase a replacement copy and if the collective has been notified).

What Cannot Be Copied under a Collective's Licence?

Equally important is what these typical licences do not cover. If the reproduction is not permitted under the terms of the licence from the collective, then it cannot be done without written authorization from the copyright owner. This rule is subject to the exceptions in the Copyright Act. See "Combining the Copyright Act with a Collective Licence," below.

Typically, the following works are not covered by comprehensive licences from CANCOPY and COPIBEC:
- unpublished works;
- published workbooks, work cards, assignment sheets, tests, and other consumables;
- printed music;
- original artistic works, including photographs or prints;
- negatives, works reproduced on slides, or other transparencies;
- commercial newsletters;

- instruction manuals, including manuals for appliances, office equipment, and computer software;
- letters to the editor and advertisements;
- business case studies;
- publications that expressly prohibit copying under a licence from a collective; and
- works by authors, artists, and publishers on an "Exclusions List."

Combining the Copyright Act with a Collective Licence

Even though the CANCOPY and COPIBEC licences do not cover any of the works listed above, limited copying can, nevertheless, take place under the Copyright Act. A collective can license only what its members authorize it to license. But the Copyright Act allows additional copying beyond what the collective is authorized to license by its members.

The relationship between collectives' licences and the copyright law is easiest to explain by examples. CANCOPY and COPIBEC do not have the authority to license the copying of instruction manuals. Therefore, under their licences, a library or its patrons are prohibited from copying any part of an instruction manual.

But we know that under the Copyright Act, copyright owners do not have the legal right to control insubstantial copying. This means that library staff and patrons can copy *insubstantial* parts of any work, including instruction manuals. To get to this result it is necessary to consider both the collective licence and the Copyright Act.

A second example is a situation in which copying is permitted under fair dealing but is prohibited under the terms of a collective's licence. In this case, the copying would be legal, because the Copyright Act overrides the terms of a licence.

A third example is federal and Ontario laws, statutes and judicial decisions. Collectives like CANCOPY and COPIBEC have no authority from the federal or Ontario governments to license copying these works. And, in fact, many CANCOPY and COPIBEC licences state that copying government works is prohibited. This is correct as far as the collective licence is concerned.

But that does not mean that these works cannot be copied. The federal and Ontario governments have declared that these works can be copied without permission (see "Government of Canada and Government of Ontario Materials" under "Works in the Public Domain," above).

The following copying is permitted by library patrons or any library staff *in addition to* the copying generally permitted by CANCOPY and COPIBEC's licences:

- "insubstantial" or small parts of any kind of work (1 or 2 per cent of the total) unless the part is a highly significant or valuable part of the work. An example often cited to illustrate this concept is an eight-word sentence taken from a four-hour movie: very small in terms of quantity, but very large in terms of significance and value. The line is "Frankly, my dear, I don't give a damn" from *Gone with the Wind.*
- fair dealing with any work for the purpose of research, private study, criticism, review;
- fair dealing with any work by a library patron (but not library staff) for news reporting;
- copying under the exception for the maintenance and management of library collections in the six situations described in the "Exceptions for Libraries" section;
- copying an article from a scientific, technical or scholarly journal at any time, or an article in a newspaper or other type of periodical, if the edition is at least 12 months old at the time of copying and provided the copy is used for research or private study;
- copying federal and Ontario laws, statutes and judicial decisions; and
- copying works in the public domain.

Copying Works of Non-Members

A frequently asked question about photocopying collectives is "What if you want to photocopy the work of someone who is not a member of a collective?"

The answer is that COPIBEC and CANCOPY generally treat all authors and publishers as members, unless the appear on an "exclusions list." This is referred to as "licensing on an exclusions basis," under which a licensee can copy any work except a work that is excluded.

A different approach is employed in a licence that authorizes copying of a specific repertoire of works. Under this type of licence, a licensee can copy only what is in the repertoire. This is referred to as an inclusions-based licence.

The inclusions licence approach is used only in the licence with the federal government. Other CANCOPY and COPIBEC licences with libraries employ the exclusions licence approach.

Exclusions List

Licences from CANCOPY and COPIBEC generally permit copying on what is called an exclusions basis. This means that a licensee can copy any material except what is excluded. A list of excluded works is provided with the licence. This "exclusions list" contains the names of countries that are not covered by the licence, individual authors and publishers, and sometimes specific works that the collective excludes from the licence.

If a work to be copied is published in an excluded country, or if a work, author or publisher is on a collective's "Exclusions List," it is necessary to contact the author or publisher directly to ask for permission to reproduce that work.

If an author or publisher is not on an "exclusions list," the collective will generally provide an indemnity to protect its licensees from lawsuits, provided that the copying complained of is within the limits set out in the licence with the collective.

Indemnity

Another important feature of a licence employing the exclusions approach is the "indemnity" offered to licensees. An indemnity is a contractual obligation that protects one person from being harmed by an act done by another person. The indemnity in the CANCOPY and COPIBEC licences protects libraries from lawsuits for copyright infringement by authors who are not members of either collective.

The indemnity applies in two ways. First, a collective will indemnify a library if it is sued for the kind of copying that falls within the terms of the licence. This would occur where a copyright owner is not on the Exclusions List and has not authorized a collective as his or her representative.

Consider the example of a library patron who copies less than 10 per cent of a book by an author who is not on a collective's Exclusions List. The author in question has not authorized any collective to license copying. The author sues the library and the patron for copyright infringement. If the library has signed a licence with either CANCOPY or COPIBEC, then the collective will assume responsibility for the lawsuit. All the legal costs and the remedies awarded by the court for the infringement will be the responsibility of the collective.

Second, the indemnity also protects the library from the consequences of infringement if a patron copies beyond the terms and conditions of the licence. To continue the same example, if a patron copies more that the authorized limit of 10 per cent of a work, the indemnity protects the library from the consequences of that infringement.

To benefit from the indemnity, the library must have made reasonable efforts to inform its staff and patrons of the terms and conditions of the licence and must have given CANCOPY or COPIBEC the opportunity to review and comment on any material the library has prepared for distribution to staff and patrons on the licence.

Copying Beyond What a Collective Licence Allows

For specific copying beyond what the licence permits (for example, more than 10 per cent of a work), it is necessary to enter into what is called a "transactional licence" with the responsible collective. CANCOPY and COPIBEC may not be able to provide every transactional licence required, but they are the best place to contact for assistance. Usually this is a simple process involving a phone call requesting permission to make the copies. The request is processed and is usually returned promptly.

WHAT IS INFRINGEMENT?

"Infringement" is the legal word for breach or violation of the rules in the copyright law. There are two kinds of infringement: direct and indirect.

Indirect infringement relates to persons who deal with infringing copies or who, without legal authority, permit a public performance of a work. These provisions usually concern commercial dealings through sales of copies, commercial distribution and trade; these are activities not commonly engaged in by libraries.

Direct infringement occurs when someone, without permission, does something only the copyright owner has the right to do or to authorize. For example, only the copyright owner has the right to make a copy or to authorize the making of a copy. When library staff members make a copy, they are doing something only the copyright owner has a right to do or to authorize. This is direct infringement unless permission is obtained or an exception applies.

Library staff members are concerned about their own personal liability for direct infringement because they make copies for patrons as part of their professional and administrative duties. Library staff members often ask who is liable if an infringement occurs. Is it the library itself, the patron who requested the copy, or the staff member who made the copy?

It is difficult to predict the outcome of any potential litigation in this area. However, there is legal precedent for assigning liability both to the person who actually does the copying and to the person who requests that the copy be made. Generally, any liability for an individual staff member is absorbed by the employer, unless the employee had been specifically directed not to do the infringing act.

What Are the Consequences of Infringing?

The last element in the regime of protection provided by the copyright law is the consequences for breaking or infringing the law. There are consequences for breaking any law. For example, there are consequences for jay walking, not paying a bill, theft, and murder. Breaking or infringing the copyright law is no different. A successful plaintiff in a copyright infringement case can be awarded "civil" remedies.

An example of a civil remedy is a court decision ordering that money be paid by a defendant as compensation for damages caused by an unauthorized use of a copyright work. This is the most common and frequently sought type of remedy. Another familiar type of civil remedy is an injunction to prevent or stop infringing activities. A court also has the authority to order the defendant to account for the profit made from infringing activities, and the court can order that all infringing copies become the property of the copyright owner.

A unique feature of the civil remedy system in the Copyright Act is a statutory limit on the amount of damages a court can award to a copyright owner who has not authorized a collective society to license the reprographic reproduction (photocopying) of his or her work. Damages are limited to the amount the copyright owner would have received from a collective, either under an agreement or under a tariff set by the Copyright Board. This feature is valuable to collectives, which, under indemnities given to licensees, are responsible for whatever damages are awarded.

Many libraries are licensed to make reprographic copies under a licence with CANCOPY or COPIBEC, the collectives administering reprography rights in published print material. A copyright owner suing a licensed library for copying published materials would receive in damages only what he or she would have been paid by CANCOPY or COPIBEC if these collectives had been authorized to license the reprography rights in the work reproduced. In practice, this amounts to a few pennies per page.

The impact of this provision is to discourage lawsuits. Litigation costing thousands of dollars will not be started when the result is limited to pennies in damages. Another impact is to encourage copyright owners to exercise their reprography rights through collectives.

Another type of consequence for infringing the copyright law is "criminal" remedies. These remedies in the Copyright Act involve fines and possible imprisonment. The Act provides for a maximum fine of $1,000,000 where the offence is a serious one.

These criminal sections in the Copyright Act are traditionally used to deal with commercial piracy. Examples most frequently encountered are copying videotapes in order to rent or sell them and selling or dealing in illegal copies of video games, compact discs, or computer programs. These criminal sanctions have not been used to deal with non-commercial activities such as those occurring in libraries.

COPYRIGHT ON THE INTERNET

The Internet is an enormous source of all kinds of information. Photographs and computer software are now routinely transmitted and accessed through the Internet. Digitized music and audiovisual material are also available, although most Internet users do not yet have the required high speed connections. The day is not far off when movies and music will be obtained through the Internet instead of a retail store.

Much of the material on the Internet is protected by copyright. Photographs, computer software, text, music, audiovisual material, news, games, stories, graphics, postings to newsgroups, and even e-mail are almost always protected by copyright. That copyright is usually owned by the person or organization that created the work.

Since material on the Internet is protected by copyright, this gives rise to legal issues that must be considered when staff or library patrons use the Internet. The Internet is used by libraries in a variety of ways: as a place for a library web site, for e-mail, as a place to participate in newsgroups, and as a library service provided to patrons.

Creating a Web Site for Your Library

Many libraries have their own web sites or have plans to create one some time in the future. A web site is an inexpensive, convenient way to promote and explain the services provided by a library. Equipped with a search feature and/or a robust table of contents, a web site can provide library patrons with a key to a broad range of web pages describing library services.

When creating a web site for your library, you will probably visit other web pages to see what others have done. It is tempting to copy and borrow the good parts from other web sites to create your own. Before starting, it is important to know what you can and cannot take without permission.

The rule is that you must get permission to use text, graphics, images, sound and video that have been created by others. If your library staff creates these items or the library already owns the copyright in them, then permission is not needed. However, there could be moral rights problems. It is best to get a moral rights waiver when you are copying or borrowing parts of works from others.

From a legal perspective, a web page is no different from any other compilation of copyright material. For example, the text, graphics, audio and video in a multimedia work are protectable by copyright. A web page is protected in a similar fashion.

The text, graphics, usenet messages, sound files, executable computer programs, and audio and video material on the web page are protectable by copyright. Each individual work will most likely be protected by copyright, and the copyright will be owned by the creator of the work.

Any original text, graphics, audio or video you create for your library's web page will be protected by copyright. You or your library will own the copyright. Your permission will be required to copy this material.

If the creator of the web page did not create the work on the page, then permission from the creator of the work should be obtained before the work is included on your library's web site. Contact the owner of the web site for permission to copy, and ask for the right to use that item on your web site.

For example, if you want to use a picture of Disney's cartoon depiction of Cinderella in the children's services part of your web page, you have to contact the Walt Disney Corporation for permission.

Permission must be in writing to be legally valid. The permission should set out the terms and conditions attaching to the permission, the circumstances where the picture will be used, and the length of time you are asking to use the image.

Public Domain Material on the Web

There are some things that are not protected by copyright. Facts, information, titles, names, slogans, ideas, plots, characters, and short word combinations are usually not protected by copyright. Neither are works in the public domain.

A work may be in the public domain because copyright has expired or because the copyright owner has given the copyright in the work to the public when the work was put on the web. You are free to download public domain works and use them on your web page.

Copyright does not protect ideas. Copyright does protect how ideas are expressed. This means that you cannot copy another web page, but you can take the ideas on a web page and express them in your own way.

If the copyright in a work on someone else's web site has expired, you are free to use it in your own web site. Since copyright lasts for quite a long time, you are not likely to find much material in the public domain on the web.

Sometimes you will find a notice from the copyright owner stating that copying is permitted. This is analogous to putting a work into the public domain. These gifts to the public vary. Sometimes there are restrictions stating the work cannot be sold or used for commercial purposes or the author must be credited whenever a copy is made. As long as you abide by the terms of the gift, you are free to download the work and use it on your web page.

Linking to Other Web Sites
Do you need someone's permission to link to his or her web site? Can you stop someone from linking to your library's site?

The value of a library's web site could be diminished by association with undesirable web sites. This is an evolving area of the law. The prevailing view is that, by putting your institution on the Internet in a web site, you implicitly give permission to others to link to your web site. This is referred to as the "implied public access theory."

A link from one web site to another is not usually considered copyright infringement, provided two "netiquette" rules are observed. First, web sites should be advised when you link to them. Secondly, a link to a web site should be removed if the owner of the linked site objects.

However, the prevailing view is being challenged in the United States, where Universal Studios has ordered a web site to remove all links to sites that have Universal servers. The links involved in the Universal dispute are known as "deep links." A deep link takes a user to specific content on a web site instead of to the home page.

Legal observers in the United States commenting on the case expressed the view that the question of who has the right to make deep links to the web site of another person or company is unsettled. Linking to a home page is fine, but deeper linking could be problematic.

Copying Link Lists
Can you reproduce a link list from another web page without infringing copyright? Hard-and-fast rules are not available to answer this question. A list may be protected by copyright, provided it is sufficiently original. A recent decision by the Federal Court of Appeal in *Tele-Direct (Publications) Inc.* v. *American Business Information Inc.* held that there was no copyright in the plaintiff's yellow pages because there was insufficient skill, judgement and labour involved in the overall arrangement of the compiled information and its arrangement according to headings. However, a list may be protected by copyright if it is sufficiently original.

Whether a link list on a particular web page is sufficiently original to be protected by copyright will depend on the degree of skill, judgement and labour involved in the selection and arrangement of the information in the list.

A suggested rule to follow is to avoid copying link lists in their entirety because that would likely infringe copyright. However, selecting links from an existing list or lists would likely be permissible.

By exercising skill, judgement and labour in compiling your own list, you will likely create a new copyright in the link list in your library's web site.

Copying from the Internet

Sending and receiving electronic information via the Internet is an increasingly important library service. Providing Internet service to library patrons is becoming increasingly important. Staff members as well as patrons need to know what can and cannot be done with information available on the Internet. And staff and patrons alike need to know if copying information from the web for one's files or sending an interesting item on the web to a colleague is permitted. From a copyright point of view, there are four rules to be aware of:

1. Most material available on the Internet is protected by copyright. This includes postings to newsgroups, e-mail messages, images, photographs, music, video clips, and computer software.

    Under the Copyright Act, reproduction and unauthorized use of a protected work are infringement. Therefore, reproduction of any work or a substantial part of any work on the Internet would infringe copyright unless you have the permission of the owner.

    The appropriateness of this is being questioned by many Internet users. An "implied licence" theory has developed. This theory holds that the act of putting a work on the Internet gives an "implied licence" to users of the Internet to copy the material and even to send it to a newsgroup or an interested colleague.

    Which uses of copyright materials from the Internet should be free of copyright restrictions is an area of the law under study in Canada and around the world. Many Internet users and service providers are asking for changes in the copyright law that would allow defined uses of works on the Internet without infringing copyright. The library community is an active participant in the work being done in this area.

2. Copyright protects only the *way* in which information is expressed, not the information itself. Copying ideas, facts or information in your own words is not copyright infringement.

3. Where a work has been placed on the Internet with the message that it can be freely copied, there is an actual licence to copy the work. Sometimes the poster will make the licence conditional.

Common conditions are that the posting cannot be used for commercial purposes, the posting must be circulated in its entirety, the posting cannot be used out of context, and the posting cannot be edited or reformatted.

If you abide by the conditions, you may copy the work without infringing copyright.

4   Any works protected by copyright that are on your library's web site require copyright clearance unless the library already owns the copyright in them. If the library does not own the copyright, then permission must be obtained from the copyright owner. The permission must be in writing.

Trade-marks

A trade-mark is a word, symbol or design, or a combination of them, used to distinguish the goods or services of one party from those of another. There are two issues you should be aware of.

The first is whether Canadian trade-mark law can be interpreted to permit linking to a web site with a trade-mark. As noted earlier, this is an evolving area of the law. There are two "netiquette" rules to be aware of. First, web sites should be advised when you link to them. Second, a link to a web site should be removed if the linked site objects. An objection could be raised on the basis of an unauthorized use of a trade-mark.

The second issue is whether you would infringe a trade-mark if you reproduce it and post it on your web page. Under the Trade-marks Act, reproduction and unauthorized use of a trade-mark are infringement. It is therefore an infringement to copy and use a trade-mark unless you have the permission of the owner.

FREQUENTLY ASKED QUESTIONS

1 What is the purpose of copyright?

The Copyright Act provides creators with the legal right to royalties, allows creators to control the use of their works, and addresses the needs of users who want access to material protected by copyright. This balance is achieved by providing creators with legal "rights" and then limiting those rights through "exceptions" for the benefit of certain users. Exceptions permit certain user groups such as libraries, archives, museums, and educational institutions to use copyright works, in specified ways, without permission and, in some cases, without paying royalties.

2 What are the rights provided to creators under the Copyright Act?

Creators are provided with economic and moral rights under the Copyright Act. Moral rights protect the integrity of a work and the reputation of its creator. Economic rights include the exclusive right to copy a creative work or to allow someone else to do so, the sole right to publish, produce or reproduce, or perform a work in public, to translate a work, to communicate a work to the public by telecommunication, to present certain artistic works at public exhibitions, and to rent sound recordings or computer programs or to authorize someone else to do so.

3 What is protected under the Copyright Act?

There are seven categories of material protected under the Copyright Act. There are four types of original works — literary, dramatic, musical, and artistic works. There are three categories of other subject matter, which includes sound recordings, performer's performances, and communication signals.

4 What is not protected by copyright?

- Titles, names, slogans and short-word combinations are usually not protected by copyright. A work protected by copyright must be something more substantial.
- Ideas are not protected. Copyright protects the expression of an idea but does not extend to the idea itself. Until an idea is expressed in some form, there is no copyright protection.
- Facts and news are not protected. It is the expression of the facts that is protected by copyright, not the facts themselves.
- Works in which the copyright has been given to the public. A work given to the public can be used in accordance with the terms of the gift. This "gift" is really a licence to use a work protected by copyright.
- Works in which copyright has expired. When the term of copyright protection ends or expires, works fall into the public domain.

5   What does "public domain" mean?
A work in the public domain belongs to the public. The work is free for everyone to use without permission or paying royalties.

6   Are tables of contents protected by copyright?
Tables of contents may be original works protected by copyright. However, library staff, in most cases, may copy contents pages. First, if your library has a licence from either CANCOPY or COPIBEC, the copying would be permitted because it constitutes less than 10 per cent of the publication. Second, the contents pages may not form a substantial part of the work. (The rights provided to copyright owners under the Copyright Act give the copyright owner the right to control reproduction of only a substantial part of the work. This means that copying an insubstantial part, like the table of contents, may not be within the legal right of a copyright owner to control.) Thirdly, from a practical perspective, little "damage" is suffered by the coypright owner or provable in this case. This is referred to as the *de minimus* principle, which means the law does not concern itself with trifles.

7   How long does copyright protection last?
In Canada the general rule is that copyright lasts for the life of the author plus 50 years. Copyright protection always ends on December 31 of the last year of protection. There are special rules for some kinds of works. These special rules are discussed in the section of this guide entitled "How Long Does Copyright Protection Last?"

8   Who owns copyright?
The general rule is that the author is the first owner of copyright, subject to any agreement between the parties that says otherwise. The owner can give, assign or license copyright in parts or in its entirety. There are special rules for works created by employees; these rules vest copyright in the employer. There are also special rules for commissioned photographs, portraits or engravings; these rules vest copyright in the person commissioning the work as long as the creator has been paid for the work.

9   What is an exception in the Copyright Act?
Creators are provided with economic and moral rights in their works. These legal rights are limited or restricted by "exceptions." An exception in the copyright law allows a work to be used in circumstances that would otherwise infringe copyright. Where an exception applies, a work can be used without the consent of its creator and without the payment of royalties.

10   What is "fair dealing"?
The Copyright Act provides that it is not an infringement of copyright to deal "fairly" with a work for the purposes of research, private study, criticism, review, and

news reporting. For the latter three purposes, the law also requires that the source and the author's name, if it is given in the source, be mentioned.

11   If I am copying for my own research and do not publish what I have copied, can I copy without infringing copyright?

The fair dealing provision allows someone to "deal" with a work as long as it is for one of the five specified purposes: research, private study, criticism, review, and news reporting. It is therefore possible that making a copy for research could be fair dealing. However, fair dealing usually involves copying a *short* extract. The legal issue to be decided is whether a particular dealing is or is not "fair." How to interpret the fair dealing provision is discussed in this guide in the "Exceptions For Non-Profit Libraries" section.

12   Is it true that I can copy anything I want as long as I don't use the copy for profit?

No. The rights of a copyright owner are not conditional on the kind of use to which copies are put. It is the act of making a copy without authorization that infringes the exclusive legal right of a copyright owner to reproduce the work or a substantial part of the work. Whether the resulting copy is used for commercial purposes or not is not a condition attaching to the rights provided under the Copyright Act.

13   How do you get permission to use a work protected by copyright?

The best place to start is with a collective administering the rights involved. The "Contacts" section of this guide identifies the different collectives and provides the information needed to contact them. If a collective cannot assist you, it will likely be able to direct you to the appropriate place. The Canadian Intellectual Property Office (CIPO) is another good source of information. Sometimes it is necessary to contact the publisher or producer directly. The work itself will be helpful in identifying the creator, publisher or producer of a work. The Copyright Board has legislative authority to issue a licence for published works when the copyright owner cannot be located. The Copyright Board has authorized CANCOPY to administer applications for the use of published print works, but the Board still decides whether a licence should be issued and on what terms.

14   What is a collective?

A collective is an organization formed and run by creators and copyright owners to administer legal rights provided under the Copyright Act. Collectives can license only what copyright owners and rights holders authorize them to license.

There are different kinds of collectives. COPIBEC and CANCOPY license photocopying. Two other collectives, Visual Education Centre (VEC) and Audio Ciné Film Inc., license the public performance of feature-length films. SOCAN licenses the public performance of music.

These licences permit copying and public performance without infringing copyright, as long as the copying or public performance remains within the negotiated limits set out in the licence.

15 Does United States copyright law apply in Canada?

Although copyright rules are the same across Canada, they do differ from one country to another. The law that applies is the law of the country in which the copyright activity takes place. Therefore, in Canada, Canadian law applies. In the United States, the United States copyright law applies, and so on. Library staff must determine whether a particular use of a work is copyright infringement by applying the rules in the Canadian Copyright Act.

16 United States government publications are in the public domain. But those of the Canadian government are protected by Crown copyright. Are United States government publications in the public domain in Canada?

This is a situation where you apply the rule set out in question 15. The law that applies is the law of the country in which the copyright activity takes place. In this question, the copyright activity is taking place in Canada. Therefore, the Canadian copyright law applies.

The Canadian copyright law provides protection to any work falling within a protected category, including works created or produced by foreign governments. The legal result is that United States government publications do not have copyright protection in their own country, but they do in Canada.

In practice, when you call a United States government office requesting permission to use a United States government publication, you are usually informed that the work is in the public domain so you don't need permission. This, in fact, is a United States citizen incorrectly assuming that the United States copyright law applies in Canada.

It is recommended that you keep a record of events: who you spoke to, what the response was, the date, and a reference to what permission was requested.

17 Are the works of foreign authors protected by copyright in Canada?

Yes. Canadian copyright law protects the works of foreign creators. This rule is illustrated by the following example. A library patron wants to copy a photograph from *National Geographic* magazine. Whether copyright is infringed in Canada is determined by the rules in the Canadian copyright law. The photograph is protected under the Canadian Copyright Act as an artistic work. One of the rights of the owner is the right to reproduce the work. Permission of the copyright owner, or a licence from the collective representing the copyright owner, would be required before making a copy of the photograph.

18 Can library staff and patrons copy laws, statutes and judicial decisions?

Anyone can copy federal laws and judicial decisions without charge and without asking for permission provided one is careful to ensure the accuracy of the material copied and to ensure that the copy is not represented as an official version. This permission is granted by an Order-In-Council of the federal government dated January 8, 1997.

The province of Ontario also permits any person to reproduce the text and images contained in the statutes, regulations and judicial decisions of Ontario without seeking permission and without charge. The materials must be reproduced accurately and must not be represented as an official version.

Copying more than small extracts from *other* provincial or territorial laws or judicial decisions requires permission from the responsible province or territory involved. However, if the copy is made for research, private study, criticism or review, it may be permitted under "fair dealing."

19 Can a library patron or library staff acting on behalf of a patron copy a periodical article?

Yes. Under the Copyright Act a non-profit library may make a single copy of an article from a scientific, technical or scholarly journal, provided the copy is used for private study or research. The library will also be able to make a single copy of an entire article in a newspaper or other type of periodical if the issue is at least 12 months old at the time of copying. The copy can be used only for research or private study. Any intermediate copy must be destroyed once the copy is delivered to the patron.

If your library has a licence with CANCOPY or COPIBEC you can copy without waiting the 12 months, and the restriction on use for research and private study does not apply. A library may make the specified copies for its own patrons or for the patrons of another library. The person receiving the copy must be given a paper, not a digital, copy. The copy must not be made "with motive of gain." A library will have a motive of gain if it recovers more than the costs, including overhead costs, associated with making the copy.

20 If a book is out of print, can library staff make a copy of it from another library's copy?

Not under the Copyright Act. The Act does not provide an exception for libraries to make a copy of out-of-print works. An exception for rare and fragile materials could apply in certain cases.

However, if your library has a CANCOPY or COPIBEC licence, you can make a replacement copy of an out-of-print work. Library licences usually permit a library with a copy of a work to assist another library needing a replacement copy of an out-of-print work, but only for publications already in the collection of the library needing the replacement copy. In other words, it must be a *replacement* copy.

Two conditions usually apply. First, the library must obtain the collective's advance confirmation that the work is out of print. Second, the library must keep a record of the copying.

If a library or a patron, in any other circumstances, wants to make a copy of an out-of-print work, the permission of the copyright owner is required. Usually permission can be obtained from the responsible collective. Which collective to contact, and how, is described in the "Contacts" section of this guide.

21 Can library staff photocopy pages in a book that has been damaged?

Insubstantial copying cannot be controlled by the copyright owner. If you need to copy only an insubstantial part of the book, then you may do so without infringing copyright. For a discussion of the meaning of "insubstantial part," see "Reproduction" under "Economic Rights."

If you need to copy a more substantial part, then you are required to buy a replacement copy if one is commercially available, as defined in the Copyright Act (see "What Does 'Commercially Available' Mean?" under "Exceptions for Non-Profit Libraries."

If a copy is not commercially available, an exception for the maintenance and management of a library's collection permits making a copy "if the original is rare or unpublished and is deteriorating, damaged or lost, or is at risk of becoming so." This exception applies to any work, not just books.

If your library has a licence with CANCOPY or COPIBEC, then up to 10 per cent of a print work can be copied under the licence. Remember that the CANCOPY and COPIBEC licences apply only to the reproduction of print materials.

If more than 10 per cent needs to be copied, then your licence permits copying missing or damaged pages for replacement purposes, provided the library first obtains the collective's advance confirmation that the work is out of print and the library keeps a record of the copying.

22 Can staff or patrons copy a photograph, drawing or illustration in a book?

If your library has a licence from CANCOPY or COPIBEC, you may copy an entire artistic work (drawings, paintings, prints, photographs, and works of sculpture or architecture) reproduced in a book or periodical.

If your library does not have a licence, the answer is more complicated. There are two likely situations. In the first situation, the copyright in the photograph, drawing or illustration is owned by the publisher of the book. Here it might be possible to argue that copying a small part of the book constitutes an "insubstantial" part of the work. The legal rights of the copyright owner do not extend to insubstantial copying.

In the second situation, the copyright in the photograph, drawing or illustration is owned by the photographer or artist, who has authorized only the use of the work in the book. Control of all other uses in this situation remains with the photographer or artist. In this case you would be copying an entire work. Copying an entire work is something only the copyright owner has the legal right to control. In this situation making the copy would likely infringe.

It is very difficult for library staff to know which situation applies to a particular photograph, drawing or illustration.

23 Can a piano teacher go to the library to photocopy music from songbooks for students? A sign concerning copyright infringement is posted on the photocopier.

Copying printed music is specifically excluded under library licences from CANCOPY and COPIBEC. Under the Copyright Act, there are two likely situations.

In the first situation, the copyright is owned by the music publisher. Here it might be possible to argue that copying one song from a songbook is a small or "insubstantial" part of the work. The legal rights of the copyright owner do not extend to insubstantial copying.

In the second situation, the copyright in the individual songs in the songbook has been retained by the individual composers whose songs comprise the volume. Copying an entire work is something only the copyright owner has the legal right to control. In this situation making the copy would likely be an infringement.

It is very difficult for library staff to know which situation applies to a particular song.

24 What are the responsibilities and liabilities of a library under the CANCOPY and COPIBEC licences?

Library licences with CANCOPY and COPIBEC usually require a library to make reasonable efforts to inform their patrons and staff of the terms and conditions of their licence. Usually this obligation can be discharged by posting a notice that summarizes the terms and conditions of the licence. Your library organization can assist you with the contents of this notice. The collectives themselves have generic information materials that can be used, or adapted, by libraries. Making a copy of this guide and the licence available for consultation by library patrons is also recommended. For library staff, some record keeping could be required. Copying out-of-print works is an example of a situation in which record keeping is required under the terms of licences with collectives.

25 A teacher tells her class of 24 students about a wonderful article on a subject being taken in class in the most recent issue of *Maclean's*. She tells the students to read it before the next class. Library staff learns of this and rushes out to the display stacks to grab the issue of *Maclean's* before it disappears. Can the library staff make several copies of the article for reserve?

An exception under the Copyright Act permits libraries to make single copies of magazine articles that are more than 12 months old. However, under the Copyright Act, multiple copying is not permitted without the permission of the copyright owner. But if your library has a licence from CANCOPY or COPIBEC, making multiple copies for reserve is often permitted. Check the terms of your library's licence.

A library in a school is usually permitted to make as many copies as are required for educational purposes. A public library is usually permitted to make multiple copies of the work, provided the copies are for "different" patrons. In this question making the copies would be permitted because they are not for the same patron, but for 24 different ones. The same reasoning would apply to making multiple copies of a chapter from a book, a poem and so on.

Remember that the copying must remain within the limits set out in the licence.

26 There are self-service copying machines in my library. If a patron uses the machine to make an infringing copy, is the library liable for copyright infringement?

It is difficult for a library to control what is copied on self-service copying machines. Because of this reality, the Copyright Act provides that a library is not legally responsible for what its patrons do on self-service photocopying machines on library premises, subject to two conditions:

1. A copyright warning is posted near the photocopying machine. The contents of this notice appears in this guide under "Exception for Libraries with a Licence from a Collective."
2. The library is participating in a licensing system available for reprographic reproduction. This condition is met if your library has a licence with CANCOPY or COPIBEC.

27 I went to the bookstore and tried to buy a copy of a certain work, but the bookstore cannot get a copy for two weeks. I need it tomorrow. Can I make a copy?

The fact that a copy is not immediately available does not alter the rules set out in the copyright law. In this question, the applicable rule is that copying a substantial part of a work without permission from the copyright owner would be an infringement of copyright.

Library staff in this situation should refer the patron to the appropriate collective, author, publisher or producer to request permission to make a copy. The "Contacts" section of this guide identifies collectives according to the works they administer and provides the information needed to contact the responsible collective. If a collective cannot provide a licence, it will likely be able to direct the inquirer to the right place. The Canadian Intellectual Property Office (CIPO) is another good source of information. Sometimes it is necessary to contact the publisher or producer directly. The work itself can be helpful in identifying and contacting the creator, publisher or producer of a work.

28 Is it an infringement of copyright to alter a work? For example, if a map is too big to print, is it permissible to manipulate it in Corel Draw? Or is it permissible to air brush a photograph?

Reproduction that entails changes to the content or appearance of a work can be an infringement of moral rights. The moral right involved here is the right to prevent distortions, mutilations, or other modifications to a work. To succeed in an action for infringement of this moral right, the creator of the work must prove that his or her reputation has been prejudiced.

The owner of the copyright also has an exclusive right to reproduce the work or a substantial part of the work. This right may also be infringed by the activities described in this question.

29 Our library has a "bestseller availability program." Can our library rent books?

Yes. In order for authors and publishers to have the legal right to control renting by libraries, they would require a right under the Copyright Act. Although there is a rental right in the Copyright Act, it applies only to computer programs and sound recordings. Since a book is neither a computer program nor a sound recording, the owner of copyright in a book has no legal right to control its rental. Exclusive rights under the Copyright Act are precise. Owners of copyright in works protected under the Act can control only those activities that the Copyright Act specifies as being within their control.

30 Can a copyright owner prevent a library renting a computer program, like a CD-ROM, or a sound recording?

Most libraries are excluded from the prohibition of unauthorized rentals of computer programs and sound recordings provided in sections 2.5 and 3(1)(h) of the Copyright Act on two grounds. First, libraries in most cases are not engaged in "renting." Renting is defined in the Copyright Act as an arrangement that "is in substance a rental having regard to all the circumstances." Most libraries lend rather than rent and therefore are not within the scope of the rental right. Second, libraries are usually non-profit entities. The rental right applies only if the rental activity is entered into with a motive of gain in relation to the overall operations of the person who rents out the computer program or sound recording. Most libraries do not make a gain on their operations and are therefore not within the scope of the rental right under the Copyright Act.

31 Our library has a great deal of difficulty with how copyright applies to videos being used. We suspect that "Home Use Videos" are being used in inappropriate ways. What are the copyright rules in this situation?

There are two types of videos in library collections. The first type has the public performance rights included with the purchase of the video. When the public performance rights have been purchased, there is no infringement when the video is performed in public. The requirement in the Copyright Act that the copyright owner's permission be obtained has been met.

With the second type ("home use"), the public performance rights have not been purchased with the video. With these videos the Copyright Act requires that the permission of the copyright owner be obtained if the work is to be performed in public.

What does performance in public mean in relation to a video? Case law has developed a basic rule that public places are places which are not domestic or home settings. Classrooms and libraries are not domestic or home settings.

For children's videos, a great reference tool for staff is the *PPR Guide*, which contains a guide to public performance rights for children's videos in Canada. It is available through Kid's Video Company. See the "Contacts" section of this guide.

32 Are there any exceptions in the Copyright Act allowing the performance of videos for educational purposes?

There are two exceptions available to educational institutions that could apply to video copies of taped radio and television programs. The Copyright Act specifically states that the exceptions for educational institutions apply to a library that forms part of an educational institution.

The first exception covers "news" and "news commentary programs." The second covers other kinds of radio and television programs. See question 33 below.

33 Can staff in a school library copy news and news commentary from radio and television programs?

Yes. An exception permits library staff in a non-profit educational institution to make a single copy of a "news program" or a "news commentary program" and to use the copy, on the premises, for educational and training purposes.

The copy can be made only at the time the program is aired. The audience must consist primarily of students of the educational institution. "Documentaries" are specifically excluded from the exception. The law does not define "news" program, "news commentary" or "documentary."

There are three conditions:
1. The copy can be made and shown without the permission of its copyright owner or the payment of a royalty an unlimited number of times for up to one year from the date the copy is made.
2. After one year, the copy must either be erased or paid for.
3. The educational institution is required to provide information relating to the making, destruction, performance and marking of the copy to the copyright owner or to a collective representing the owner.

Copies that are not destroyed after one year are subject to payment, terms and conditions relating to the use of the copy.

The Copyright Board, an independent tribunal established by the Copyright Act, has the authority to set the amount of the payment and the terms and conditions of use. In copyright law this is called a "tariff." The Copyright Board will approve a tariff after holding hearings, if necessary, to listen to the views of educational institutions and copyright owners.

34 Can staff in a school library copy other kinds of radio and television programs without permission from the copyright owner?

Yes. Library staff in a non-profit educational institution may make a single copy of all other types of broadcast programs (i.e., those that are not "news programs" or "news commentary programs"). The copy can be made only at the time the program is aired.

Three conditions apply:
1. The copy may be examined for up to 30 days to determine whether the copy will be used on the premises of an educational institution for educational purposes. After 30 days the copy must either be erased or paid for.
2. A royalty must be paid if the copy is shown to students. It may be viewed only by an audience consisting primarily of students of the educational institution.
3. The educational institution is required to provide information relating to the making, destruction, performance and marking of the copy to the copyright owner or to a collective representing the owner.

Copies that are not destroyed after 30 days will be subject to payment, terms and conditions relating to the use of the copy.

The Copyright Board, an independent tribunal established by the Copyright Act, has the authority to set the amount of the payment and the terms and conditions of use. In copyright law this is called a "tariff." The Copyright Board will approve a tariff after holding hearings, if necessary, to listen to the views of educational institutions and copyright owners.

35 If a work does not have a © symbol, does that mean it is not protected by copyright?

No. Under international copyright agreements, copyright marking consists of a small "c" in a circle, the name of the copyright owner, and the year the work is first published. In Canada there is no requirement to mark your work because copyright comes into existence automatically when a work is created. Some countries that are members of the Universal Copyright Convention require marking. Where it is required, placing the small "c" in a circle, the name of the copyright owner, and the year the work is first published meets this requirement.

36 What do collectives do with the money paid to them by libraries?

The money received by collectives is sent to creators in accordance with formulas established by them, less the administrative costs of the collectives.

37 How do collectives know which creators to pay?

Collective licences are negotiated based on detailed surveys of the use being licensed. These surveys help to establish who gets paid. In addition, some copying in libraries is subject to record keeping. These records are also used in distribution. Libraries are also asked to provide detailed collections information from time to time. All of these methods help collectives to determine which creators receive payment and how much they get when funds are distributed.

GLOSSARY

Artistic work: Visual representation, such as a painting, drawing, map, photograph, sculpture, engraving, or architectural plan.

Assigning copyright: Transfer of copyright ownership from one party to another party.

Author: The creator of an original literary, dramatic, musical, or artistic work.

Berne Convention for the Protection of Literary and Artistic Works: An international treaty extending copyright protection in member countries to nationals of other member countries. Canada is a signatory to this treaty.

CANCOPY (Canadian Copyright Licensing Agency): A reprography collective that grants licences to photocopy print works to users anywhere in Canada except Quebec and collects fees on behalf of its members.

Canadian Intellectual Property Office (CIPO): Federal agency responsible for the administration of intellectual property laws (includes the Copyright Office).

Collective: An organization that carries on the business of collective administration of legal rights granted by the Copyright Act on behalf of copyright owners, who authorize that organization to administer copyright on their behalf.

COPIBEC: A reprography collective that grants licences to photocopy print works to users in Quebec and collects fees on behalf of its members. COPIBEC was formerly known as UNEQ (Union des écrivaines et écrivains québécois).

Copyright: A number of moral and economic rights provided to creators of works. Economic rights include the right to publish, produce, reproduce, translate, communicate to the public by telecommunication, and, in some cases, rent a work, the right to perform in public and, under certain conditions, to exhibit an artistic work in public. Moral rights permit an author to maintain the integrity of a work and to protect the honour or reputation of its creator.

Copyright Act: Federal legislation governing copyright in Canada.

Copyright Board of Canada: A tribunal that reviews and approves all tariffs for the public performance of music, for retransmission, for private copying of sound recordings, and for off-air taping by educational institutions, that functions as an arbitrator of rates in certain cases, and that grants licences for use of works when the copyright owner cannot be located.

Copyright infringement: Violation of copyright through unauthorized copying or use of a work protected by copyright.

Crown copyright: Copyright in works prepared for or published by federal or provincial/territorial governments.

Dramatic work: Includes plays, screenplays, scripts, films, videos, choreographic works, and translations of such works.

Exclusive distributor: A person who has been appointed as the only distributor of a book in Canada.

Fair dealing: Use of works for purposes of private study, research, criticism, review, or news reporting that does not constitute infringement of copyright.

Fair use: A term found in United States copyright law, not to be confused with the fair dealing provision found in the Canadian Copyright Act.

Insubstantial copying: The right of a copyright owner to control the reproduction of a work or of a substantial part of a work does not include the right to control the reproduction of an insubstantial part of the work. "Insubstantial copying" is not defined in the Copyright Act.

Intellectual property: There are five types of intellectual property, each of which is a form of creative endeavour: copyright, patent, trade-mark, industrial design, and integrated circuit topography.

Licence: Legal agreement granting someone permission to use a work for certain purposes or under certain conditions. A licence does not constitute a change in ownership of the copyright.

Literary work: Works consisting of text; includes magazines, books, novels, poems, catalogues, reports, tables, and computer programs.

Moral rights: Rights an author maintains over the integrity of a work: includes the right to be named as its author even after sale or transfer of the copyright, and the right to prevent use of a work in association with products, services, causes, or institutions in ways that are prejudicial to its creator's honour or reputation.

Musical work: Work that consists of music alone or music and lyrics.

Nom de plume: A fictitious name or pseudonym assumed by an author for a time. Sometimes also called a pen name.

Plagiarism: Copying the work (or part of it) of another person and claiming it as your own. Under the Copyright Act, this might be considered a moral rights infringement.

Netiquette: The written and unwritten rules of behaviour on the Internet.

Newsgroup: An Internet protocol and service that provides users with access to other users in a group, which shares information and materials related to specific topics.

Public domain: Copyright protection has a set time limit. When the time ends, the work falls into the public domain. Works then belong to the public and anyone may use them without permission or the payment of royalties.

Publication: Making copies of a work or a sound recording available to the public. The construction of an architectural work and the incorporation of an artistic work into an architectural work are considered publication. Communication to the public by telecommunication and the exhibition in public of an artistic work do not constitute publication for the purposes of the Copyright Act.

Reprographic reproduction: Making copies by photocopying, xerography, duplicating, and other analogous methods of reproduction.

Royalty: A sum paid to copyright owners for the sale or use of their works.

Sound recording: A device such as a cassette, record, or CD that reproduces sounds.

Tariff: A standard charge for the use of copyright works. Tariffs are used to pay for the use of musical works, for the rebroadcast of programs by cable companies, for the taping of radio and television programs for educational use, and for the private copying of sound recordings.

Trade-mark: A word, symbol or design, or a combination of them, used to distinguish the goods or services of one party from those of another.

Universal Copyright Convention: An international treaty extending copyright protection in member countries to nationals of other member countries. Canada is a signatory to this treaty.

World Trade Organization: An international organization dealing with trade in goods and services, including copyright, between member countries.

CONTACTS
Artistic Works
Canadian Artists' Representation
401 Richmond Street West, Suite 402
Toronto, Ontario M5V 3A8
Tel: (416) 595-0045
Fax: (416) 340-8458
E-mail: carfac@carfac.ca
Web site: www.carfac.ca/

SODART (Société de droits d'auteur en arts visuels)
Montreal Office
460, rue Sainte-Catherine ouest
Montréal, Québec H3B 1A7

Quebec Office
640, côte d'Abraham
Québec, Québec G1R 1A1

SODRAC (Société du droit de reproduction des auteurs, compositeurs et éditeurs du Canada)
759, carré Victoria
Bureau 420
Montréal, Québec H2Y 2J7

VIS-ART Copyright Collective
3575 St. Laurent Boulevard
Montreal, Québec H2X 2T7
Tel: (514) 845-6061
Fax: (514) 845-6240

Crown Copyright
Canada Communication Group
Ottawa, Ontario K1A 0S9
Tel: (819) 990-8254
Fax: (819) 994-1498
Web site: publications.pwgsc.gc.ca/

Films, Videos, Sound Recordings
Children's videos
Kid's Video Company
C.V.S.- Children's Video Services)
40 Scollard Street
Toronto, Ontario M5R 3S1
Tel: (416) 925-5857 or
   1-800-263-1258
Fax: (416) 925-6436
E-mail: kidvideo@total.net

Feature-length Films
Audio Ciné Films Inc. (ACF)
8462 Sherbrooke Street East
Montreal, Quebec H1L 1B2
Tel: 1-800-289-8887
Fax: (514) 493-9058

Visual Education Centre (VEC)
Head Office
41 Horner Avenue, Unit 3
Toronto, Ontario M8Z 4X4
Tel: 1-800-668-0749
Fax: (416) 251-3720

Montreal Office
7810 Jarry Street, Unit J
Anjou, Québec H1G 2A1
Tel: 1-800-361-2788
Fax: (514) 356-1499

Vancouver Office
7218 Progress Way, Unit 7
Delta, B.C. V4G 1H2
Tel: 1-800-663-0991
Fax: (604) 940-9541

Music Videos and Sound Recordings
Audio Video Licensing Agency (AVLA)
1250 Bay Street, Suite 400
Toronto, Ontario M5R 2B1
Tel: (416) 922-8727
Fax: (416) 967-9415
E-mail: cria@interlog.com
Web site: www.cria.com/

General Information
Canadian Intellectual Property Office (CIPO)
Industry Canada
Place du Portage, Phase I
50 Victoria Street
Hull, Québec K1A 0C9
Tel: (819) 997-1936
Fax: (819) 953-7620
or 1-900-565-2476 (English); 1-900- 565-6742 (French)
There is a $3.00 charge per call.
Web site: info.gc.ca/ic-data/marketplace/cipo/

Library Associations
ASTED
3414, avenue du Parc
Bureau 202
Montréal, Québec H2X 2H5
Tel: (514) 281-5012
Fax: (514) 281-8219
E-mail: info@asted.org

Canadian Association of Research Libraries
Room 139, Morrissette Hall
University of Ottawa
65 University Private
Ottawa, Ontario K1N 9A5
Tel: (613) 562-5800 ext. 3652
Fax: (613) 562-5195
E-mail: carl@uottawa.ca
Web site: www.uottawa.ca/library/carl/

Canadian Library Association
200 Elgin Street, Suite 602
Ottawa, Ontario K2P 1L5
Tel: (613) 232-9625, ext. 306
Fax: (613) 563-9895
E-mail: vwhitmell@cla.ca
Web site: www.cla.ca/

Music

Society of Composers, Authors and Music Publishers of Canada (SOCAN)
Head Office
41 Valleybrook Drive
Don Mills, Ontario M3B 2S6
Tel: (416) 445-8700
or 1-800-55-SOCAN (1-800-557-6226)
Fax: (416) 445-7108
E-mail: socan@socan.ca
Web site: www.socan.ca/

Photocopying
Anywhere in Canada except Quebec
Canadian Copyright Licensing Agency (CANCOPY)
1 Yonge Street
Suite 1900
Toronto, Ontario M5E 1E5
Tel: (416) 868-1620 or
1-800-893-5777
Fax: (416) 868-1621
E-mail: admin@cancopy.com
Web site: www.cancopy.com/

Quebec only
COPIBEC
1290, rue Saint-Denis, 7th Floor
Montréal, Québec H2X 3J7
Tel: (514) 288-1664
Tel: 1-800-717-2022
Fax: (514) 288-1669
E-mail: info@copibec.qc.ca
Web site: www.copibec.qc.ca/

Tariffs
Copyright Board
56 Sparks Street, Suite 800
Ottawa, Ontario K1A 0C9
Tel: (613) 952-8621
FAX: (613) 952-8630
E mail: laflammej@smtp.gc.ca

Revised Statutes of Canada 1985
Chapter C-42, as amended

An Act respecting copyright

SHORT TITLE

Short title
1. This Act may be cited as the *Copyright Act*.

INTERPRETATION

Definitions
2. In this Act,
"architectural work" means any building or structure or any model of a building or structure; [S.C. 1993, c. 44, s. 53(2)]
"artistic work" includes paintings, drawings, maps, charts, plans, photographs, engravings, sculptures, works of artistic craftsmanship, architectural works, and compilations of artistic works; [S.C. 1993, c. 44, s. 53(2)]
"Berne Convention country" means a country that is part of the Convention for the Protection of Literary and Artistic Works concluded at Berne on September 9, 1886, or any one of its revisions, including the Paris Act of 1971; [S.C. 1993, c. 44, s. 53(2)]
"Board" means the Copyright Board established by subsection 66(1); [R.S.C. 1985, c. 10 (4th Supp.), s. 1(3)]
"book" means a volume or a part or division of a volume, in printed form, but does not include
(*a*) a pamphlet
(*b*) a newspaper, review, magazine or other periodical,
(*c*) a map, chart, plan or sheet music where the map, chart, plan or sheet music is separately published, and
(*d*) an instruction or repair manual that accompanies a product or that is supplied as an accessory to a service; [S.C. 1997, c. 24, s.1(2)]
"broadcaster" means a body that, in the course of operating a broadcasting undertaking, broadcasts a communication signal in accordance with the law of the country in which the broadcasting undertaking is carried on, but excludes a body whose primary activity in relation to communication signals is their retransmission; [S.C. 1997, c. 24, s. 1(5)]
"choreographic work" includes any work of choreography, whether or not it has any story line; [R.S.C. 1985, c. 10 (4th Supp.), s. 1(3)]
"cinematographic work" includes any work expressed by any process analogous to cinematography, whether or not accompanied by a soundtrack; [S.C. 1997, c. 24, s. 1(2)]

"collective society" means a society, association or corporation that carries on the business of collective administration of copyright or of the remuneration right conferred by section 19 or 81 for the benefit of those who, by assignment, grant of licence, appointment of it as their agent or otherwise, authorize it to act on their behalf in relation to that collective administration, and
(*a*) operates a licensing scheme, applicable in relation to a repertoire of works, performer's performances, sound recordings or communication signals of more than one author, performer, sound recording maker or broadcaster, pursuant to which the society, association or corporation sets out classes of uses that it agrees to authorize under this Act, and the royalties and terms and conditions on which it agrees to authorize those classes of uses, or
(*b*) carries on the business of collecting and distributing royalties or levies payable pursuant to this Act;
[S.C. 1997, c. 24, s. 1(5)]
"collective work" means
(*a*) an encyclopaedia, dictionary, year book or similar work,
(*b*) a newspaper, review, magazine or similar periodical, and
(*c*) any work written in distinct parts by different authors, or in which works or parts of works of different authors are incorporated;
"commercially available" means, in relation to a work or other subject-matter
(*a*) available on the Canadian market within a reasonable time and for a reasonable price and may be located with reasonable effort, or
(*b*) for which a licence to reproduce, perform in public or communicate to the public by telecommunication is available from a collective society within a reasonable time and for a reasonable price and may be located with reasonable effort;
[S.C. 1997, c. 24, s. 1(5)]
"communication signal" means radio waves transmitted through space without any artificial guide, for reception by the public; [S.C. 1997, c. 24, s. 1(5)]
"compilation" means
(*a*) a work resulting from the selection or arrangement of literary, dramatic, musical or artistic works or of parts thereof, or

(*b*) a work resulting from the selection or arrangement of data;
[S.C. 1993, c. 44, s. 53(2)]
"computer program" means a set of instructions or statements, expressed, fixed, embodied or stored in any manner, that is to be used directly or indirectly in a computer in order to bring about a specific result; [R.S.C. 1985, c. 10 (4th Supp.), s. 1(3)]
"copyright" means the rights described in
(*a*) section 3, in the case of a work,
(*b*) sections 15 and 26, in the case of a performer's performance,
(*c*) section 18, in the case of a sound recording, or
(*d*) section 21, in the case of a communication signal;
[S.C. 1997, c. 24, s. 1(5)]
"country" includes any territory;
[S.C. 1997, c. 24, s. 1(5)]
"defendant" includes a respondent to an application;
[S.C. 1997, c. 24, s. 1(5)]
"delivery" [Repealed by S.C. 1997, c. 24, s.1(1).]
"dramatic work" includes
(*a*) any piece for recitation, choreographic work or mime, the scenic arrangement or acting form of which is fixed in writing or otherwise,
(*b*) any cinematographic work, and [S.C. 1997, c. 24, s. 1(4)]
(*c*) any compilation of dramatic works; [S.C. 1993, c. 44, s. 53(2)]
"educational institution" means
(*a*) a non-profit institution licensed or recognized by or under an Act of Parliament or the legislature of a province to provide pre-school, elementary, secondary or post-secondary education,
(*b*) a non-profit institution that is directed or controlled by a board of education regulated by or under an Act of the legislature of a province and that provides continuing, professional or vocational education or training,
(*c*) a department or agency of any order of government, or any non-profit body, that controls or supervises education or training referred to in paragraph (*a*) or (*b*), or
(*d*) any other non-profit institution prescribed by regulation; [S.C. 1997, c. 24, ss. 1(5) and 62(1)]
"engravings" includes etchings, lithographs, woodcuts, prints and other similar works, not being photographs;
"every original literary, dramatic, musical and artistic work" includes every original production in the literary, scientific or artistic domain, whatever may be the mode or form of its expression, such as compilations, books, pamphlets and other writings, lectures, dramatic or dramatico-musical works, musical works, translations, illustrations, sketches, and plastic works relative to geography, topography, architecture or science; [S.C. 1993, c. 44, s. 53(2)]

"exclusive distributor" means, in relation to a book, a person who
(*a*) has, before or after the coming into force of this definition, been appointed in writing, by the owner or exclusive licensee of the copyright in the book in Canada, as
(i) the only distributor of the book in Canada or any part of Canada, or
(ii) the only distributor of the book in Canada or any part of Canada in respect of a particular sector of the market, and
(*b*) meets the criteria established by regulations made under section 2.6,
and, for greater certainty, if there are no regulations made under section 2.6, then no person qualifies under this definition as an "exclusive distributor";
[S.C. 1997, c. 24, ss. 1(5) and 62(1)]
"Her Majesty's Realms and Territories" [Repealed by S.C. 1997, c. 24, s. 1(1)]
"infringing" means
(*a*) in relation to a work in which copyright subsists, any copy, including any colourable imitation, made or dealt with in contravention of this Act,
(*b*) in relation to a performer's performance in respect of which copyright subsists, any fixation or copy of a fixation of it made or dealt with in contravention of this Act,
(*c*) in relation to a sound recording in respect of which copyright subsists, any copy of it made or dealt with in contravention of this Act, or
(*d*) in relation to a communication signal in respect of which copyright subsists, any fixation or copy of a fixation of it made or dealt with in contravention of this Act.
The definition includes a copy that is imported in the circumstances set out in paragraph 27(2)(*e*) and section 27.1 but does not otherwise include a copy made with the consent of the owner of the copyright in the country where the copy was made;
[S.C. 1994, c. 47, s. 56(1); S.C. 1997, c. 24, s. 1(2)]
"lecture" includes address, speech and sermon;
"legal representatives" includes heirs, executors, administrators, successors and assigns, or agents or attorneys who are thereunto duly authorized in writing;
"library, archive or museum" means
(*a*) an institution, whether or not incorporated, that is not established or conducted for profit or that does not form a part of, or is not administered or directly or indirectly controlled by, a body that is established or conducted for profit, in which is held and maintained a collection of documents and other materials that is open to the public or to researchers, or
(*b*) any other non-profit institution prescribed by regulation;
[S.C. 1997, c. 24, ss. 1(5) and 62]

"literary work" includes tables, computer programs, and compilations of literary works; [S.C. 1993, c. 44, s. 53(2)]

"maker" means
(*a*) in relation to a cinematographic work, the person by whom the arrangements necessary for the making of the work are undertaken, or
(*b*) in relation to a sound recording, the person by whom the arrangements necessary for the first fixation of the sounds are undertaken;
[S.C. 1993, c. 44, s. 53(3); S.C. 1997, c. 24, s. 1(2)]

"Minister", except in section 44.1, means the Minister of Industry; [S.C. 1993, c. 44, s. 53(2); S.C. 1995, c. 1, s. 62]

"moral rights" means the rights described in subsection 14.1(1); [S.C. 1993, c. 44, s. 53(2)]

"musical work" means any work of music or musical composition, with or without words, and includes any compilation thereof; [S.C. 1993, c. 44, s. 53(2)]

"perceptual disability" means a disability that prevents or inhibits a person from reading or hearing a literary, dramatic, musical or artistic work in its original format, and includes such a disability resulting from
(*a*) severe or total impairment of sight or hearing or the inability to focus or move one's eyes,
(*b*) the inability to hold or manipulate a book, or
(*c*) an impairment relating to comprehension;
[S.C. 1997, c. 24, s. 1(5)]

"performance" means any acoustic or visual representation of a work, performer's performance, sound recording or communication signal, including a representation made by means of any mechanical instrument, radio receiving set or television receiving set;
[S.C. 1994, c. 47, s. 56(1); S.C. 1997, c. 24, s. 1(2)]

"performer's performance" means any of the following when done by a performer:
(*a*) a performance of an artistic work, dramatic work or musical work, whether or not the work was previously fixed in any material form, and whether or not the work's term of copyright protection under this Act has expired,
(*b*) a recitation or reading of a literary work, whether or not the work's term of copyright protection under this Act has expired, or
(*c*) an improvisation of a dramatic work, musical work or literary work, whether or not the improvised work is based on a pre-existing work;
[S.C. 1994, c. 47, s. 56(3); S.C. 1997, c. 24, s. 1(2)]

"photograph" includes photo-lithograph and any work expressed by any process analogous to photography; [S.C. 1993, c. 44, s. 53(2)]

"plaintiff" includes an applicant; [S.C. 1997, c. 24, s. 1(5)]

"plate" includes
(*a*) any stereotype or other plate, stone, block, mould, matrix, transfer or negative used or intended to be used for printing or reproducing copies of any work, and
(*b*) any matrix or other appliance used or intended to be used for making or reproducing sound recordings, performer's performances or communication signals;
[S.C. 1997, c. 24, s. 1(2)]

"premises" means, in relation to an educational institution, a place where education or training referred to in the definition "educational institution" is provided, controlled or supervised by the educational institution; [S.C. 1997, c. 24, s. 1(5)]

"receiving device" [Repealed by S.C. 1993, c. 44, s. 79(1)]

"Rome Convention country" means a country that is a party to the International Convention for the Protection of Performers, Producers of Phonograms and Broadcasting Organisations, done at Rome on October 26, 1961; [S.C. 1997, c. 24, s. 1(5)]

"sculpture" includes a cast or model; [S.C. 1997, c. 24, s. 1(5)]

"sound recording" means a recording, fixed in any material form, consisting of sounds, whether or not of a performance of a work, but excludes any soundtrack of a cinematographic work where it accompanies the cinematographic work; [S.C. 1997, c. 24, s. 1(5)]

"telecommunication" means any transmission of signs, signals, writing, images or sounds or intelligence of any nature by wire, radio, visual, optical or other electromagnetic system; [S.C. 1988, c. 65, s. 61]

"treaty country" means a Berne Convention country, UCC country or WTO Member; [S.C. 1994, c. 47, s. 56(3)]

"UCC country" means a country that is a party to the Universal Copyright Convention, adopted on September 6, 1952 in Geneva, Switzerland, or to that Convention as revised in Paris, France on July 24, 1971; [S.C. 1994, c. 47, s. 56(3)]

"work" includes the title thereof when such title is original and distinctive;

"work of joint authorship" means a work produced by the collaboration of two or more authors in which the contribution of one author is not distinct from the contribution of the other author or authors;

"work of sculpture" [Repealed by S.C. 1997, c. 24, s. 1(1)]

"WTO Member" means a Member of the World Trade Organization as defined in subsection 2(1) of the *World Trade Organization Agreement Implementation Act*. [S.C. 1994, c. 47, s. 56(3)]

Compilations
2.1 (1) A compilation containing two or more of the categories of literary, dramatic, musical or artistic works shall be deemed to be a compilation of the category making up the most substantial part of the compilation.
(2) *Idem.* — The mere fact that a work is included in a compilation does not increase, decrease or otherwise affect the protection conferred by this Act in respect of the copyright in the work or the moral rights in respect of the work. [S.C. 1993, c. 44, s. 54]

Definitions of "Maker"
2.11 For greater certainty, the arrangements referred to in paragraph (*b*) of the definition "maker" in section 2, as that term is used in section 19 and in the definition "eligible maker" in section 79, include arrangements for entering into contracts with performers, financial arrangements and technical arrangements required for the first fixation of the sounds for a sound recording. [S.C. 1997, c. 24, s. 2]

Definition of "Publication"
2.2 (1) For the purposes of this Act, "publication" means
(*a*) in relation to any works
(i) making copies of a work available to the public,
(ii) the construction of an architectural work, and
(iii) the incorporation of an artistic work into an architectural work, and
(*b*) in relation to sound recordings, making copies of a sound recording available to the public,
but does not include
(*c*) the performance in public, or the communication to the public by telecommunication, of a literary, dramatic, musical or artistic work or a sound recording, or
(*d*) the exhibition in public of an artistic work.
(2) *Issue of photographs and engravings.* — For the purpose of subsection (1), the issue of photographs and engravings of sculptures and architectural works is not deemed to be publication of those works.
(3) *Where no consent of copyright owner.* — For the purposes of this Act, other than in respect of infringement of copyright, a work or other subject-matter is not deemed to be published or performed in public or communicated to the public by telecommunication if that act is done without the consent of the owner of the copyright.
(4) *Unpublished works.* — Where, in the case of an unpublished work, the making of the work is extended over a considerable period, the conditions of this Act conferring copyright shall be deemed to have been complied with if the author was, during any substantial part of that period, a subject or citizen of, or a person ordinarily resident in, a country to which this Act extends. [S.C. 1997, c. 24, s. 2]

Telecommunication
2.3 A person who communicates a work or other subject-matter to the public by telecommunication does not by that act alone perform it in public, nor by that act alone is deemed to authorize its performance in public. [S.C. 1997, c. 24, s. 2]

Communication to the Public by Telecommunication
2.4 (1) For the purposes of communication to the public by telecommunication,
(*a*) persons who occupy apartments, hotel rooms or dwelling units situated in the same building are part of the public, and a communication intended to be received exclusively by such persons is a communication to the public;
(*b*) a person whose only act in respect of the communication of a work or other subject-matter to the public consists of providing the means of telecommunication necessary for another person to so communicate the work or other subject-matter does not communicate that work or other subject-matter to the public; and
(*c*) where a person, as part of
(i) a network, within the meaning of the *Broadcasting Act*, whose operations result in the communication of works or other subject-matter to the public, or
(ii) any programming undertaking whose operations result in the communication of works or other subject-matter to the public,
transmits by telecommunication a work or other subject-matter that is communicated to the public by another person who is not a retransmitter of a signal within the meaning of subsection 31(1), the transmission and communication of that work or other subject-matter by those persons constitute a single communication to the public for which those persons are jointly and severally liable.
(2) *Regulations.* — The Governor in Council may make regulations defining "programming undertaking" for the purpose of paragraph (1)(*c*).
(3) *Exception.* — A work is not communicated in the manner described in paragraph (1)(*c*) or 3(1)(*f*) where a signal carrying the work is retransmitted to a person who is a retransmitter to whom section 31 applies. [S.C. 1997, c. 24, s. 2]

What Constitutes Rental
2.5 (1) For the purposes of paragraphs 3(1)(*h*) and (*i*), 15(1)(*c*) and 18(1)(*c*), an arrangement, whatever its form, constitutes a rental of a computer program or sound recording if, and only if,
(*a*) it is in substance a rental, having regard to all the circumstances; and

(*b*) it is entered into with motive of gain in relation to the overall operations of the person who rents out the computer program or sound recording, as the case may be.
(2) *Motive of gain.* — For the purpose of paragraph (1)(*b*), a person who rents out a computer program or sound recording with the intention of recovering no more than the costs, including overhead, associated with the rental operations does not by that act alone have a motive of gain in relation to the rental operations.
[S.C. 1997, c. 24, s. 2]

Exclusive Distributor

2.6 The Governor in Council may make regulations establishing distribution criteria for the purpose of paragraph (*b*) of the definition "exclusive distributor" in section 2. [S.C. 1997, c. 24, ss. 2 and 62(1)]

Exclusive Licence

2.7 For the purposes of this Act, an exclusive licence is an authorization to do any act that is subject to copyright to the exclusion of all others including the copyright owner, whether the authorization is granted by the owner or an exclusive licensee claiming under the owner. [S.C. 1997, c. 24, s. 2]

PART I
COPYRIGHT AND MORAL RIGHTS IN WORKS
[S.C. 1997, c 24, s. 2]

Copyright in Works

3. (1) For the purposes of this Act, "copyright", in relation to a work, means the sole right to produce or reproduce the work or any substantial part thereof in any material form whatever, to perform the work or any substantial part thereof in public or, if the work is unpublished, to publish the work or any substantial part thereof, and includes the sole right [S.C. 1997, c. 24, s. 3(1)]
(*a*) to produce, reproduce, perform or publish any translation of the work,
(*b*) in the case of a dramatic work, to convert it into a novel or other non-dramatic work,
(*c*) in the case of a novel or other non-dramatic work, or of an artistic work, to convert it into a dramatic work, by way of performance in public or otherwise,
(*d*) in the case of a literary, dramatic or musical work, to make any sound recording, cinematograph film or other contrivance by means of which the work may be mechanically reproduced or performed, [S.C. 1997, c. 24, s. 3(2)]
(*e*) in the case of any literary, dramatic, musical or artistic work, to reproduce, adapt and publicly present the work as a cinematographic work, [S.C. 1993, c. 44, s. 55(1); S.C. 1997, c. 24, s. 3(2)]
(*f*) in the case of any literary, dramatic, musical or artistic work, to communicate the work to the public by telecommunication, [S.C. 1988, c. 65, s. 62(1)]
(*g*) to present at a public exhibition, for a purpose other than sale or hire, an artistic work created after June 7, 1988, other than a map, chart or plan, [S.C. 1993, c. 44, s. 55(2)]
(*h*) in the case of a computer program that can be reproduced in the ordinary course of its use, other than by a reproduction during its execution in conjunction with a machine, device or computer, to rent out the computer program, and [S.C. 1993, c. 44, s. 55(2)]
(*i*) in the case of a musical work, to rent out a sound recording in which the work is embodied, [S.C. 1997, c. 24, s. 3(3)]
and to authorize any such acts.
(1.1) *Simultaneous fixing.* — A work that is communicated in the manner described in paragraph (1)(*f*) is fixed even if it is fixed simultaneously with its communication. [S.C. 1988, c. 65, s. 62(2)]
(1.2) to (4) Repealed. [S.C. 1997, c. 24, s. 3(4)]

4. [Repealed by S.C. 1997, c. 24, s. 4]

WORKS IN WHICH COPYRIGHT MAY SUBSIST

Conditions for Subsistence of Copyright

5. (1) Subject to this Act, copyright shall subsist in Canada, for the term hereinafter mentioned, in every original literary, dramatic, musical and artistic work if any one of the following conditions is met:
(*a*) in the case of any work, whether published or unpublished, including a cinematographic work, the author was, at the date of the making of the work, a citizen or subject of, or a person ordinarily resident in, a treaty country,
(*b*) in the case of a cinematographic work, whether published or unpublished, the maker, at the date of the making of the cinematographic work,
(i) if a corporation, had its headquarters in a treaty country, or
(ii) if a natural person, was a citizen or subject of, or a person ordinarily resident in, a treaty country, or
(*c*) in the case of a published work, including a cinematographic work,
(i) in relation to subparagraph 2.2(1)(*a*)(i), the first publication in such a quantity as to satisfy the reasonable demands of the public, having regard to the nature of the work, occurred in a treaty country, or
(ii) in relation to subparagraph 2.2(1)(*a*)(ii) or (iii), the first publication occurred in a treaty country.
[S.C. 1997, c. 24, s. 5(1)]

(1.01) *Protection for older works.* — For the purposes of subsection (1), a country that becomes a Berne Convention country or a WTO Member after the date of the making or publication of a work shall, as of becoming a Berne Convention country or WTO Member, as the case may be, be deemed to have been a Berne Convention country or WTO Member at the date of the making or publication of the work, subject to subsection (1.02) and section 29.

(1.02) *Limitation* — Subsection (1.01) does not confer copyright protection in Canada on a work whose term of copyright protection in the country referred to in that subsection had expired before that country became a Berne Convention country or WTO Member, as the case may be. [S.C. 1994, c. 47, s. 57(1)]

(1.03) *Application of subsections (1.01) and (1.02).* — Subsections (1.01) and (1.02) apply, and are deemed to have applied, regardless of whether the country in question became a Berne Convention country or a WTO Member before or after the coming into force of those subsections. [S.C. 1997, c. 24, s. 5(2)]

(1.1) *First publication.* — The first publication described in subparagraph (1)(*c*)(i) or (ii) is deemed to have occurred in a treaty country notwithstanding that it in fact occurred previously elsewhere, if the interval between those two publications did not exceed thirty days. [S.C. 1994, c. 47, s. 57(1); S.C.1997, c. 24, s. 5(2)]

(1.2) *Idem.* — Copyright shall not subsist in Canada otherwise than as provided by subsection (1), except in so far as the protection conferred by this Act is extended as hereinafter provided to foreign countries to which this Act does not extend. [S.C. 1993, c. 44, s. 57(1)]

(2) *Minister may extend copyright to other countries.* — Where the Minister certifies by notice, published in the *Canada Gazette*, that any country that is not a treaty country grants or has undertaken to grant, either by treaty, convention, agreement or law, to citizens of Canada, the benefit of copyright on substantially the same basis as to its own citizens or copyright protection substantially equal to that conferred by this Act, the country shall, for the purpose of the rights conferred by this Act, be treated as if it were a country to which this Act extends, and the Minister may give a certificate, notwithstanding that the remedies for enforcing the rights, or the restrictions on the importation of copies of works, under the law of such country, differ from those in this Act. [S.C. 1994, c. 47, s. 57(2)]

(3) to (6) [Repealed by S.C. 1997, c. 24, s. 5(3)]

(7) *Reciprocity protection preserved.* — For greater certainty, the protection to which a work is entitled by virtue of a notice published under subsection (2), or under that subsection as it read at any time before the coming into force of this subsection, is not affected by reason only of the country in question becoming a treaty country. [S.C. 1994, c. 47, s. 57(3)]

TERM OF COPYRIGHT

Term of Copyright
6. The term for which copyright shall subsist shall, except as otherwise expressly provided by this Act, be the life of the author, the remainder of the calendar year in which the author dies, and a period of fifty years following the end of that calendar year. [S.C. 1993, c. 44, s. 58]

Anonymous and Pseudonymous Works
6.1 Except as provided in section 6.2, where the identity of the author of a work is unknown, copyright in the work shall subsist for whichever of the following terms ends earlier:
(*a*) a term consisting of the remainder of the calendar year of the first publication of the work and a period of fifty years following the end of that calendar year, and
(*b*) a term consisting of the remainder of the calendar year of the making of the work and a period of seventy-five years following the end of that calendar year,
but where, during that term, the author's identity becomes commonly known, the term provided in section 6 applies. [S.C. 1993, c. 44, s. 58]

Anonymous and Pseudonymous Works of Joint Authorship
6.2 Where the identity of all the authors of a work of joint authorship is unknown, copyright in the work shall subsist for whichever of the following terms ends earlier:
(*a*) a term consisting of the remainder of the calendar year of the first publication of the work and a period of fifty years following the end of that calendar year, and
(*b*) a term consisting of the remainder of the calendar year of the making of the work and a period of seventy-five years following the end of a that calendar year,
but where, during that term, the identity of one or more of the authors becomes commonly known, copyright shall subsist for the life of whichever of those authors dies last, the remainder of the calendar year in which that author dies, and a period of fifty years following the end of that calendar year. [S.C. 1993, c. 44, s. 58]

Term of Copyright in Posthumous Works
7. (1) Subject to subsection (2), in the case of a literary, dramatic or musical works or an engraving, in which copyright subsists at the date of the death of the author

or, in the case of a work of joint authorship, at or immediately before the date of the death of the author who dies last, but which has not been published or, in the case of a lecture or a dramatic or musical work, been performed in public or communicated to the public by telecommunication, before that date, copyright shall subsist until publication, or performance in public or communication to the public by telecommunication, whichever may first happen, for the remainder of the calendar year of the publication or of the performance in public or communication to the public by telecommunication, as the case may be, and for a period of fifty years following the end of that calendar year.

(2) *Application of subsection (1).* — Subsection (1) applies only where the work in question was published or performed in public or communicated to the public by telecommunication, as the case may be, before the coming into force of this section.

(3) *Transitional provision.* — Where

(*a*) a work has not, at the coming into force of this section, been published or performed in public or communicated to the public by telecommunication,

(*b*) subsection (1) would apply to that work if it had been published or performed in public or communicated to the public by telecommunication before the coming into force of this section, and

(*c*) the relevant death referred to in subsection (1) occurred during the period of fifty years immediately before the coming into force of this section,

copyright shall subsist in the work for the remainder of the calendar year in which this section comes into force and for a period of fifty years following the end of that calendar year, whether or not the work is published or performed in public or communicated to the public by telecommunication after the coming into force of this section.

(4) *Transitional provision.* — Where

(*a*) a work has not, at the coming into force of this section, been published or performed in public or communicated to the public by telecommunication,

(*b*) subsection (1) would apply to that work if it had been published or performed in public or communicated to the public by telecommunication before the coming into force of this section, and

(*c*) the relevant death referred to in subsection (1) occurred more than fifty years before the coming into force of this section,

copyright shall subsist in the work for the remainder of the calendar year in which this section comes into force and for a period of five years following the end of that calendar year, whether or not the work is published or performed in public or communicated to the public by telecommunication after the coming into force of this section. [S.C. 1997, c. 24, s. 6]

8. [Repealed S.C. 1993, c. 44, s. 59]

Cases of Joint Authorship

9. (1) In the case of a work of joint authorship, except as provided in section 6.2, copyright shall subsist during the life of the author who dies last, for the remainder of the calendar year of that author's death, and for a period of fifty years following the end of that calendar year, and references in this Act to the period after the expiration of any specified number of years from the end of the calendar year of the death of the author shall be construed as references to the period after the expiration of the like number of years from the end of the calendar year of the death of the author who dies last.

(2) *Nationals of other countries.* — Authors who are nationals of any country, other than a country that is a party to the North American Free Trade Agreement, that grants a term of protection shorter than that mentioned in subsection (1) are not entitled to claim a longer term of protection in Canada. [S.C. 1993, c. 44, s. 60(1)]

Term of Copyright in Photographs

10. (1) Where the owner referred to in subsection (2) is a corporation, the term for which copyright subsists in a photograph shall be the remainder of the year of the making of the initial negative or plate from which the photograph was derived or, if there is no negative or plate, of the initial photograph, plus a period of fifty years.

(1.1) *Where author majority shareholder.* — Where the owner is a corporation, the majority of the voting shares of which are owned by a natural person who would have qualified as the author of the photograph except for subsection (2), the term of copyright is the term set out in section 6.

(2) *Author of photograph.* — The person who

(*a*) was the owner of the initial negative or other plate at the time when that negative or other plate was made, or

(*b*) was the owner of the initial photograph at the time when that photograph was made, where there was no negative or other plate,

is deemed to be the author of the photograph and, where that owner is a body corporate, the body corporate is deemed for the purposes of this Act to be ordinarily resident in a treaty country if it has established a place of business therein. [S.C. 1997, c. 24, s. 7]

11. [Repealed by S.C. 1997, c. 24, s. 8]

Cinematographic Works

11.1 Except for cinematographic works in which the arrangement or acting form or the combination of incidents represented give the work a dramatic character, copyright

in a cinematographic work or a compilation of cinematographic works shall subsist
(*a*) for the remainder of the calendar year of the first publication of the cinematographic work or of the compilation, and for a period of fifty years following the end of that calendar year; or
(*b*) if the cinematographic work or compilation is not published before the expiration of fifty years following the end of the calendar year of its making, for the remainder of that calendar year and for a period of fifty years following the end of that calendar year.
[S.C. 1993, c. 44, s. 60(1); S.C. 1997, c. 24, s. 9(2)]

Where the Copyright Belongs to Her Majesty
12. Without prejudice to any rights or privileges of the Crown, where any work is, or has been, prepared or published by or under the direction or control of Her Majesty or any government department, the copyright in the work shall, subject to any agreement with the author, belong to Her Majesty and in that case shall continue for the remainder of the calendar year of the first publication of the work and for a period of fifty years following the end of that calendar year. [S.C. 1993, c. 44, s. 60(1)]

OWNERSHIP OF COPYRIGHT

Ownership of Copyright
13. (1) Subject to this Act, the author of a work shall be the first owner of the copyright therein.
(2) *Engraving, photograph or portrait.* — Where, in the case of an engraving, photograph or portrait, the plate or other original was ordered by some other person and was made for valuable consideration, and the consideration was paid, in pursuance of that order, in the absence of any agreement to the contrary, the person by whom the plate or other original was ordered shall be the first owner of the copyright. [S.C. 1997, c. 24, s. 10(1)]
(3) *Work made in the course of employment.* — Where the author of a work was in the employment of some other person under a contract of service or apprenticeship and the work was made in the course of his employment by that person, the person by whom the author was employed shall, in the absence of any agreement to the contrary, be the first owner of the copyright, but where the work is an article or other contribution to a newspaper, magazine or similar periodical, there shall, in the absence of any agreement to the contrary, be deemed to be reserved to the author a right to restrain the publication of the work, otherwise than as part of a newspaper, magazine or similar periodical.

(4) *Assignments and licences.* — The owner of the copyright in any work may assign the right, either wholly or partially, and either generally or subject to limitations relating to territory, medium or sector of the market or other limitations relating to the scope of the assignment, and either for the whole term of the copyright or for any other part thereof, and may grant any interest in the right by licence, but no assignment or grant is valid unless it is in writing signed by the owner of the right in respect of which the assignment or grant is made, or by the owner's duly authorized agent.
(5) *Ownership in case of partial assignment.* — Where, under any partial assignment of copyright, the assignee becomes entitled to any right comprised in copyright, the assignee, with respect to the rights so assigned, and the assignor, with respect to the rights not assigned, shall be treated for the purposes of this Act as the owner of the copyright, and this Act has effect accordingly.
(6) *Assignment of right of action.* — For greater certainty, it is deemed always to have been the law that a right of action for infringement of copyright may be assigned in association with the assignment of the copyright or the grant of interest in the copyright by licence.
(7) *Exclusive licence.* — For greater certainty, it is deemed always to have been the law that a grant of an exclusive licence in a copyright constitutes the grant of an interest in the copyright by licence. [S.C. 1977, c. 24, s. 10(2)]

Limitation Where Author is First Owner of Copyright
14. (1) Where the author of a work is the first owner of the copyright therein, no assignment of the copyright and no grant of any interest therein, made by him, otherwise than by will, after June 4, 1921, is operative to vest in the assignee or grantee any rights with respect to the copyright in the work beyond the expiration of twenty-five years from the death of the author, and the reversionary interest in the copyright expectant on the termination of that period shall, on the death of the author, notwithstanding any agreement to the contrary, devolve on his legal representatives as part of the estate of the author, and any agreement entered into by the author as to the disposition of such reversionary interest is void.
(2) *Restriction.* — Nothing in subsection (1) shall be construed as applying to the assignment of the copyright in a collective work or a licence to publish a work or part of a work as part of a collective work.
(3) [Repealed by S.C. 1997, c. 24, s. 11]
(4) [Repealed by R.S.C. 1985, c. 10 (4th Supp.), s. 3]

14.01 [Repealed by S.C. 1997, c. 24, s. 12]

MORAL RIGHTS

Moral Rights
14.1 (1) The author of a work has, subject to section 28.2, the right to the integrity of the work and, in connection with an act mentioned in section 3, the right, where reasonable in the circumstances, to be associated with the work as its author by name or under a pseudonym and the right to remain anonymous.
(2) *No assignment of moral rights.* — Moral rights may not be assigned but may be waived in whole or in part.
(3) *No waiver by assignment.* — An assignment of copyright in a work does not by that act alone constitute a waiver of any moral rights.
(4) *Effect of waiver.* — Where a waiver of any moral right is made in favour of an owner or a licensee of copyright, it may be invoked by any person authorized by the owner or licensee to use the work, unless there is an indication to the contrary in the waiver.
[R.S.C. 1985, c. 10 (4th Supp.), s. 4]

Term
14.2 (1) Moral rights in respect of a work subsist for the same term as the copyright in the work.
(2) *Succession.* — The moral rights in respect of a work pass, on the death of its author, to
(*a*) the person to whom those rights are specifically bequeathed;
(*b*) where there is no specific bequest of those moral rights and the author dies testate in respect of the copyright in the work, the person to whom that copyright is bequeathed; or
(*c*) where there is no person described in paragraph (*a*) or (*b*), the person entitled to any other property in respect of which the author dies intestate. [R.S.C. 1985, c. 10 (4th Supp.), s. 4]
(3) *Subsequent succession.* — Subsection (2) applies, with such modifications as the circumstances require, on the death of any person who holds moral rights.
[S.C. 1997, c. 24, s. 13]

PART II
COPYRIGHT IN PERFORMER'S PERFORMANCES, SOUND RECORDINGS AND COMMUNICATION SIGNALS
[S.C. 1997, c. 24. s. 14]

PERFORMERS' RIGHTS

Copyright in Performers' Performance
15. (1) Subject to subsection (2), a performer has a copyright in the performer's performance, consisting of the sole right to do the following in relation to the performer's performance or any substantial part thereof:
(*a*) if it is not fixed,
(i) to communicate it to the public by telecommunication,
(ii) to perform it in public, where it is communicated to the public by telecommunication otherwise than by communication signal, and
(iii) to fix it in any material form,
(*b*) if it is fixed,
(i) to reproduce any fixation that was made without the performer's authorization,
(ii) where the performer authorized a fixation, to reproduce any reproduction of that fixation, if the reproduction being reproduced was made for a purpose other than that for which the performer's authorization was given, and
(iii) where a fixation was permitted under Part III or VIII, to reproduce any reproduction of that fixation, if the reproduction being reproduced was made for a purpose other than one permitted under Part III or VIII, and
(*c*) to rent out a sound recording of it,
and to authorize any such acts.
(2) *Conditions.* — Subsection (1) applies only if the performer's performance
(*a*) takes place in Canada or in a Rome Convention country;
(*b*) is fixed in
(i) a sound recording whose maker, at the time of the first fixation,
(A) if a natural person, was a Canadian citizen or permanent resident of Canada within the meaning of the *Immigration Act*, or a citizen or permanent resident of a Rome Convention country, or
(B) if a corporation, had its headquarters in Canada or in a Rome Convention country, or
(ii) a sound recording whose first publication in such a quantity as to satisfy the reasonable demands of the public occurred in Canada or in a Rome Convention country; or
(*c*) is transmitted at the time of the performer's performance by a communication signal broadcast from Canada or a Rome Convention country by a broadcaster that has its headquarters in the country of broadcast.
(3) *Publication.* — The first publication is deemed to have occurred in a country referred to in paragraph (2)(*b*) notwithstanding that it in fact occurred previously elsewhere, if the interval between those two publications does not exceed thirty days.
[S.C. 1993, c.44, s. 61; S.C. 1997, c. 24, s. 14]

Contractual Arrangements
16. Nothing in section 15 prevents the performer from entering into a contract governing the use of the performer's performance for the purpose of broadcasting, fixation or retransmission. [S.C. 1994, c. 47, s. 59; S.C. 1997, c. 24, s. 14]

Cinematographic Works

17. (1) Where the performer authorizes the embodiment of the performer's performance in a cinematographic work, the performer may no longer exercise, in relation to the performance where embodied in that cinematographic work, the copyright referred to in subsection 15(1).

(2) *Right to remuneration.* — Where there is an agreement governing the embodiment referred to in subsection (1) and that agreement provides for a right to remuneration for the reproduction, performance in public or communication to the public by telecommunication of the cinematographic work, the performer may enforce that right against

(*a*) the other party to the agreement or, if that party assigns the agreement, the assignee, and

(*b*) any other person who

(i) owns the copyright in the cinematographic work governing the reproduction of the cinematographic work, its performance in public or its communication to the public by telecommunication, and

(ii) reproduces the cinematographic work, performs it in public or communicates it to the public by telecommunication,

and persons referred to in paragraphs (*a*) and (*b*) are jointly and severally liable to the performer in respect of the remuneration relating to that copyright.

(3) *Application of subsection (2).* — Subsection (2) applies only if the performer's performance is embodied in a prescribed cinematographic work.

(4) *Exception.* — If so requested by a country that is a party to the North American Free Trade Agreement, the Minister may, by a statement published in the *Canada Gazette*, grant the benefits conferred by this section, subject to any terms and conditions specified in the statement, to performers who are nationals of that country or another country that is a party to the Agreement or are Canadian citizens or permanent residents within the meaning of the *Immigration Act* and whose performer's performances are embodied in works other than the prescribed cinematographic works referred to in subsection (3).

[S.C. 1994, c. 47, s. 59; S.C. 1997, c. 24, s. 14]

RIGHTS OF SOUND RECORDING MAKERS

Copyright in Sound Recordings

18. (1) Subject to subsection (2), the maker of a sound recording has a copyright in the sound recording, consisting of the sole right to do the following in relation to the sound recording or any substantial part thereof:

(*a*) to publish it for the first time,

(*b*) to reproduce it in any material form, and

(*c*) to rent it out,

and to authorize any such acts.

(2) *Conditions for copyright.* — Subsection (1) applies only if

(*a*) the maker of the sound recording was a Canadian citizen or permanent resident of Canada within the meaning of the *Immigration Act*, or a citizen or permanent resident of a Berne Convention country, a Rome Convention country or a country that is a WTO Member, or, if a corporation, had its headquarters in one of the foregoing countries,

(i) at the date of the first fixation, or

(ii) if that first fixation was extended over a considerable period, during any substantial part of that period; or

(*b*) the first publication of the sound recording in such a quantity as to satisfy the reasonable demands of the public occurred in any country referred to in paragraph (*a*).

(3) *Publication.* — The first publication is deemed to have occurred in a country referred to in paragraph (2)(*a*) notwithstanding that it in fact occurred previously elsewhere, if the interval between those two publications does not exceed thirty days.

[S.C. 1994, c. 47, s. 59; S.C. 1997, c. 24, s. 14]

PROVISIONS APPLICABLE TO BOTH PERFORMERS AND SOUND RECORDING MAKERS

Right to Remuneration

19. (1) Where a sound recording has been published, the performer and maker are entitled, subject to section 20, to be paid equitable remuneration for its performance in public or its communication to the public by telecommunication, except for any retransmission.

(2) *Royalties.* — For the purpose of providing the remuneration mentioned in subsection (1), a person who performs a published sound recording in public or communicates it to the public by telecommunication is liable to pay royalties

(*a*) in the case of a sound recording of a musical work, to the collective society authorized under Part VII to collect them; or

(*b*) in the case of a sound recording of a literary work or dramatic work, to either the maker of the sound recording or the performer.

(3) *Division of royalties.* — The royalties, once paid pursuant to paragraph (2)(*a*) or (*b*), shall be divided so that

(*a*) the performer or performers receive in aggregate fifty per cent; and

(*b*) the maker or makers receive in aggregate fifty per cent.

[S.C. 1994, c. 47, s. 59; S.C. 1997, c. 24, s. 14]

Conditions
20. (1) The right to remuneration conferred by section 19 applies only if
(*a*) the maker was, at the date of the first fixation, a Canadian citizen or permanent resident of Canada within the meaning of the *Immigration Act*, or a citizen or permanent resident of a Rome Convention country, or, if a corporation, had its headquarters in one of the foregoing countries; or
(*b*) all the fixations done for the sound recording occurred in Canada or in a Rome Convention country.
(2) *Exception.* — Notwithstanding subsection (1), if the Minister is of the opinion that a Rome Convention country does not grant a right to remuneration, similar in scope and duration to that provided by section 19, for the performance in public or the communication to the public of a sound recording whose maker, at the date of its first fixation, was a Canadian citizen or permanent resident of Canada within the meaning of the *Immigration Act* or, if a corporation, had its headquarters in Canada, the Minister may, by a statement published in the *Canada Gazette*, limit the scope and duration of the protection for sound recordings whose first fixation is done by a maker who is a citizen or permanent resident of that country or, if a corporation, has its headquarters in that country.
(3) *Exception.* — If so requested by a country that is a party to the North American Free Trade Agreement, the Minister may, by a statement published in the *Canada Gazette*, grant the right to remuneration conferred by section 19 to performers or makers who are nationals of that country and whose sound recordings embody dramatic or literary works.
(4) *Application of section 19.* — Where a statement is published under subsection (3), section 19 applies
(*a*) in respect of nationals of a country mentioned in that statement, as if they were citizens of Canada or, in the case of corporations, had their headquarters in Canada; and
(*b*) as if the fixations made for the purpose of their sound recordings had been made in Canada.
[S.C. 1994, c. 47, s. 59; S.C. 1997, c. 24, s. 14]

RIGHTS OF BROADCASTERS

Copyright in Communication Signals
21. (1) Subject to subsection (2), a broadcaster has a copyright in the communication signals that it broadcasts, consisting of the sole right to do the following in relation to the communication signal or any substantial part thereof:
(*a*) to fix it,
(*b*) to reproduce any fixation of it that was made without the broadcaster's consent,
(*c*) to authorize another broadcaster to retransmit it to the public simultaneously with its broadcast, and
(*d*) in the case of a television communication signal, to perform it in a place open to the public on payment of an entrance fee,
and to authorize any act described in paragraph (*a*), (*b*) or (*d*).
(2) *Conditions for copyright.* — Subsection (1) applies only if the broadcaster
(*a*) at the time of the broadcast, had its headquarters in Canada, in a country that is a WTO Member or in a Rome Convention country; and
(*b*) broadcasts the communication signal from that country.
(3) *Exception.* — Notwithstanding subsection (2), if the Minister is of the opinion that a Rome Convention country or a country that is a WTO Member does not grant the right mentioned in paragraph (1)(*d*), the Minister may, by a statement published in the *Canada Gazette*, declare that broadcasters that have their headquarters in that country are not entitled to that right.
[S.C. 1994, c. 47, s. 59; S.C. 1997, c. 24, s. 14]

RECIPROCITY

Reciprocity
22. (1) Where the Minister is of the opinion that a country other than a Rome Convention country grants or has undertaken to grant
(*a*) to performers and to makers of sound recordings, or
(*b*) to broadcasters
that are Canadian citizens or permanent residents of Canada within the meaning of the *Immigration Act* or, if corporations, have their headquarters in Canada, as the case may be, whether by treaty, convention, agreement or law, benefits substantially equivalent to those conferred by this Part, the Minister may, by a statement published in the *Canada Gazette*,
(*c*) grant the benefits conferred by this Part
(i) to performers and to makers of sound recordings, or
(ii) to broadcasters
as the case may be, that are citizens, subjects or permanent residents of or, if corporations, have their headquarters in that country, and
(*d*) declare that that country shall, as regards those benefits, be treated as if it were a country to which this Part extends.
(2) *Reciprocity.* — Where the Minister is of the opinion that a country other than a Rome Convention country neither grants nor has undertaken to grant
(*a*) to performers, and to makers of sound recordings, or
(*b*) to broadcasters
that are Canadian citizens or permanent residents of Canada within the meaning of the *Immigration Act* or,

if corporations, have their headquarters in Canada, as the case may be, whether by treaty, convention, agreement or law, benefits substantially equivalent to those conferred by this Part, the Minister may, by a statement published in the *Canada Gazette*,
(*c*) grant the benefits conferred by this Part to performers, makers of sound recordings or broadcasters that are citizens, subjects or permanent residents of or, if corporations, have their headquarters in that country, as the case may be, to the extent that that country grants those benefits to performers, makers of sound recordings or broadcasters that are Canadian citizens or permanent residents of Canada within the meaning of the *Immigration Act* or, if corporations, have their headquarters in Canada, and
(*d*) declare that that country shall, as regards those benefits, be treated as if it were a country to which this Part extends.
(3) *Application of Act.* — Any provision of this Act that the Minister specifies in a statement referred to in subsection (1) or (2)
(*a*) applies in respect of performers, makers of sound recordings or broadcasters covered by that statement, as if they were citizens of or, if corporations, had their headquarters in Canada; and
(*b*) applies in respect of a country covered by that statement, as if that country were Canada.
(4) *Application of Act.* — Subject to any exceptions that the Minister may specify in a statement referred to in subsection (1) or (2), the other provisions of this Act also apply in the way described in subsection (3).
[S.C. 1994, c. 47, s. 59; S.C. 1997, c. 24, s. 14]

TERM OF RIGHTS

Term of Rights
23. (1) Subject to this Act, the rights conferred by sections 15, 18 and 21 terminate fifty years after the end of the calendar year in which
(*a*) in the case of a performer's performance,
(i) its first fixation in a sound recording, or
(ii) its performance, if it is not fixed in a sound recording, occurred;
(*b*) in the case of a sound recording, the first fixation occurred; or
(*c*) in the case of a communication signal, it was broadcast.
(2) *Term of right to remuneration.* — The rights to remuneration conferred on performers and makers by section 19 have the same terms, respectively, as those provided by paragraphs (1)(*a*) and (*b*).
(3) *Application of subsections (1) and (2).* — Subsections (1) and (2) apply whether the fixation, performance or broadcast occurred before or after the coming into force of this Part.

(4) *Berne Convention countries, Rome Convention countries, WTO Members.* — Where the performer's performance, sound recording or communication signal meets the requirements set out in section 15, 18 or 21, as the case may be, a country that becomes a Berne Convention country, a Rome Convention country or a WTO Member after the date of the fixation, performance or broadcast is, as of becoming a Berne Convention country, Rome Convention country or WTO Member, as the case may be, deemed to have been such at the date of the fixation, performance or broadcast.
(5) *Where term of protection expired.* — Subsection (4) does not confer any protection in Canada where the term of protection in the country referred to in that subsection had expired before that country became a Berne Convention country, Rome Convention country or WTO Member, as the case may be.
[S.C. 1994, c. 47, s. 59; S.C. 1997, c. 24, s. 14]

OWNERSHIP OF COPYRIGHT

Ownership of Copyright
24. The first owner of the copyright
(*a*) in a performer's performance, is the performer;
(*b*) in a sound recording, is the maker; or
(*c*) in a communication signal, is the broadcaster that broadcasts it.
[S.C. 1994, c. 47, s. 59; S.C. 1997, c. 24, s. 14]

Assignment of Rights
25. Subsections 13(4) to (7) apply, with such modifications as the circumstances require, in respect of the rights conferred by this Part on performers, makers of sound recordings and broadcasters. [S.C. 1994, c. 47, s. 59; S.C. 1997, c. 24, s. 14]

PERFORMER'S RIGHTS — WTO COUNTRIES

Performer's Performance in WTO Country
26. (1) Where a performer's performance takes place on or after January 1, 1996 in a country that is a WTO Member, the performer has, as of the date of the performer's performance, a copyright in the performer's performance, consisting of the sole right to do the following in relation to the performer's performance or any substantial part thereof;
(*a*) if it is not fixed, to communicate it to the public by telecommunication and to fix it in a sound recording, and
(*b*) if it has been fixed in a sound recording without the performer's authorization, to reproduce the fixation or any substantial part thereof
and to authorize any such acts.

(2) *Where country joins WTO after Jan. 1, 1996.* — Where a performer's performance takes place on or after January 1, 1996 in a country that becomes a WTO Member after the date of the performer's performance, the performer has the copyright described in subsection (1) as of the date the country becomes a WTO Member.
(3) *Performer's performances before Jan. 1, 1996.* — Where a performer's performance takes place before January 1, 1996 in a country that is a WTO Member, the performer has, as of January 1, 1996, the sole right to do and to authorize the act described in paragraph (1)(*b*).
(4) *Where country joins WTO after Jan. 1, 1996.* — Where a performer's performance takes place before January 1, 1996 in a country that becomes a WTO Member on or after January 1, 1996, the performer has the right described in subsection (3) as of the date the country becomes a WTO Member.
(5) *Term of performer's rights.* — The rights conferred by this section subsist for the remainder of the calendar year in which the performer's performance takes place and a period of fifty years following the end of that calendar year.
(6) *Assignment of rights.* — Subsections 13(4) to (7) apply, with such modifications as the circumstances require, in respect of a performer's rights conferred by this section.
(7) *Limitation.* — Notwithstanding an assignment of a performer's right conferred by this section, the performer, as well as the assignee, may
(*a*) prevent the reproduction of
(i) any fixation of the performer's performance, or
(ii) any substantial part of such a fixation,
where the fixation was made without the performer's consent or the assignee's consent; and
(*b*) prevent the importation of any fixation of the performer's performance, or any reproduction of such a fixation, that the importer knows or ought to have known was made without the performer's consent or the assignee's consent.
[S.C. 1994, c. 47, s. 59; S.C. 1997, c. 24, s. 14]

PART III
INFRINGEMENT OF COPYRIGHT AND MORAL RIGHTS AND EXCEPTIONS TO INFRINGEMENT
[S.C. 1997, c. 24, s. 15]

INFRINGEMENT OF COPYRIGHT

General

Infringement Generally
27. (1) It is an infringement of copyright for any person to do, without the consent of the owner of the copyright, anything that by this Act only the owner of the copyright has the right to do.

(2) *Secondary infringement.* — It is an infringement of copyright for any person to
(*a*) sell or rent out,
(*b*) distribute to such an extent as to affect prejudicially the owner of the copyright,
(*c*) by way of trade distribute, expose or offer for sale or rental, or exhibit in public,
(*d*) possess for the purpose of doing anything referred to in paragraphs (*a*) to (*c*), or
(*e*) import into Canada for the purpose of doing anything referred to in paragraphs (*a*) to (*c*),
a copy of a work, sound recording or fixation of a performer's performance or of a communication signal that the person knows or should have known infringes copyright or would infringe copyright if it had been made in Canada by the person who made it.
(3) *Knowledge of importer.* — In determining whether there is an infringement under subsection (2) in the case of an activity referred to in any of paragraphs (2)(*a*) to (*d*) in relation to a copy that was imported in the circumstances referred to in paragraph (2)(*e*), it is irrelevant whether the importer knew or should have known that the importation of the copy infringed copyright.
(4) *Plates.* — It is an infringement of copyright for any person to make or possess a plate that has been specifically designed or adapted for the purpose of making infringing copies of a work or other subject-matter.
(5) *Public performance for profit.* — It is an infringement of copyright for any person, for profit, to permit a theatre or other place of entertainment to be used for the performance in public of a work or other subject-matter without the consent of the owner of the copyright unless that person was not aware, and had no reasonable ground for suspecting, that the performance would be an infringement of copyright.
[R.S.C. 1985, c. 1 (3rd Supp.), s. 13; R.S.C. 1985, c. 10 (4th Supp.), s. 5; S.C. 1993, c. 44, s. 64; S.C. 1997, c. 24, s. 15]

Parallel Importation of Books

Importation of Books
27.1 (1) Subject to any regulations made under subsection (6), it is an infringement of copyright in a book for any person to import the book where
(*a*) copies of the book were made with the consent of the owner of the copyright in the book in the country where the copies were made, but were imported without the consent of the owner of the copyright in the book in Canada; and
(*b*) the person knows or should have known that the book would infringe copyright if it was made in Canada by the importer.

(2) *Secondary infringement.* — Subject to any regulations made under subsection (6), where the circumstances described in paragraph (1)(*a*) exist, it is an infringement of copyright in an imported book for any person who knew or should have known that the book would infringe copyright if it was made in Canada by the importer to
(*a*) sell or rent out the book;
(*b*) by way of trade, distribute, expose or offer for sale or rental, or exhibit in public, the book; or
(*c*) possess the book for the purpose of any of the activities referred to in paragraph (*a*) or (*b*).
(3) *Limitation.* — Subsections (1) and (2) only apply where there is an exclusive distributor of the book and the acts described in those subsections take place in the part of Canada or in respect of the particular sector of the market for which the person is the exclusive distributor.
(4) *Exclusive distributor.* — An exclusive distributor is deemed, for the purposes of entitlement to any of the remedies under Part IV in relation to an infringement under this section, to derive an interest in the copyright in question by licence.
(5) *Notice.* — No exclusive distributor, copyright owner or exclusive licensee is entitled to a remedy under Part IV in relation to an infringement under this section unless, before the infringement occurred, notice has been given within the prescribed time and in the prescribed manner to the person referred to in subsections (1) or (2), as the case may be, that there is an exclusive distributor of the book.
(6) *Regulations.* — The Governor in Council may, by regulation, establish terms and conditions for the importation of certain categories of books, including remaindered books, books intended solely for re-export and books imported by special order. [S.C. 1997, c. 24, ss. 15 and 62(1)]

28. [Repealed by S.C. 1997, c. 24, s. 15]

28.01 [Renumbered as section 31 by S.C. 1997, c. 24, s. 16 and repositioned accordingly]

28.02 and **28.03** [Repealed by S.C. 1997, c. 24, s. 17]

MORAL RIGHTS INFRINGEMENT

Infringement Generally
28.1 Any act or omission that is contrary to any of the moral rights of the author of a work is, in the absence of consent by the author, an infringement of the moral rights. [R.S.C. 1985, c. 10 (4th Supp.), s. 6]

Nature of Right of Integrity
28.2 (1) The author's right to the integrity of a work is infringed only if the work is, to the prejudice of the honour or reputation of the author,
(*a*) distorted, mutilated or otherwise modified; or
(*b*) used in association with a product, service, cause or institution.
(2) *Where prejudice deemed.* — In the case of a painting, sculpture or engraving, the prejudice referred to in subsection (1) shall be deemed to have occurred as a result of any distortion, mutilation or other modification of the work.
(3) *When work not distorted, etc.* — For the purposes of this section,
(*a*) a change in the location of a work, the physical means by which a work is exposed or the physical structure containing a work, or
(*b*) steps taken in good faith to restore or preserve the work shall not, by that act alone, constitute a distortion, mutilation or other modification of the work. [R.S.C. 1985, c. 10 (4th Supp.), s. 6]

EXCEPTIONS
[S.C. 1997, c. 24, s. 18(1)]

Fair Dealing

Research or Private Study
29. Fair dealing for the purpose of research or private study does not infringe copyright. [S.C. 1997, c. 24, s. 18(1)]

Criticism or Review
29.1 Fair dealing for the purpose of criticism or review does not infringe copyright if the following are mentioned:
(*a*) the source; and
(*b*) if given in the source, the name of the
(i) author, in the case of a work,
(ii) performer, in the case of a performer's performance,
(iii) maker, in the case of a sound recording, or
(iv) broadcaster, in the case of a communication signal.
[S.C. 1997, c. 24, s. 18(1)]

News Reporting
29.2 Fair dealing for the purpose of news reporting does not infringe copyright if the following are mentioned:
(*a*) the source; and
(*b*) if given in the source, the name of the
(i) author, in the case of a work,
(ii) performer, in the case of a performer's performance,
(iii) maker, in the case of a sound recording, or
(iv) broadcaster, in the case of a communication signal.
[S.C. 1997, c. 24, s. 18(1)]

Acts Undertaken without Motive of Gain

Motive of Gain
29.3 (1) No action referred to in section 29.4, 29.5, 30.2 or 30.21 may be carried out with motive of gain.
(2) *Cost recovery.* — An educational institution, library, archive or museum, or person acting under its authority does not have a motive of gain where it or the person acting under its authority, does anything referred to in section 29.4, 29.5, 30.2 or 30.21 and recovers no more than the costs, including overhead costs, associated with doing that act.
[S.C. 1997, c. 24, s. 18(1)]

Educational Institutions

Reproduction for Instruction
29.4 (1) It is not an infringement of copyright for an educational institution or a person acting under its authority
(*a*) to make a manual reproduction of a work onto a dry-erase board, flip chart or other similar surface intended for displaying handwritten material, or
(*b*) to make a copy of a work to be used to project an image of that copy using an overhead projector or similar device
for the purposes of education or training on the premises of an educational institution.
(2) *Reproduction for examinations, etc.* — It is not an infringement of copyright for an educational institution or a person acting under its authority to
(*a*) reproduce, translate or perform in public on the premises of the educational institution, or
(*b*) communicate by telecommunication to the public situated on the premises of the educational institution
a work or other subject-matter as required for a test or examination.
(3) *Where work commercially available.* — Except in the case of manual reproduction, the exemption from copyright infringement provided by paragraph (1)(*b*) and subsection (2) does not apply if the work or other subject-matter is commercially available in a medium that is appropriate for the purpose referred to in that paragraph or subsection, as the case may be.
[S.C. 1997, c. 24, s. 18(1)]

Performances
29.5 It is not an infringement of copyright for an educational institution or a person acting under its authority to do the following acts if they are done on the premises of an educational institution for educational or training purposes and not for profit, before an audience consisting primarily of students of the educational institution, instructors acting under the authority of the educational institution or any person who is directly responsible for setting a curriculum for the educational institution:
(*a*) the live performance in public, primarily by students of the educational institution, of a work;
(*b*) the performance in public of a sound recording or of a work or performer's performance that is embodied in a sound recording; and
(*c*) the performance in public of a work or other subject-matter at the time of its communication to the public by telecommunication.
[S.C. 1997, c. 24, s. 18(1)]

News and Commentary
29.6 (1) Subject to subsection (2) and section 29.9, it is not an infringement of copyright for an educational institution or a person acting under its authority to
(*a*) make, at the time of its communication to the public by telecommunication, a single copy of a news program or a news commentary program, excluding documentaries, for the purposes of performing the copy for the students of the educational institution for educational or training purposes; and
(*b*) perform the copy in public, at any time or times within one year after the making of a copy under paragraph (*a*), before an audience consisting primarily of students of the educational institution on its premises for educational or training purposes.
(2) *Royalties for reproduction and performance.* — The educational institution must
(*a*) on the expiration of one year after making a copy under paragraph (1)(*a*), pay the royalties and comply with any terms and conditions fixed under this Act for the making of the copy or destroy the copy; and
(*b*) where it has paid the royalties referred to in paragraph (*a*), pay the royalties and comply with any terms and conditions fixed under this Act for any performance in public of the copy after the expiration of that year.
[S.C. 1997, c. 24, s. 18(1)]

Reproduction of Broadcast
29.7 (1) Subject to subsection (2) and section 29.9, it is not an infringement of copyright for an educational institution or a person acting under its authority to
(*a*) make a single copy of a work or other subject-matter at the time that it is communicated to the public by telecommunication; and
(*b*) keep the copy for up to thirty days to decide whether to perform the copy for educational or training purposes.
(2) *Royalties for performance.* — An educational institution that has not destroyed the copy by the expiration of

the thirty days infringes copyright in the work or other subject-matter unless it pays any royalties, and complies with any terms and conditions, fixed under this Act for the making of the copy.

(3) *Royalties for performance.* — It is not an infringement of copyright for the educational institution or a person acting under its authority to perform the copy in public for educational or training purposes on the premises of the educational institution before an audience consisting primarily of students of the educational institution if the educational institution pays the royalties and complies with any terms and conditions fixed under this Act for the performance in public.
[S.C. 1997, c. 24, s. 18(1)]

Unlawful Reception
29.8 The exceptions to infringement of copyright provided for under sections 29.5 to 29.7 do not apply where the communication to the public by telecommunication was received by unlawful means. [S.C. 1997, c. 24, s. 18(1)]

Records and Marking
29.9 (1) Where an educational institution or person acting under its authority
(*a*) makes a copy of a news program or a news commentary program and performs it pursuant to section 29.6, or
(*b*) makes a copy of a work or other subject-matter communicated to the public by telecommunication and performs it pursuant to section 29.7,
the educational institution shall keep a record of the information prescribed by regulation in relation to the making of the copy, the destruction of it or any performance in public of it for which royalties are payable under this Act and shall, in addition, mark the copy in the manner prescribed by regulation.
(2) *Regulations.* — The Board may, with the approval of the Governor in Council, make regulations
(*a*) prescribing the information in relation to the making, destruction, performance and marking of copies that must be kept under subsection (1),
(*b*) prescribing the manner and form in which records referred to in that subsection must be kept and copies destroyed or marked, and
(*c*) respecting the sending of information to collective societies referred to in section 71.
[S.C. 1997, c. 24, s. 18(1)]

Literary Collections
30. The publication in a collection, mainly composed of non-copyright matter, intended for the use of educational institutions, and so described in the title and in any advertisements issued by the publisher, of short passages from published literary works in which copyright subsists and not themselves published for the use of educational institutions, does not infringe copyright in those published literary works if
(*a*) not more than two passages from works by the same author are published by the same publisher within five years;
(*b*) the source from which the passages are taken is acknowledged; and
(*c*) the name of the author, if given in the source, is mentioned.
[S.C. 1997, c. 24, s. 18(1)]

Libraries, Archives and Museums

Management and Maintenance of Collection
30.1 (1) It is not an infringement of copyright for a library, archive or museum or a person acting under the authority of a library, archive or museum to make, for the maintenance or management of its permanent collection or the permanent collection of another library, archive or museum, a copy of a work or other subject-matter, whether published or unpublished, in its permanent collection
(*a*) if the original is rare or unpublished and is
(i) deteriorating, damaged or lost, or
(ii) at risk of deterioration or becoming damaged or lost;
(*b*) for the purposes of on-site consultation if the original cannot be viewed, handled or listened to because of its condition or because of the atmospheric conditions in which it must be kept;
(*c*) in an alternative format if the original is currently in an obsolete format or the technology required to use the original is unavailable;
(*d*) for the purposes of internal record-keeping and cataloguing;
(*e*) for insurance purposes or police investigations; or
(*f*) if necessary for restoration.
(2) *Limitation.* — Paragraphs (1)(*a*) to (*c*) do not apply where an appropriate copy is commercially available in a medium and of a quality that is appropriate for the purposes of subsection (1).
(3) *Destruction of intermediate copies.* — If a person must make an intermediate copy in order to make a copy under subsection (1), the person must destroy the intermediate copy as soon as it is no longer needed.
(4) *Regulations.* — The Governor in Council may make regulations with respect to the procedure for making copies under subsection (1).
[S.C. 1997, c. 24, s. 18(1)]

Research or Private Study
30.2 (1) It is not an infringement of copyright for a library, archive or museum or a person acting under its authority to do anything on behalf of any person that the person may do personally under section 29 or 29.1.
(2) *Copies of articles for research, etc.* — It is not an infringement of copyright for a library, archive or museum or a person acting under the authority of a library, archive or museum to make, by reprographic reproduction, for any person requesting to use the copy for research or private study, a copy of a work that is, or that is contained in, an article published in
(*a*) a scholarly, scientific or technical periodical; or
(*b*) a newspaper or periodical, other than a scholarly, scientific or technical periodical, if the newspaper or periodical was published more than one year before the copy is made.
(3) *Restriction.* — Paragraph (2)(*b*) does not apply in respect of a work of fiction or poetry or a dramatic or musical work.
(4) *Conditions.* — A library, archive or museum may make a copy under subsection (2) only on condition that
(*a*) the person for whom the copy will be made has satisfied the library, archive or museum that the person will not use the copy for a purpose other than research or private study; and
(*b*) the person is provided with a single copy of the work.
(5) *Patrons of other libraries, etc.* — A library, archive or museum or a person acting under the authority of a library, archive or museum may do, on behalf of a person who is a patron of another library, archive or museum, anything under subsection (1) or (2) in relation to printed matter that it is authorized by this section to do on behalf of a person who is one of its patrons, but the copy given to the patron must not be in digital form.
(5.1) *Destruction of intermediate copies.* — Where an intermediate copy is made in order to copy a work referred to in subsection (5), once the copy is given to the patron, the intermediate copy must be destroyed.
(6) *Regulations.* — The Governor in Council may, for the purposes of this section, make regulations
(*a*) defining "newspaper" and "periodical";
(*b*) defining scholarly, scientific and technical periodicals;
(*c*) prescribing the information to be recorded about any action taken under subsection (1) or (5) and the manner and form in which the information is to be kept; and
(*d*) prescribing the manner and form in which the conditions set out in subsection (4) are to be met.
[S.C. 1997, c. 24, s. 18(1)]

Copying Works Deposited in an Archive
30.21 (1) It is not an infringement of copyright for an archive to make a copy, in accordance with subsection (3), of an unpublished work that is deposited in the archive after the coming into force of this section.
(2) *Notice.* — When a person deposits a work in an archive, the archive must give the person notice that it may copy the work in accordance with this section.
(3) *Conditions for copying of works.* — The archive may only copy the work if
(*a*) the person who deposited the work, if a copyright owner, does not at the time the work is deposited prohibit its copying;
(*b*) copying has not been prohibited by any other owner of copyright in the work; and
(*c*) the archive is satisfied that the person for whom it is made will use the copy only for purposes of research or private study and makes only one copy for that person.
(4) *Regulations.* — The Governor in Council may prescribe the manner and form in which the conditions in subsection (3) may be met.
(5) *Where copyright owner cannot be found.* — Where an archive requires the consent of the copyright owner to copy an unpublished work deposited in the archive before the coming into force of this section but is unable to locate the owner, the archive may copy the work in accordance with subsection (3).
(6) *Notice.* — The archive must make a record of any copy made under subsection (5), and keep it available for public inspection, as prescribed.
(7) *Posthumous works.* — It is not an infringement of copyright for an archive to make a copy, in accordance with subsection (3), of any work to which subsection 7(4) applies, if it was in the archive on the date of coming into force of this section.
[S.C. 1997, c. 24, s. 18(1)]

Machines Installed in Educational Institutions, Libraries, Archives and Museums

No Infringement by Educational Institution, etc.
30.3 (1) An educational institution or a library, archive or museum does not infringe copyright where
(*a*) a copy of a work is made using a machine for the making, by reprographic reproduction, of copies of works in printed form;
(*b*) the machine is installed by or with the approval of the educational institution, library, archive or museum on its premises for use by students, instructors or staff at the educational institution or by persons using the library, archive or museum; and

(*c*) there is affixed in the prescribed manner and location a notice warning of infringement of copyright.
(2) *Applications.* — Subsection (1) only applies if, in respect of a reprographic reproduction,
(*a*) the educational institution, library, archive or museum has entered into an agreement with a collective society that is authorized by copyright owners to grant licences on their behalf;
(*b*) the Board has, in accordance with section 70.2, fixed the royalties and related terms and conditions in respect of a licence;
(*c*) a tariff has been approved in accordance with section 70.15; or
(*d*) a collective society has filed a proposed tariff in accordance with section 70.13.
(3) *Order.* — Where a collective society offers to negotiate or has begun to negotiate an agreement referred to in paragraph (2)(*a*), the Board may, at the request of either party, order that the educational institution, library, archive or museum be treated as an institution to which subsection (1) applies, during the period specified in the order.
(4) *Agreement with copyright owner.* — Where an educational institution, library, archive or museum has entered into an agreement with a copyright owner other than a collective society respecting reprographic reproduction, subsection (1) applies only in respect of the works of the copyright owner that are covered by the agreement.
(5) *Regulations.* — The Governor in Council may, for the purposes of paragraph 1(*c*), prescribe by regulation the manner of affixing and location of notices and the dimensions, form and contents of notices. [S.C. 1997, c. 24, s. 18(1)]

Libraries, Archives and Museums in Educational Institutions

Application to Libraries, etc., within Educational Institutions
30.4 For greater certainty, the exceptions to infringement of copyright provided for under sections 29.4 to 30.3 and 45 also apply in respect of a library, archive or museum that forms part of an educational institution. [S.C. 1997, c. 24, s. 18(1)]

National Archives of Canada

Copies for Archival Purposes
30.5 The National Archives of Canada may
(*a*) make a copy of a recording, as defined in section 8 of the *National Archives Act*, for the purposes of that section; and

(*b*) at the time that a broadcasting undertaking, within the meaning of subsection 2(1) of the *Broadcasting Act*, communicates a work or other subject-matter to the public by telecommunication, make a copy for archival purposes of the work or other subject-matter that is included in that communication.
[S.C. 1997, c. 24, s. 18(1)]

Computer Programs

Permitted Acts
30.6 It is not an infringement of copyright in a computer program for a person who owns a copy of the computer program that is authorized by the owner of the copyright to
(*a*) make a single reproduction of the copy by adapting, modifying or converting the computer program or translating it into another computer language if the person proves that the reproduced copy is
(i) essential for the compatibility of the computer program with a particular computer,
(ii) solely for the person's own use, and
(iii) destroyed immediately after the person ceases to be the owner of the copy; or
(*b*) make a single reproduction for backup purposes of the copy or of a reproduced copy referred to in paragraph (*a*) if the person proves that the reproduction for backup purposes is destroyed immediately when the person ceases to be the owner of the copy of the computer program.
[S.C. 1997, c. 24, s. 18(1)]

Incidental Inclusion

Incidental Use
30.7 It is not an infringement of copyright to incidentally and not deliberately
(*a*) include a work or other subject-matter in another work or other subject-matter; or
(*b*) do any act in relation to a work or other subject-matter that is incidentally and not deliberately included in another work or other subject-matter.
[S.C. 1997, c. 24, s. 18(1)]

Ephemeral Recordings

Ephemeral Recordings
30.8 (1) It is not an infringement of copyright for a programming undertaking to fix or reproduce in accordance with this section a performer's performance or work, other than a cinematographic work, that is performed live or a sound recording that is performed at the same time as the performer's performance or work, if the undertaking

(*a*) is authorized to communicate the performer's performance, work or sound recording to the public by telecommunication;
(*b*) makes the fixation or the reproduction itself, for its own broadcasts;
(*c*) does not synchronize the fixation or reproduction with all or part of another recording, performer's performance or work; and
(*d*) does not cause the fixation or reproduction to be used in an advertisement intended to sell or promote, as the case may be, a product, service, cause or institution.
(2) *Record keeping.* — The programming undertaking must record the dates of the making and destruction of all fixations and reproductions and any other prescribed information about the fixation or reproduction, and keep the record current.
(3) *Right of access by copyright owners.* — The programming undertaking must make the record referred to in subsection (2) available to owners of copyright in the works, sound recordings or performer's performances, or their representatives, within twenty-four hours after receiving a request.
(4) *Destruction.* — The programming undertaking must destroy the fixation or reproduction within thirty days after making it, unless
(*a*) the copyright owner authorizes its retention; or
(*b*) it is deposited in an archive, in accordance with subsection (6).
(5) *Royalties.* — Where the copyright owner authorizes the fixation or reproduction to be retained after the thirty days, the programming undertaking must pay any applicable royalty.
(6) *Archive.* — Where the programming undertaking considers a fixation or reproduction to be of an exceptional documentary character, the undertaking may, with the consent of an official archive, deposit it in the official archive and must notify the copyright owner, within thirty days, of the deposit of the fixation or reproduction.
(7) *Definition of "official archive".* — In subsection (6), "official archive" means the National Archives of Canada or any archive established under the law of a province for the preservation of the official archives of the province.
(8) *Application.* — This section does not apply where a licence is available from a collective society to make the fixation or reproduction of the performer's performance, work or sound recording.
(9) *Telecommunication by networks.* — A broadcasting undertaking, as defined in the *Broadcasting Act*, may make a single reproduction of a fixation or reproduction made by a programming undertaking and communicate it to the public by telecommunication, within the period referred to in subsection (4), if the broadcasting undertaking meets the conditions set out in subsection (1) and is part of a prescribed network that includes the programming undertaking.
(10) *Limitations.* — The reproduction and communication to the public by telecommunication must be made
(*a*) in accordance with subsections (2) to (6); and
(*b*) within thirty days after the day on which the programming undertaking made the fixation or reproduction.
(11) *Definition of "programming undertaking".* — In this section, "programming undertaking" means
(*a*) a programming undertaking as defined in the *Broadcasting Act*;
(*b*) a programming undertaking described in paragraph (*a*) that originates programs within a network, as defined in the *Broadcasting Act*; or
(*c*) a distribution undertaking as defined in the *Broadcasting Act*, in respect of the programs that it originates.
The undertaking must hold a broadcasting licence issued by the Canadian Radio-television and Telecommunications Commission under the *Broadcasting Act*.
[S.C. 1997, c. 24, s. 18(1)]

Pre-Recorded Recordings
30.9 (1) It is not an infringement of copyright for a broadcasting undertaking to reproduce in accordance with this section a sound recording, or a performer's performance or work that is embodied in a sound recording, solely for the purpose of transferring it to a format appropriate for broadcasting, if the undertaking
(*a*) owns the copy of the sound recording, performer's performance or work and that copy is authorized by the owner of the copyright;
(*b*) is authorized to communicate the sound recording, performer's performance or work to the public by telecommunication;
(*c*) makes the reproduction itself, for its own broadcasts;
(*d*) does not synchronize the reproduction with all or part of another recording, performer's performance or work; and
(*e*) does not cause the reproduction to be used in an advertisement intended to sell or promote, as the case may be, a product, service, cause or institution.
(2) *Record keeping.* — The broadcasting undertaking must record the dates of the making and destruction of all reproductions and any other prescribed information about the reproduction, and keep the record current.
(3) *Right of access by copyright owners.* — The broadcasting undertaking must make the record referred to in subsection (2) available to owners of copyright in the sound recordings, performer's performances or works, or their representatives, within twenty-four hours after receiving a request.

(4) *Destruction.* — The broadcasting undertaking must destroy the reproduction when it no longer possesses the sound recording or performer's performance or work embodied in the sound recording, or at the latest within thirty days after making the reproduction, unless the copyright owner authorizes the reproduction to be retained.
(5) *Royalty.* — If the copyright owner authorizes the reproduction to be retained, the broadcasting undertaking must pay any applicable royalty.
(6) *Applications.* — This section does not apply if a licence is available from a collective society to reproduce the sound recording, performer's performance or work.
(7) *Definition of "broadcasting undertaking".* — In this section, "broadcasting undertaking" means a broadcasting undertaking as defined in the *Broadcasting Act* that holds a broadcasting licence issued by the Canadian Radio-television and Telecommunications Commission under that Act.
[S.C. 1997, c. 24, s. 18(1)]

Retransmission

Interpretation
31. (1) In this section,
"retransmitter" does not include a person who uses Hertzian waves to retransmit a signal but does not perform a function comparable to that of a cable retransmission system;
"signal" means a signal that carries a literary, dramatic, musical or artistic work and is transmitted for free reception by the public by a terrestrial radio or terrestrial television station.
(2) *Retransmission of local signals.* — It is not an infringement of copyright to communicate to the public by telecommunication any literary, dramatic, musical or artistic work if
(*a*) the communication is a retransmission of a local or distant signal;
(*b*) the retransmission is lawful under the *Broadcasting Act*;
(*c*) the signal is retransmitted simultaneously and in its entirety, except as otherwise required or permitted by or under the laws of Canada; and
(*d*) in the case of the retransmission of a distant signal, the retransmitter has paid any royalties, and complied with any terms and conditions, fixed under this Act.
(3) *Regulations.* — The Governor in Council may make regulations defining "local signal" and "distant signal" for the purposes of this section. [S.C. 1988, c. 65, s. 63; 1997, c. 24, s. 16]

Persons with Perceptual Disabilities

Reproduction in Alternate Format
32. (1) It is not an infringement of copyright for a person, at the request of a person with a perceptual disability, or for a non-profit organization acting for his or her benefit, to
(*a*) make a copy or sound recording of a literary, musical, artistic or dramatic work, other than a cinematographic work, in a format specially designed for persons with a perceptual disability;
(*b*) translate, adapt or reproduce in sign language a literary or dramatic work, other than a cinematographic work, in a format specially designed for persons with a perceptual disability; or
(*c*) perform in public a literary or dramatic work, other than a cinematographic work, in sign language, either live or in a format specially designed for persons with a perceptual disability.
(2) *Limitation.* — Subsection (1) does not authorize the making of a large print book.
(3) *Limitation.* — Subsection (1) does not apply where the work or sound recording is commercially available in a format specially designed to meet the needs of any person referred to in that subsection, within the meaning of paragraph (*a*) of the definition "commercially available".
[S.C. 1997, c. 24, s. 19]

Statutory Obligations

No Infringement
32.1 (1) It is not an infringement of copyright for any person
(*a*) to disclose, pursuant to the *Access to Information Act*, a record within the meaning of that Act, or to disclose, pursuant to any like Act of the legislature of a province, like material;
(*b*) to disclose, pursuant to the *Privacy Act*, personal information within the meaning of that Act, or to disclose, pursuant to any like Act of the legislature of a province, like information;
(*c*) to make a copy of an object referred to in section 14 of the *Cultural Property Export and Import Act*, for deposit in an institution pursuant to a direction under that section; and
(*d*) to make a fixation or copy of a work or other subject-matter in order to comply with the *Broadcasting Act* or any rule, regulation or other instrument made under it.
(2) *Limitation.* — Nothing in paragraph (1)(*a*) or (*b*) authorizes a person to whom a record or information is disclosed to do anything that, by this Act, only the owner of the copyright in the record, personal information or like information, as the case may be, has a right to do.

(3) *Destruction of fixation or copy.* — Unless the *Broadcasting Act* otherwise provides, a person who makes a fixation or copy under paragraph (1)(*d*) shall destroy it immediately on the expiration of the period for which it must be kept pursuant to that Act, rule, regulation or other instrument. [S.C. 1997, c. 24, s. 19]

Miscellaneous

Permitted Acts

32.2 (1) It is not an infringement of copyright
(*a*) for an author of an artistic work who is not the owner of the copyright in the work to use any mould, cast, sketch, plan, model or study made by the author for the purpose of the work, if the author does not thereby repeat or imitate the main design of the work;
(*b*) for any person to reproduce, in a painting, drawing, engraving, photograph or cinematographic work
(i) an architectural work, provided the copy is not in the nature of an architectural drawing or plan, or
(ii) a sculpture or work of artistic craftsmanship or a cast or model of a sculpture or work of artistic craftsmanship, that is permanently situated in a public place or building;
(*c*) for any person to make or publish, for the purposes of news reporting or news summary, a report of a lecture given in public, unless the report is prohibited by conspicuous written or printed notice affixed before and maintained during the lecture at or about the main entrance of the building in which the lecture is given, and, except while the building is being used for public worship, in a position near the lecturer;
(*d*) for any person to read or recite in public a reasonable extract from a published work; or
(*e*) for any person to make or publish, for the purposes of news reporting or news summary, a report of an address of a political nature given at a public meeting.
(2) *Further permitted acts.* — It is not an infringement of copyright for a person to do any of the following acts without motive of gain at any agricultural or agricultural-industrial exhibition or fair that receives a grant from or is held by its directors under federal, provincial or municipal authority:
(*a*) the live performance in public of a musical work;
(*b*) the performance in public of a sound recording embodying a musical work or a performer's performance of a musical work; or
(*c*) the performance in public of a communication signal carrying
(i) the live performance in public of a musical work, or
(ii) a sound recording embodying a musical work or a performer's performance of a musical work.

(3) *Further permitted acts.* — No religious organization or institution, educational institution and no charitable or fraternal organization shall be held liable to pay any compensation for doing any of the following acts in furtherance of a religious, educational or charitable object:
(*a*) the live performance in public of a musical work;
(*b*) the performance in public of a sound recording embodying a musical work or a performer's performance of a musical work; or
(*c*) the performance in public of a communication signal carrying
(i) the live performance in public of a musical work, or
(ii) a sound recording embodying a musical work or a performer's performance of a musical work.
[S.C. 1997, c. 24, s. 19]

INTERPRETATION

No Right to Equitable Remuneration

32.3 For the purposes of sections 29 to 32.2, an act that does not infringe copyright does not give rise to a right to remuneration conferred by section 19. [S.C. 1997, c. 24, s. 19]

COMPENSATION FOR ACTS DONE BEFORE RECOGNITION OF COPYRIGHT OF PERFORMERS AND BROADCASTERS

Certain Rights and Interests Protected

32.4 (1) Notwithstanding section 27, where a person has, before the later of January 1, 1996 and the day on which a country becomes a WTO Member, incurred an expenditure or liability in connection with, or in preparation for, the doing of an act that would have infringed copyright under section 26 commencing on the later of those days, had that country been a WTO Member, any right or interest of that person that
(*a*) arises from or in connection with the doing of that act, and
(*b*) is subsisting and valuable on the later of those days is not prejudiced or diminished by reason only that that country has become a WTO Member, except as provided by an order of the Board made under subsection 78(3).
(2) *Compensation.* — Notwithstanding subsection (1), a person's right or interest that is protected by that subsection terminates if and when the owner of the copyright pays that person such compensation as is agreed to between the parties or, failing agreement, as is determined by the Board in accordance with section 78.
(3) *Limitation.* — Nothing in subsections (1) and (2) affects any right of a performer available in law or equity. [S.C. 1997, c. 24, s. 19]

Certain Rights and Interests Protected
32.5 (1) Notwithstanding section 27, where a person has, before the later of the coming into force of Part II and the day on which a country becomes a Rome Convention country, incurred an expenditure or liability in connection with, or in preparation for, the doing of an act that would have infringed copyright under section 15 or 21 commencing on the later of those days, had Part II been in force or had that country been a Rome Convention country, any right or interest of that person that
(*a*) arises from or in connection with the doing of that act, and
(*b*) is subsisting and valuable on the later of those days
is not prejudiced or diminished by reason only that Part II has come into force or that the country has become a Rome Convention country, except as provided by an order of the Board made under subsection 78(3).
(2) *Compensation.* — Notwithstanding subsection (1), a person's right or interest that is protected by that subsection terminates if and when the owner of the copyright pays that person such compensation as is agreed to between the parties or, failing agreement, as is determined by the Board in accordance with section 78.
(3) *Limitation.* — Nothing in subsections (1) and (2) affects any right of a performer available in law or equity. [S.C. 1997, c. 24, s. 19]

COMPENSATION FOR ACTS DONE BEFORE RECOGNITION OF COPYRIGHT OR MORAL RIGHTS

Certain Rights and Interests Protected
33. (1) Notwithstanding subsections 27(1), (2) and (4) and sections 27.1, 28.1 and 28.2, where a person has, before the later of January 1, 1996 and the day on which a country becomes a treaty country, incurred an expenditure or liability in connection with, or in preparation for, the doing of an act that would have infringed a copyright owner's copyright or an author's moral rights had that country been a treaty country, any right or interest of that person that
(*a*) arises from or in connection with the doing of that act, and
(*b*) is subsisting and valuable on the latest of those days
is not prejudiced or diminished by reason only that that country has become a treaty country, except as provided by an order of the Board made under subsection 78(3).
(2) *Compensation.* — Notwithstanding subsection (1), a person's right or interest that is protected by that subsection terminates, as against the copyright owner or author, if and when that copyright owner or the author, as the case may be, pays that person such compensation as is agreed to between the parties or, failing agreement, as is determined by the Board in accordance with section 78. [S.C. 1997, c. 24, s. 19]

PART IV
REMEDIES
[S.C. 1997, c. 24, s. 19]

Copyright
34. (1) Where copyright has been infringed, the owner of the copyright is, subject to this Act, entitled to all remedies by way of injunction, damages, accounts, delivery up and otherwise that are or may be conferred by law for the infringement of a right.
(1.01-1.03 and 1.1) [Repealed by S.C. 1997, c. 24, s. 20(1)]
(2) *Moral rights.* — In any proceedings for an infringement of a moral right of an author, the court may grant to the author or to the person who holds the moral rights by virtue of subsection 14.2(2) or (3), as the case may be, all remedies by way of injunction, damages, accounts, delivery up and otherwise that are or may be conferred by law for the infringement of a right.
(3) *Costs.* — The costs of all parties in any proceedings in respect of the infringement of a right conferred by this Act shall be in the discretion of the court.
(4) *Summary proceedings.* — The following proceedings may be commenced or proceeded with by way of application or action and shall, in the case of an application, be heard and determined without delay and in a summary way:
(*a*) proceedings for infringement of copyright or moral rights;
(*b*) proceedings taken under section 44.1, 44.2 or 44.4; and
(*c*) proceedings taken in respect of
(i) a tariff certified by the Board under Part VII or VIII, or
(ii) agreements referred to in section 70.12.
(5) *Practice and procedure.* — The rules of practice and procedure, in civil matters, of the court in which proceedings are commenced by way of application apply to those proceedings, but where those rules do not provide for the proceedings to be heard and determined without delay and in a summary way, the court may give such directions as it considers necessary in order to so provide.
(6) *Actions.* — The court in which proceedings are instituted by way of application may, where it considers it appropriate, direct that the proceeding be proceeded with as an action.
(7) *Meaning of "application".* — In this section, "application" means a proceeding that is commenced other than by way of a writ or statement of claim.
[S.C. 1997, c. 24, s. 20(1)]

Presumptions Respecting Copyright and Ownership
34.1 (1) In any proceedings for infringement of copyright in which the defendant puts in issue either the existence of the copyright or the title of the plaintiff thereto,
(*a*) copyright shall be presumed, unless the contrary is proved, to subsist in the work, performer's performance, sound recording or communication signal, as the case may be; and
(*b*) the author, performer, maker or broadcaster, as the case may be, shall, unless the contrary is proved, be presumed to be the owner of the copyright.
(2) *Where no grant registered.* — Where any matter referred to in subsection (1) is at issue and no assignment of the copyright, or licence granting an interest in the copyright, has been registered under this Act,
(*a*) if a name purporting to be that of
(i) the author of the work,
(ii) the performer of the performer's performance,
(iii) the maker of the sound recording, or
(iv) the broadcaster of the communication signal
is printed or otherwise indicated thereon in the usual manner, the person whose name is so printed or indicated shall, unless the contrary is proved, be presumed to be the author, performer, maker or broadcaster;
(*b*) if
(i) no name is so printed or indicated, or if the name so printed or indicated is not the true name of the author, performer, maker or broadcaster or the name by which that person is commonly known, and
(ii) a name purporting to be that of the publisher or owner of the work, performer's performance, sound recording or communication signal is printed or otherwise indicated thereon in the usual manner,
the person whose name is printed or indicated as described in subparagraph (ii) shall, unless the contrary is proved, be presumed to be the owner of the copyright in question; and
(*c*) if, on a cinematographic work, a name purporting to be that of the maker of the cinematographic work appears in the usual manner, the person so named shall, unless the contrary is proved, be presumed to be the maker of the cinematographic work.
[S.C. 1997, c. 24, s. 20(1)]

Liability for Infringement
35. (1) Where a person infringes copyright, the person is liable to pay such damages to the owner of the copyright as the owner has suffered due to the infringement and, in addition to those damages, such part of the profits that the infringer has made from the infringement and that were not taken into account in calculating the damages as the court considers just.

(2) *Proof of profits.* — In proving profits
(*a*) the plaintiff shall be required to prove only receipts or revenues derived from the infringement; and
(*b*) the defendant shall be required to prove every element of cost that the defendant claims.
[S.C. 1997, c. 24, s. 20(1)]

Protection of Separate Rights
36. (1) Subject to this section, the owner of any copyright, or any person or persons deriving any right, title or interest by assignment or grant in writing from the owner, may individually for himself or herself, as a party to the proceedings in his or her own name, protect and enforce any right that he or she holds, and, to the extent of that right, title and interest, is entitled to the remedies provided by this Act.
(2) *Where copyright owner to be made party.* — Where proceedings referred to in subsection (1) are taken by a person other than the copyright owner, the copyright owner must be made a party to those proceedings, except
(*a*) in respect of proceedings taken under section 44.1, 44.2 or 44.4;
(*b*) in respect of interlocutory proceedings unless the court is of the opinion that the interests of justice require the copyright owner to be a party; and
(*c*) in any other case, if the court is of the opinion that the interests of justice do not require the copyright owner to be a party.
(3) *Owner's liability for costs.* — A copyright owner who is made a party to proceedings pursuant to subsection (2) is not liable for any costs unless the copyright owner takes part in the proceedings.
(4) *Apportionment of damages, profits.* — Where a copyright owner is made a party to proceedings pursuant to subsection (2), the court, in awarding damages or profits, shall, subject to any agreement between the person who took the proceedings and the copyright owner, apportion the damages or profits referred to in subsection 35(1) between them as the court considers appropriate. [S.C. 1997, c. 24, s. 20(1)]

Concurrent Jurisdiction of Federal Court
37. The Federal Court has concurrent jurisdiction with provincial courts to hear and determine all proceedings, other than the prosecution of offences under section 42 and 43, for the enforcement of a provision of this Act or of the civil remedies provided by this Act. [S.C. 1997, c. 24, s. 20(1)]

Recovery of Possession of Copies, Plates

38. (1) Subject to subsection (2), the owner of the copyright in a work or other subject-matter may

(*a*) recover possession of all infringing copies of that work or other subject-matter, and of all plates used or intended to be used for the production of infringing copies, and

(*b*) take proceedings for seizure of those copies or plates before judgment if, under the law of Canada or of the province in which those proceedings are taken, a person is entitled to take such proceedings,

as if those copies or plates were the property of the copyright owner.

(2) *Powers of court.* — On application by

(*a*) a person from whom the copyright owner has recovered possession of copies or plates referred to in subsection (1),

(*b*) a person against whom proceedings for seizure before judgment of copies or plates referred to in subsection (1) have been taken, or

(*c*) any other person who has an interest in those copies or plates,

a court may order that those copies or plates be destroyed, or may make any other order that it considers appropriate in the circumstances.

(3) *Notice to interested persons.* — Before making an order under subsection (2), the court shall direct that notice be given to any person who has an interest in the copies or plates in question, unless the court is of the opinion that the interests of justice do not require such notice to be given.

(4) *Circumstances court to consider.* — In making an order under subsection (2), the court shall have regard to all the circumstances, including

(*a*) the proportion, importance and value of the infringing copy or plate, as compared to the substrate or carrier embodying it; and

(*b*) the extent to which the infringing copy or plate is severable from, or a distinct part of, the substrate or carrier embodying it.

(5) *Limitation.* — Nothing in this Act entitles the copyright owner to damages in respect of the possession or conversion of the infringing copies or plates. [S.C. 1997, c. 24, s. 20(1)]

Statutory Damages

38.1 (1) Subject to this section, a copyright owner may elect, at any time before final judgment is rendered, to recover, instead of damages and profits referred to in subsection 35(1), an award of statutory damages for all infringements involved in the proceedings, with respect to any one work or other subject-matter, for which any one infringer is liable individually, or for which any two or more infringers are liable jointly and severally, in a sum of not less than $500 or more than $20,000 as the court considers just.

(2) *Where defendant unaware of infringement.* — Where a copyright owner has made an election under subsection (1) and the defendant satisfies the court that the defendant was not aware and had no reasonable grounds to believe that the defendant had infringed copyright, the court may reduce the amount of the award to less than $500, but not less than $200.

(3) *Special case.* — Where

(*a*) there is more than one work or other subject-matter in a single medium, and

(*b*) the awarding of even the minimum amount referred to in subsection (1) or (2) would result in a total award that, in the court's opinion, is grossly out of proportion to the infringement,

the court may award, with respect to each work or other subject-matter, such lower amount than $500 or $200, as the case may be, as the court considers just.

(4) *Collective societies.* — Where the defendant has not paid applicable royalties, a collective society referred to in section 67 may only make an election under this section to recover, in lieu of any other remedy of a monetary nature provided by this Act, an award of statutory damages in a sum of not less than three and not more than ten times the amount of the applicable royalties, as the court considers just.

(5) *Factors to consider.* — In exercising its discretion under subsections (1) to (4), the court shall consider all relevant factors, including

(*a*) the good faith or bad faith of the defendant;

(*b*) the conduct of the parties before and during the proceedings; and

(*c*) the need to deter other infringements of the copyright in question.

(6) *No award.* — No statutory damages may be awarded against

(*a*) an educational institution or a person acting under its authority that has committed an act referred to in section 29.6 or 29.7 and has not paid any royalties or complied with any terms and conditions fixed under this Act in relation to the commission of the act;

(*b*) an educational institution, library, archive or museum that is sued in the circumstances referred to in section 38.2; or

(*c*) a person who infringes copyright under paragraph 27(2)(*e*) or section 27.1, where the copy in question was made with the consent of the copyright owner in the country where the copy was made.

(7) *Exemplary or punitive damages not affected.* — An election under subsection (1) does not affect any right that the copyright owner may have to exemplary or punitive damages.

[S.C. 1997, c. 24, s. 20(1)]

Maximum Amount That May Be Recovered
38.2 (1) An owner of copyright in a work who has not authorized a collective society to authorize its reprographic reproduction may recover, in proceedings against an educational institution, library, archive or museum that has reproduced the work, a maximum amount equal to the amount of royalties that would have been payable to the society in respect of the reprographic reproduction, if it were authorized, either
(*a*) under any agreement entered into with the collective society; or
(*b*) under a tariff certified by the Board pursuant to section 70.15.
(2) *Agreements with more than one collective society.* — Where agreements respecting reprographic reproduction have been signed with more than one collective society or where more than one tariff applies or where both agreements and tariffs apply, the maximum amount that the copyright owner may recover is the largest amount of the royalties provided for in any of those agreements or tariffs.
(3) *Application.* — Subsections (1) and (2) apply only where
(*a*) the collective society is entitled to authorize, or the tariff provides for the payment of royalties in respect of, the reprographic reproduction of that category of work; and
(*b*) copying of that general nature and extent is covered by the agreement or tariff.
[S.C. 1997, c. 24, s. 20(1)]

Injunction Only Remedy When Defendant Not Aware of Copyright
39. (1) Subject to subsection (2), in any proceedings for infringement of copyright, the plaintiff is not entitled to any remedy other than an injunction in respect of the infringement if the defendant proves that, at the date of the infringement, the defendant was not aware and had no reasonable ground for suspecting that copyright subsisted in the work or other subject-matter in question.
(2) *Exception where copyright registered.* — Subsection (1) does not apply if, at the date of the infringement, the copyright was duly registered under this Act.
[S.C. 1997, c. 24, s. 20(1)]

Wide Injunction
39.1 (1) When granting an injunction in respect of an infringement of copyright in a work or other subject-matter, the court may further enjoin the defendant from infringing the copyright in any other work or subject-matter if
(*a*) the plaintiff is the owner of the copyright or the person to whom an interest in the copyright has been granted by licence; and
(*b*) the plaintiff satisfies the court that the defendant will likely infringe the copyright in those other works or subject-matter unless enjoined by the court from doing so.
(2) *Application of injunction.* — An injunction granted under subsection (1) may extend to works or other subject-matter
(*a*) in respect of which the plaintiff was not, at the time the proceedings were commenced, the owner of the copyright or the person to whom an interest in the copyright has been granted by licence; or
(*b*) that did not exist at the time the proceedings were commenced.
[S.C. 1997, c. 24, s. 20(1)]

No Injunction in Case of a Building
40. (1) Where the construction of a building or other structure that infringes or that, if completed, would infringe the copyright in some other work has been commenced, the owner of the copyright is not entitled to obtain an injunction in respect of the construction of that building or structure or to order its demolition.
(2) *Certain remedies inapplicable.* — Sections 38 and 42 do not apply in any case in respect of which subsection (1) applies. [S.C. 1997, c. 24, s. 21]

Limitation Period for Civil Remedies
41. (1) Subject to subsection (2), a court may not award a remedy in relation to an infringement unless
(*a*) in the case where the plaintiff knew, or could reasonably have been expected to know, of the infringement at the time it occurred, the proceedings for infringement are commenced within three years after the infringement occurred; or
(*b*) in the case where the plaintiff did not know, and could not reasonably have been expected to know, of the infringement at the time it occurred, the proceedings for infringement are commenced within three years after the time when the plaintiff first knew, or could reasonably have been expected to know, of the infringement.
(2) *Restriction.* — The court shall apply the limitation period set out in paragraph (1)(*a*) or (*b*) only in respect of a party who pleads a limitation period.
[R.S.C. 1985, c. 10 (4th Supp.), s. 9, S.C. 1997, c. 24, s. 22(1)]

CRIMINAL REMEDIES
[S.C. 1997, c. 24, s. 23]

Offences and Punishment
42. (1) Every person who knowingly
(*a*) makes for sale or rental any infringing copy of a work or other subject-matter in which copyright subsists,

(*b*) sells or rents out, or by way of trade exposes or offers for sale or rental, an infringing copy of a work or other subject-matter in which copyright subsists,
(*c*) distributes infringing copies of a work or other subject-matter in which copyright subsists, either for the purpose of trade or to such an extent as to affect prejudicially the owner of the copyright,
(*d*) by way of trade exhibits in public an infringing copy of any work or other subject-matter in which copyright subsists, or
(*e*) imports for sale or rental into Canada any infringing copy of a work or other subject-matter in which copyright subsists [S.C. 1997, c. 24, s. 24(1)]
is guilty of an offence and liable
(*f*) on summary conviction, to a fine not exceeding twenty-five thousand dollars or to imprisonment for a term not exceeding six months, or to both, or
(*g*) on conviction on indictment, to a fine not exceeding one million dollars or to imprisonment for a term not exceeding five years, or to both.
[R.S.C. 1985, c. 10 (4th Supp.), s. 10]
(2) *Possession and performance offences and punishment.* — Every person who knowingly
(*a*) makes or possesses any plate that is specifically designed or adapted for the purpose of making infringing copies of any work or other subject-matter in which copyright subsists, or
(*b*) for private profit causes to be performed in public, without the consent of the owner of the copyright, any work or other subject-matter in which copyright subsists [S.C. 1997, c. 24, s. 24(2)]
is guilty of an offence and liable
(*c*) on summary conviction, to a fine not exceeding twenty-five thousand dollars or to imprisonment for a term not exceeding six months or to both, or
(*d*) on conviction on indictment, to a fine not exceeding one million dollars or to imprisonment for a term not exceeding five years or to both.
[R.S.C. 1985, c. 10 (4th Supp.), s. 10]
(3) *Power of court to deal with copies or plates.* — The court before which any proceedings under this section are taken may, on conviction, order that all copies of the work or other subject-matter that appear to it to be infringing copies, or all plates in the possession of the offender predominantly used for making infringing copies, be destroyed or delivered up to the owner of the copyright or otherwise dealt with as the court may think fit.
(4) *Limitation period.* — Proceedings by summary conviction in respect of an offence under this section may be instituted at any time within, but not later than, two years after the time when the offence was committed.

(5) *Parallel importation of books.* — No person may be prosecuted under this section for importing a book or dealing with an imported book in the manner described in section 27.1. [S.C. 1985, c. 10 (4th Supp.), s. 10; S.C. 1997, c. 24 s. 24(3)]

Infringement in Case of Dramatic, Operatic or Musical Work
43. (1) Any person who, without the written consent of the owner of the copyright or of the legal representative of the owner, knowingly performs or causes to be performed in public and for private profit the whole or any part, constituting an infringement of any dramatic or operatic work or musical composition in which copyright subsists in Canada is guilty of an offence and liable on summary conviction to a fine not exceeding two hundred and fifty dollars and, in the case of a second or subsequent offence, either to that fine or to imprisonment for a term not exceeding two months or to both.
(2) *Change or suppression of title or author's name.* — Any person who makes or causes to be made any change in or suppression of the title, or the name of the author, of any dramatic or operatic work or musical composition in which copyright subsists in Canada, or who makes or causes to be made any change in the work or composition itself without the written consent of the author or of his legal representative, in order that the work or composition may be performed in whole or in part in public for private profit, is guilty of an offence and liable on summary conviction to a fine not exceeding five hundred dollars and, in the case of a second or subsequent offence, either to that fine or to imprisonment for a term not exceeding four months or to both.

43.1 [Repealed by S.C. 1997, c. 24, s. 25]

IMPORTATION

Importation of Certain Copyright Works Prohibited
44. Copies made out of Canada of any work in which copyright subsists that if made in Canada would infringe copyright and as to which the owner of the copyright gives notice in writing to the Department of National Revenue that the owner desires that the copies not be so imported into Canada, shall not be so imported, and shall be deemed to be included in tariff item No. 9897.00.00 in the List of Tariff Provisions set out in the schedule to the *Customs Tariff* and section 136 of that Act applies accordingly. [R.S.C. 1985, c. 41 (3rd Supp.), s. 116; S.C. 1997, c. 36, s. 205]

Definitions
44.1 (1) In this section and sections 44.2 and 44.3, [S.C. 1997, c. 24, s. 27(1)]
"court" means the Federal Court or the superior court of a province;
"duties" has the same meaning as in the *Customs Act*;
"Minister" means the Minister of National Revenue;
"release" has the same meaning as in the *Customs Act*.
[S.C. 1993, c. 44, s.s. 66]
(2) *power of court.* — A court may make an order described in subsection (3) where the court is satisfied that
(*a*) copies of the work are about to be imported into Canada, or have been imported into Canada but have not yet been released;
(*b*) either
(i) copies of the work were made without the consent of the person who then owned the copyright in the country where the copies were made, or
(ii) the copies were made elsewhere than in a country to which this Act extends; and
(*c*) the copies would infringe copyright if they were made in Canada by the importer and the importer knows or should have known this.
[S.C. 1993, c. 44, s. 66, S.C. 1997, c. 24, s. 27(2)]
(2.1) *Who may apply.* — A court may make an order described in subsection (3) on application by the owner or exclusive licensee of copyright in a work in Canada. [S.C. 1997, c. 24, s. 27(2)]
(3) *Order of court.* — The order referred to in subsection (2) is an order
(*a*) directing the Minister
(i) to take reasonable measures, on the basis of information reasonably required by the Minister and provided by the applicant, to detain the work, and
(ii) to notify the applicant and the importer, forthwith after detaining the work, of the detention and the reasons therefor; and
(*b*) providing for such other matters as the court considers appropriate. [S.C. 1993, c. 44, s. 66]
(4) *How applications made.* — An application for an order made under subsection (2) may be made in an action or otherwise, and either on notice or *ex parte*, except that it must always be made on notice to the Minister. [S.C. 1993, c. 44, s. 66; S.C. 1997, c. 24, s. 27(3)]
(5) *Court may require security.* — Before making an order under subsection (2), the court may require the applicant to furnish security, in an amount fixed by the court,
(*a*) to cover duties, storage and handling charges, and any other amount that may become chargeable against the work; and

(*b*) to answer any damages that may by reason of the order be incurred by the owner, importer or consignee of the work. [S.C. 1993, c. 44, s. 66]
(6) *Application for directions.* — The Minister may apply to the court for directions in implementing an order made under subsection (2). [S.C. 1993, c. 44, s. 66]
(7) *Minister may allow inspection.* — The Minister may give the applicant or the importer an opportunity to inspect the detained work for the purpose of substantiating or refuting, as the case may be, the applicant's claim. [S.C. 1993, c. 44, s. 66]
(8) *Where applicant fails to commence an action.* — Unless an order made under subsection (2) provides otherwise, the Minister shall, subject to the *Customs Act* and to any other Act of Parliament that prohibits, controls or regulates the importation or exportation of goods, release the copies of the work without further notice to the applicant if, two weeks after the applicant has been notified under subparagraph (3)(*a*)(ii), the applicant has not notified the Minister that the applicant has commenced a proceeding for a final determination by the court of the issues referred to in paragraphs (2)(*b*) and (*c*). [S.C. 1993, c. 44, s. 66; S.C. 1997, c. 24, s. 27(4)]
(9) *Where court finds in plaintiff's favour.* — Where, in a proceeding commenced under this section, the court finds that the circumstances referred to in paragraphs (2)(*b*) and (*c*) existed, the court may make any order that it considers appropriate in the circumstances, including an order that the copies of the work be destroyed, or that they be delivered up to the plaintiff as the plaintiff's property absolutely. [S.C. 1993, c. 44, s. 66; S.C. 1997, c. 24, s. 27(4)]
(10) *Other remedies not affected.* — For greater certainty, nothing in this section affects any remedy available under any other provision of this Act or any other Act of Parliament. [S.C. 1993, c. 44, s. 66]

Importation of Books
44.2 (1) A court may, subject to this section, make an order described in subsection 44.1(3) in relation to a book where the court is satisfied that
(*a*) copies of the book are about to be imported into Canada, or have been imported into Canada but have not yet been released;
(*b*) copies of the book were made with the consent of the owner of the copyright in the book in the country where the copies were made, but were imported without the consent of the owner in Canada of the copyright in the book; and
(*c*) the copies would infringe copyright if they were made in Canada by the importer and the importer knows or should have known this.

(2) *Who may apply.* — A court may make an order described in subsection 44.1(3) in relation to a book on application by
(*a*) the owner of the copyright in the book in Canada;
(*b*) the exclusive licensee of the copyright in the book in Canada;
(*c*) the exclusive distributor of the book.
(3) *Limitation.* — Subsections (1) and (2) only apply where there is an exclusive distributor of the book and the acts described in those subsections take place in the part of Canada or in respect of the particular sector of the market for which the person is the exclusive distributor.
(4) *Application of certain provisions.* — Subsections 44.1(3) to (10) apply, with such modifications as the circumstances require, in respect of an order made under subsection (1).
[S.C 1994, c. 47, s. 66; S.C. 1997, c. 24, s. 28]

Limitation
44.3 No exclusive licensee of the copyright in a book in Canada, and no exclusive distributor of a book, may obtain an order under section 44.2 against another exclusive licensee of the copyright in that book in Canada or against another exclusive distributor of that book. [S.C. 1997, c. 24, s. 28]

Importation of Other Subject-Matter
44.4 Section 44.1 applies, with such modifications as the circumstances require, in respect of a sound recording, performer's performance or communication signal, where a fixation or a reproduction of a fixation of it
(*a*) is about to be imported into Canada, or has been imported into Canada but has not yet been released;
(*b*) either
(i) was made without the consent of the person who then owned the copyright in the sound recording, performer's performance or communication signal, as the case may be, in the country where the fixation or reproduction was made, or
(ii) was made elsewhere than in a country to which Part II extends; and
(*c*) would infringe the right of the owner of copyright in the sound recording, performer's performance or communication signal if it was made in Canada by the importer and the importer knows or should have known this.
[S.C. 1997, c. 24, s. 28]

Exceptions
45. (1) Notwithstanding anything in this Act, it is lawful for a person
(*a*) to import for their own use not more than two copies of a work or other subject-matter made with the consent of the owner of the copyright in the country where it was made;
(*b*) to import for use by a department of the Government of Canada or a province copies of a work or other subject-matter made with the consent of the owner of the copyright in the country where it was made;
(*c*) at any time before copies of a work or other subject-matter are made in Canada, to import any copies, except copies of a book, made with the consent of the owner of the copyright in the country where the copies were made, that are required for the use of a library, archive, museum or educational institution;
(*d*) to import, for the use of a library, archive, museum or educational institution, not more than one copy of a book that is made with the consent of the owner of the copyright in the country where the book was made; and
(*e*) to import copies, made with the consent of the owner of the copyright in the country where they were made, of any used books, except textbooks of a scientific, technical or scholarly nature for use within an educational institution in a course of instruction.
(2) *Satisfactory evidence.* — An officer of customs may, in the officer's discretion, require a person seeking to import a copy of a work or other subject-matter under this section to produce satisfactory evidence of the facts necessary to establish the person's right to import the copy.
[1994, c. 47, s. 67(4); S.C. 1997, c. 24, ss. 28 and 62(1)]

PART V
ADMINISTRATION
[S.C. 1997, c. 24, s. 29]

COPYRIGHT OFFICE

Copyright Office
46. The Copyright Office shall be attached to the Patent Office.

Powers of Commissioner and Registrar
47. The Commissioner of Patents shall exercise the powers conferred and perform the duties imposed on him by this Act under the direction of the Minister, and, in the absence of the Commissioner of Patents or if the Commissioner is unable to act, the Registrar of Copyrights or other officer temporarily appointed by the Minister may, as Acting Commissioner, exercise those powers and perform those duties under the direction of the Minister.

Registrar
48. There shall be a Registrar of Copyrights.

Register of Copyrights Certificates and Certified Copies

49. The Commissioner of Patents, the Registrar of Copyrights or an officer, clerk or employee of the Copyright Office may sign certificates and certified copies of the Register of Copyrights. [S.C. 1992, c. 1, s. 47; S.C. 1993, c. 15, s. 4]

Other Duties of Registrar

50. The Registrar of Copyrights shall perform such other duties in connection with the administration of this Act as may be assigned to him by the Commissioner of Patents.

51. [Repealed by S.C. 1992, c. 1, s. 48]

Control of Business and Officials

52. The Commissioner of Patents shall, subject to the Minister, oversee and direct the officers, clerks and employees of the Copyright Office, have general control of the business thereof and perform such other duties as are assigned to him by the Governor in Council.

Register to Be Evidence

53. (1) The Register of Copyrights is evidence of the particulars entered in it, and a copy of an entry in the Register is evidence of the particulars of the entry if it is certified by the Commissioner of Patents, the Registrar of Copyrights or an officer, clerk or employee of the Copyright Office as a true copy. [S.C. 1992, c. 1, s. 49; S.C. 1993, c. 15, s. 5(1)]
(2) *Owner of copyright.* — A certificate of registration of copyright is evidence that copyright subsists and that the person registered is the owner of the copyright. [S.C. 1997, c. 24, s. 30]
(2.1) *Assignee.* — A certificate of registration of an assignment of copyright is evidence that the right recorded on the certificate has been assigned and that the assignee registered is the owner of that right. [S.C. 1997, c. 24, s. 30]
(2.2) *Licensee.* — A certificate of registration of a licence granting an interest in a copyright is evidence that the interest recorded on the certificate has been granted and that the licensee registered is the holder of that interest. [S.C. 1997, c. 24, s. 30]
(3) *Admissibility.* — A certified copy or certificate appearing to have been issued under this section is admissible in all courts without proof of the signature or official character of the person appearing to have signed it. [S.C. 1993, c. 15, s. 5(2)]

REGISTRATION

Register of Copyrights

54. (1) The Minister shall cause to be kept at the Copyright Office a register to be called the Register of Copyrights in which may be entered
(*a*) the names or titles of works and of other subject-matter in which copyright subsists;
(*b*) the names and addresses of authors, performers, makers of sound recordings, broadcasters, owners of copyright, assignees of copyright, and persons to whom an interest in copyright has been granted by licence; and
(*c*) such other particulars as may be prescribed by regulation.
[S.C. 1997, c. 24, s. 31(1)]
(2) [Repealed by S.C. 1997, c. 24, s. 31(1)]
(3) *Single entry sufficient.* — In the case of an encyclopaedia, newspaper, review, magazine or other periodical work, or work published in a series of books or parts, it is not necessary to make a separate entry for each number or part, but a single entry for the whole work is sufficient.
(4) *Indices.* — There shall also be kept at the Copyright Office such indices of the Register established under this section as may be prescribed by regulation. [S.C. 1997, c. 24, s. 31(2)]
(5) *Inspection and extracts.* — The Register and indices established under this section shall at all reasonable times be open to inspection, and any person is entitled to make copies of or take extracts from the Register. [S.C. 1997, c. 24, s. 31(2)]
(6) *Former registration effective.* — Any registration made under the *Copyright Act*, chapter 70 of the Revised Statutes of Canada, 1906, has the same force and effect as if made under this Act.
(7) *Subsisting copyright.* — Any work in which copyright, operative in Canada, subsisted immediately before January 1, 1924 is registrable under this Act.

Copyright in Works

55. (1) Application for the registration of a copyright in a work may be made by or on behalf of the author of the work, the owner of the copyright in the work, an assignee of the copyright, or a person to whom an interest in the copyright has been granted by licence.
(2) *Application for registration.* — An application under subsection (1) must be filed with the Copyright Office, be accompanied by the fee prescribed by or determined under the regulations, and contain the following information:
(*a*) the name and address of the owner of the copyright in the work;

(*b*) a declaration that the applicant is the author of the work, the owner of the copyright in the work, an assignee of the copyright, or a person to whom an interest in the copyright has been granted by licence;
(*c*) the category of the work;
(*d*) the title of the work;
(*e*) the name of the author and, if the author is dead, the date of the author's death, if known;
(*f*) in the case of a published work, the date and place of the first publication; and
(*g*) any additional information prescribed by regulation. [S.C. 1997, c. 24, s. 32]

Copyright in Subject-Matter Other Than Works
56. (1) Application for the registration of a copyright in subject-matter other than a work may be made by or on behalf of the owner of the copyright in the subject-matter, an assignee of the copyright, or a person to whom an interest in the copyright has been granted by licence.
(2) *Application for registration.* — An application under subsection (1) must be filed with the Copyright Office, be accompanied by the fee prescribed by or determined under the regulations, and contain the following information:
(*a*) the name and address of the owner of the copyright in the subject-matter;
(*b*) a declaration that the applicant is the owner of the copyright in the subject-matter, an assignee of the copyright, or a person to whom an interest in the copyright has been granted by licence;
(*c*) whether the subject-matter is a performer's performance, a sound recording or a communication signal;
(*d*) the title, if any, of the subject-matter;
(*e*) the date of
(i) in the case of a performer's performance, its first fixation in a sound recording or, if it is not fixed in a sound recording, its first performance,
(ii) in the case of a sound recording, the first fixation, or
(iii) in the case of a communication signal, its broadcast; and
(*f*) any additional information prescribed by regulation. [S.C. 1993, c. 15, s. 6; S.C. 1997, c. 24, s. 32]

Recovery of Damages
56.1 Where a person purports to have the authority to apply for the registration of a copyright under section 55 or 56 on behalf of another person, any damage caused by a fraudulent or erroneous assumption of such authority is recoverable in any court of competent jurisdiction. [S.C. 1997, c. 24, s. 32]

Registration of Assignment or Licence
57. (1) The Registrar of Copyrights shall register an assignment of copyright, or a licence granting an interest in a copyright, on being furnished with
(*a*) the original instrument or a certified copy of it, or other evidence satisfactory to the Registrar of the assignment or licence; and
(*b*) the fee prescribed by or determined under the regulations.
[S.C. 1997, c. 24, s. 33(1)]
(2) [Repealed by S.C. 1992, c. 1, s. 51(l)]
(3) *When assignment or licence is void.* — Any assignment of copyright, or any licence granting an interest in a copyright, shall be adjudged void against any subsequent assignee or licensee for valuable consideration without actual notice, unless the prior assignment or licence is registered in the manner prescribed by this Act before the registering of the instrument under which the subsequent assignee or licensee claims. [S.C. 1997, c. 24, s. 33(2)]
(4) *Rectification of Register by the Court.* — The Federal Court may, on application of the Registrar of Copyrights or of any interested person, order the rectification of Register of Copyrights by
(*a*) the making of any entry wrongly omitted to be made in the Register,
(*b*) the expunging of any entry wrongly made in or remaining on the Register, or
(*c*) the correction of any error or defect in the Register, and any rectification of the Register under this subsection shall be retroactive from such date as the Court may order. [R.S.C. 1985, c. 10 (2nd Supp.), s. 64; S.C. 1992. c. 1, s. 51; S.C. 1993, c. 15, s. 7]

Execution of Instruments
58. (1) Any assignment of copyright, or any licence granting an interest in a copyright, may be executed, subscribed or acknowledged at any place in a treaty country or a Rome Convention country by the assignor, licensor or mortgagor, before any notary public, commissioner or other official or the judge of any court, who is authorized by law to administer oaths or perform notarial acts in that place, and who also subscribes their signature and affixes thereto or impresses thereon their official seal or the seal of the court of which they are such judge.
(2) *Execution of instruments.* — Any assignment of copyright, or any licence granting an interest in a copyright, may be executed, subscribed or acknowledged by the assignor, licensor or mortgagor, in any other foreign country before any notary public, commissioner or other official or the judge of any court of the foreign country, who is authorized to administer oaths or perform notarial

acts in that foreign country and whose authority shall be proved by the certificate of a diplomatic or consular officer of Canada performing their functions in that foreign country. [S.C. 1997, c. 24, s. 34(1)]

(3) *Seals to be evidence.* — The official seal or seal of the court or the certificate of a diplomatic or consular officer is evidence of the execution of the instrument, and the instrument with the seal or certificate affixed or attached thereto is admissible as evidence in any action or proceeding brought under this Act without further proof.

(4) *Other testimony.* — The provisions of subsections (1) and (2) shall be deemed to be permissive only, and the execution of any assignment of copyright, or any licence granting an interest in a copyright, may in any case be proved in accordance with the applicable rules of evidence. [S.C. 1997, c. 24, s. 34(2)]

FEES

Fees Regulations

59. The Governor in Council may make regulations
(*a*) prescribing fees, or the manner of determining fees, to be paid for anything required or authorized to be done in the administration of this Act; and
(*b*) prescribing the time and manner in which the fees must be paid.
[S.C. 1993, c. 15, s. 8]

PART VI
MISCELLANEOUS PROVISIONS
[S.C. 1997, c. 24, s. 35]

Substituted Right

60. (1) Where any person is immediately before January 1, 1924 entitled to any right in any work that is set out in column I of Schedule I, or to any interest in such a right, he is, as from that date, entitled to the substituted right set out in column II of that Schedule, or to the same interest in the substituted right, and to no other right or interest, and the substituted right shall subsist for the term for which it would have subsisted if this Act had been in force at the date when the work was made, and the work had been one entitled to copyright thereunder.

(2) *Where author has assigned the right.* — Where the author of any work in which any right that is set out in column I of Schedule I subsists on January 1, 1924 has, before that date, assigned the right or granted any interest therein for the whole term of the right, then at the date when, but for the passing of this Act, the right would have expired, the substituted right conferred by this section shall, in the absence of express agreement, pass to the author of the work, and any interest therein created before January 1, 1924 and then subsisting shall determine, but the person who immediately before the date at which the right would have expired was the owner of the right or interest is entitled at his option either
(*a*) on giving such notice as is hereinafter mentioned, to an assignment of the right or the grant of a similar interest therein for the remainder of the term of the right for such consideration as, failing agreement, may be determined by arbitration, or
(*b*) without any assignment or grant, to continue to reproduce or perform the work in like manner as theretofore subject to the payment, if demanded by the author within three years after the date at which the right would have expired, of such royalties to the author as, failing agreement, may be determined by arbitration, or, where the work is incorporated in a collective work and the owner of the right or interest is the proprietor of that collective work, without any payment,

and the notice referred to in paragraph (*a*) must be given not more than one year or less than six months before the date at which the right would have expired, and must be sent by registered post to the author, or, if he cannot with reasonable diligence be found, advertised in the *Canada Gazette*.

(3) *Definition of "author".* — For the purposes of this section, "author" includes the legal representatives of a deceased author.

(4) *Works made before this Act in force.* — Subject to this Act, copyright shall not subsist in any work made before January 1, 1924 otherwise than under and in accordance with the provisions of this section.
[S.C. 1993, c. 15, s. 9]

CLERICAL ERRORS
[S.C. 1997, C. 24, s. 36]

Clerical Errors Do Not Invalidate

61. Clerical errors in any instrument of record in the Copyright Office do not invalidate the instrument, but they may be corrected under the authority of the Registrar of Copyrights. [S.C. 1992, c. 1, s. 52; S.C. 1993, c. 15, s. 10]

REGULATIONS

Regulations

62. (1) The Governor in Council may make regulations
(*a*) prescribing anything that by this Act is to be prescribed by regulation; and
(*b*) generally for carrying out the purposes and provisions of this Act.
[S.C. 1997, c. 24, s. 37(2)]

(2) *Rights saved.* — The Governor in Council may make orders for altering, revoking or varying any order in council made under this Act, but any order made under this section does not affect prejudicially any rights or interests acquired or accrued at the date when the order comes into operation, and shall provide for the protection of those rights and interests.

INDUSTRIAL DESIGNS AND TOPOGRAPHIES
[S.C. 1997, c. 24, s. 38]

63. [Repealed by S.C. 1997, c. 24, s. 38]

Interpretation
64. (1) In this section and section 64.1,
"article" means any thing that is made by hand, tool or machine;
"design" means features of shape, configuration, pattern or ornament and any combination of those features that, in a finished article, appeal to and are judged solely by the eye;
"useful article" means an article that has a utilitarian function and includes a model of any such article;
"utilitarian function", in respect of an article, means a function other than merely serving as a substrate or carrier for artistic or literary matter.
(2) *Non-infringement re certain designs.* — Where copyright subsists in a design applied to a useful article or in an artistic work from which the design is derived and, by or under the authority of any person who owns the copyright in Canada or who owns the copyright elsewhere,
(*a*) the article is reproduced in a quantity of more than fifty, or
(*b*) where the article is a plate, engraving or cast, the article is used for producing more than fifty useful articles,
it shall not thereafter be an infringement of the copyright or the moral rights for anyone
(*c*) to reproduce the design of the article or a design not differing substantially from the design of the article by
(i) making the article, or
(ii) making a drawing or other reproduction in any material form of the article, or
(*d*) to do with an article, drawing or reproduction that is made as described in paragraph (*c*) anything that the owner of the copyright has the sole right to do with the design or artistic work in which the copyright subsists.
(3) *Exception.* — Subsection (2) does not apply in respect of the copyright or the moral rights in an artistic work in so far as the work is used as or for
(*a*) a graphic or photographic representation that is applied to the face of an article;
(*b*) a trade-mark or a representation thereof or a label;
(*c*) material that has a woven or knitted pattern or that is suitable for piece goods or surface coverings or for making wearing apparel;
(*d*) an architectural work that is a building or a model of a building; [S.C. 1993, c. 44, s. 68]
(*e*) a representation of a real or fictitious being, event or place that is applied to an article as a feature of shape, configuration, pattern or ornament;
(*f*) articles that are sold as a set, unless more than fifty sets are made; or
(*g*) such other work or article as may be prescribed by regulation. [S.C. 1997, c. 24, s. 39]
(4) *Idem.* — Subsections (2) and (3) apply only in respect of designs created after the coming into force of this subsection, and section 64 of this Act and the *Industrial Design Act*, as they read immediately before the coming into force of this subsection, as well as the rules made under them, continue to apply in respect of designs created before that coming into force. [R.S.C. 1985, c. 10 (4th Supp.), s. 11]

Non-Infringement Re Useful Article Features
64.1 (1) The following acts do not constitute an infringement of the copyright or moral rights in a work:
(*a*) applying to a useful article features that are dictated solely by a utilitarian function of the article;
(*b*) by reference solely to a useful article, making a drawing or other reproduction in any material form of any features of the article that are dictated solely by a utilitarian function of the article;
(*c*) doing with a useful article having only features described in paragraph (*a*), or with a drawing or reproduction made as described in paragraph (*b*), anything that the owner of the copyright has the sole right to do with the work; and
(*d*) using any method or principle of manufacture or construction.
(2) *Exception.* — Nothing in subsection (1) affects
(*a*) the copyright, or
(*b*) the moral rights, if any,
in any sound recording, cinematograph film or other contrivance by means of which a work may be mechanically reproduced or performed.
[R.S.C. 1985, c. 10 (4th Supp.), s. 11; S.C. 1997, c. 24, s. 40]

Application of Act to Topographies
64.2 (1) *Application of Act to topographies.* — This Act does not apply, and shall be deemed never to have applied, to any topography or to any design, however expressed, that is intended to generate all or part of a topography.

(2) *Computer programs.* — For greater certainty, the incorporation of a computer program into an integrated circuit product or the incorporation of a work unto such a computer program may constitute an infringement of the copyright or moral rights in a work.
(3) *Definitions.* — In this section, "topography" and "integrated circuit product" have the same meaning as in the *Integrated Circuit Topography Act*. [S.C. 1990, c. 37, s. 33]

65. [Repealed by S.C. 1993, c. 44, s. 69]

PART VII

COPYRIGHT BOARD AND COLLECTIVE ADMINISTRATION OF COPYRIGHT
[S.C. 1997, c. 24, s. 41]

COPYRIGHT BOARD

Establishment
66. (1) There is hereby established a Board, to be known as the Copyright Board, consisting of not more than five members, including a chairman and a vice-chairman, to be appointed by the Governor in Council.
(2) *Service.* — The members of the Board shall be appointed to serve either full-time or part-time.
(3) *Chairman.* — The chairman must be a judge, either sitting or retired, of a superior, county or district court.
(4) *Tenure.* — Each member of the Board shall hold office during good behaviour for a term not exceeding five years, but may be removed at any time by the Governor in Council for cause.
(5) *Re-appointment.* — A member of the Board is eligible to be re-appointed once only.
(6) *Prohibition.* — A member of the Board shall not be employed in the Public Service within the meaning of the *Public Service Staff Relations Act* during the member's term of office.
(7) *Members deemed public service employees.* — A full-time member of the Board, other than the chairman, shall be deemed to be employed in
(*a*) the Public Service for the purposes of the *Public Service Superannuation Act*; and
(*b*) the public service of Canada for the purposes of any regulations made pursuant to section 9 of the *Aeronautics Act*. [R.S.C. 1985, c. 10 (4th Supp.), s. 12]

Duties of Chairman
66.1 (1) The chairman shall direct the work of the Board and apportion its work among the members of the Board.

(2) *Absence or incapacity of chairman.* — If the chairman is absent or incapacitated or if the office of chairman is vacant, the vice-chairman has all the powers and functions of the chairman during the absence, incapacity or vacancy.
(3) *Duties of vice-chairman.* — The vice-chairman is the chief executive officer of the Board and has supervision over and direction of the Board and its staff. [R.S.C. 1985, c. 10 (4th Supp.), s. 12]

Remuneration and Expenses
66.2 The members of the Board shall be paid such remuneration as may be fixed by the Governor in Council and are entitled to be paid reasonable travel and living expenses incurred by them in the course of their duties under this Act while absent from their ordinary place of residence. [R.S.C. 1985, c. 10 (4th Supp.), s. 12]

Conflict of Interest Prohibited
66.3 (1) A member of the Board shall not, directly or indirectly, engage in any activity, have any interest in a business or accept or engage in any office or employment that is inconsistent with the member's duties.
(2) *Termination of conflict of interest.* — Where a member of the Board becomes aware that he is in a conflict of interest contrary to subsection (1), the member shall, within one hundred and twenty days, terminate the conflict or resign. [R.S.C. 1985, c. 10 (4th Supp.), s. 12]

Staff
66.4 (1) Such officers and employees as are necessary for the proper conduct of the work of the Board shall be appointed in accordance with the *Public Service Employment Act*.
(2) *Idem.* — The officers and employees referred to in subsection (1) shall be deemed to be employed in the Public Service for the purposes of the *Public Service Superannuation Act*.
(3) *Technical assistance.* — The Board may engage on a temporary basis the services of persons having technical or specialized knowledge to advise and assist in the performance of its duties and the Board may, in accordance with Treasury Board directives, fix and pay the remuneration and expenses of those persons. [R.S.C. 1985, c. 10 (4th Supp.), s. 12]

Concluding Matters After Membership Expires
66.5 (1) A member of the Board whose term expires may conclude the matters that the member has begun to consider.
(2) *Decisions.* — Matters before the Board shall be decided by a majority of the members of the Board and the presiding member shall have a second vote in the case of a tie. [R.S.C. 1985, c. 10 (4th Supp.), s.12]

Interim Decisions

66.51 The Board may, on application, make an interim decision. [R.S.C. 1985, c. 10 (4th Supp.), s. 12]

Variation of Decisions

66.52 A decision of the Board respecting royalties or their related terms and conditions that is made under subsection 68(3), sections 68.1 or 70.15 or subsections 70.2(2), 70.6(1), 73(1) or 83(8) may, on application, be varied by the Board if, in its opinion, there has been a material change in circumstances since the decision was made. [R.S.C. 1985, c. 10 (4th Supp.), s. 12; S.C. 1998, c. 65, s. 64; S.C. 1997, c. 24, s. 42]

Regulations

66.6 (1) The Board may, with the approval of the Governor in Counsil, make regulations governing

(*a*) the practice and procedure in respect of the Board's hearings, including the number of members of the Board that constitutes a quorum;

(*b*) the time and manner in which applications and notices must be made or given;

(*c*) the establishment of forms for the making or giving of applications and notices; and

(*d*) the carrying out of the work of the Board, the management of its internal affairs and the duties of its officers and employees.

(2) *Publication of proposed regulations.* — A copy of each regulation that the Board proposes to make under subsection (1) shall be published in the *Canada Gazette* at least sixty days before the proposed effective date thereof and a reasonable opportunity shall be given to interested persons to make representations with respect thereto.

(3) *Exception.* — No proposed regulation that has been published pursuant to subsection (2) need again be published under that subsection, whether or not it has been altered as a result of representations made with respect thereto. [R.S.C. 1985, c. 10 (4th Supp.), s. 12]

General Powers, etc.

66.7 (1) The Board has, with respect to the attendance, swearing and examination of witnesses, the production and inspection of documents, the enforcement of its decisions and other matters necessary or proper for the due exercise of its jurisdiction, all such powers, rights and privileges as are vested in a superior court of record.

(2) *Enforcement of decisions.* — Any decision of the Board may, for the purposes of its enforcement, be made an order of the Federal Court or of any superior court and is enforceable in the same manner as an order thereof.

(3) *Procedure.* — To make a decision of the Board an order of a court, the usual practice and procedure of the court in such matters may be followed or a certified copy of the decision may be filed with the registrar of the court and thereupon the decision becomes an order of the court.

(4) *Effect of variation of decision.* — Where a decision of the Board that has been made an order of a court is varied by a subsequent decision of the Board, the order of the court shall be deemed to have been varied accordingly and the subsequent decision may, in the same manner, be made an order of the court. [R.S.C.1985, c. 10 (4th Supp.), s. 12]

Distribution, Publication of Notices

66.71 Independently of any other provision of this Act relating to the distribution or publication of information or documents by the Board, the Board may at any time cause to be distributed or published, in any manner and on any terms and conditions that it sees fit, any notice that it sees fit to be distributed or published. [S.C. 1997, c. 24, s. 43]

Studies

66.8 The Board shall conduct such studies with respect to the exercise of its powers as are requested by the Minister. [R.S.C. 1985, c. 10 (4th Supp.), s. 12]

Report

66.9 (1) The Board shall, not later than August 31 each year, submit to the Governor in Council through the Minister an annual report on the Board's activities for the preceding year describing briefly the applications made to the Board, the Board's decisions and any other matter that the Board considers relevant.

(2) *Tabling.* — The Minister shall cause a copy of each annual report to be laid before each House of Parliament on any of the first fifteen days on which that House is sitting after the Minister receives the report. [R.S.C. 1985, c. 10 (4th Supp.), s. 12]

Regulations

66.91 The Governor in Council may make regulations issuing policy directions to the Board and establishing general criteria to be applied by the Board or to which the Board must have regard

(*a*) in establishing fair and equitable royalties to be paid pursuant to this Act; and

(*b*) in rendering its decisions in any matter within its jurisdiction.
[S.C. 1997, c. 24, s. 44]

COLLECTIVE ADMINISTRATION OF PERFORMING RIGHTS AND OF COMMUNICATION RIGHTS
[S.C. 1997, c. 24, s. 45]

Public Access to Repertoires
67. Each collective society that carries on
(*a*) the business of granting licences or collecting royalties for the performance in public of musical works, dramatico-musical works, performer's performances of such works, or sound recordings embodying such works, or
(*b*) the business of granting licences or collecting royalties for the communication to the public by telecommunication of musical works, dramatico-musical works, performer's performances of such works, or sound recordings embodying such works, other than the communication of musical works or dramatico-musical works in a manner described in subsection 31(2),
must answer within a reasonable time all reasonable requests from the public for information about its repertoire of works, performer's performances or sound recordings, that are in current use. [S.C. 1997, c. 24, s. 45]

Filing of Proposed Tariffs
67.1 (1) Each collective society referred to in section 67 shall, on or before the March 31 immediately before the date when its last tariff approved pursuant to subsection 68(3) expires, file with the Board a proposed tariff, in both official languages, of all royalties to be collected by the collective society.
(2) *Where no previous tariff.* — A collective society referred to in subsection (1) in respect of which no tariff has been approved pursuant to subsection 68(3) shall file with the Board its proposed tariff, in both official languages, of all royalties to be collected by it, on or before the March 31 immediately before its proposed effective date. [S.C. 1993, c. 23, s. 3; S.C. 1997, c. 24, s. 45]
(3) *Effective period of tariffs.* — A proposed tariff must provide that the royalties are to be effective for periods of one or more calendar years.
(4) *Prohibition of enforcement.* — Where a proposed tariff is not filed with respect to the work, performer's performance or sound recording in question, no action may be commenced, without the written consent of the Minister, for
(*a*) the infringement of the rights, referred to in section 3, to perform in public or to communicate to the public by telecommunication, the work, performer's performance or sound recording; or
(*b*) the recovery of royalties referred to in section 19.
[R.S.C. 1985, c. 10 (4th Supp.), s. 12; S.C. 1993, c. 23, s. 3; S.C. 1997, c. 24, s. 45]

(5) *Publication of proposed tariffs.* — As soon as practicable after the receipt of a proposed tariff filed pursuant to subsection (1), the Board shall publish it in the *Canada Gazette* and shall give notice that, within sixty days after the publication of the tariff, prospective users or their representatives may file written objections to the tariff with the Board. [S.C. 1997, c. 24, s. 45]

67.2 [Repealed by S.C. 1997, c. 24, s. 45]

67.3 [Repealed by S.C. 1997, c. 24, s. 45]

Board to Consider Proposed Tariffs and Objections
68. (1) The Board shall, as soon as practicable, consider a proposed tariff and any objections thereto referred to in subsection 67.1(5) or raised by the Board, and
(*a*) send to the collective society concerned a copy of the objections so as to permit it to reply; and
(*b*) send to the persons who filed the objections a copy of any reply thereto. [R.S.C. 1985, c. 10 (4th Supp.), s. 12; S.C. 1997, c. 24, s. 45]
(2) *Criteria and factors.* — In examining a proposed tariff for the performance in public or the communication to the public by telecommunication of performer's performances of musical works, or of sound recordings embodying such performer's performances, the Board
(*a*) shall ensure that
(i) the tariff applies in respect of performer's performances and sound recordings only in the situations referred to in subsections 20(1) and (2),
(ii) the tariff does not, because of linguistic and content requirements of Canada's broadcasting policy set out in section 3 of the *Broadcasting Act*, place some users that are subject to that Act at a greater financial disadvantage than others, and
(iii) the payment of royalties by users pursuant to section 19 will be made in a single payment; and
(*b*) may take into account any factor that it considers appropriate.
(3) *Certification.* — The Board shall certify the tariffs as approved, with such alterations to the royalties and to the terms and conditions related thereto as the Board considers necessary, having regard to
(*a*) any objections to the tariffs under subsection 67.1(5); and
(*b*) the matters referred to in subsection (2).
(4) *Publication of approved tariffs.* — The Board shall
(*a*) publish the approved tariffs in the *Canada Gazette* as soon as practicable; and
(*b*) send a copy of each approved tariff, together with the reasons for the Board's decision, to each collective society that filed a proposed tariff and to any person who filed an objection.
[S.C. 1997, c. 24, s. 45]

Special and Transitional Royalty Rates
68.1 (1) Notwithstanding the tariffs approved by the Board under subsection 68(3) for the performance in public or the communication to the public by telecommunication of performer's performances of musical works, or of sound recordings embodying such performer's performances,
(*a*) wireless transmission systems, except community systems and public transmission systems, shall pay royalties as follows:
(i) in respect of each year, $100 on the first 1.25 million dollars of annual advertising revenues, and
(ii) on any portion of annual advertising revenues exceeding 1.25 million dollars,
(*A*) for the first year following the coming into force of this section, thirty-three and one third per cent of the royalties set out in the approved tariff for that year,
(*B*) for the second year following the coming into force of this section, sixty-six and two thirds per cent of the royalties set out in the approved tariff for that year, and
(*C*) for the third year following the coming into force of this section, one hundred per cent of the royalties set out in the approved tariff for that year;
(*b*) community systems shall pay royalties of $100 in respect of each year; and
(*c*) public transmission systems shall pay royalties, in respect of each of the first three years following the coming into force of this section, as follows:
(i) for the first year following the coming into force of this section, thirty-three and one third per cent of the royalties set out in the approved tariff for that year,
(ii) for the second year following the coming into force of this section, sixty-six and two thirds per cent of the royalties set out in the approved tariff for that year, and
(iii) for the third year following the coming into force of this section, one hundred per cent of the royalties set out in the approved tariff for that year.
(2) *Effect of paying royalties.* — The payment of the royalties set out in subsection (1) fully discharges all liabilities of the system in question in respect of the approved tariffs.
(3) *Definition of "advertising revenues".* — The Board may, by regulation, define "advertising revenues" for the purposes of subsection (1).
(4) *Preferential royalty rates.* — The Board shall, in certifying a tariff as approved under subsection 68(3), ensure that there is a preferential royalty rate for small cable transmission systems.
(5) *Regulations.* — The Governor in Council may make regulations defining "small cable transmission system", "community system", "public transmission system" and "wireless transmission system" for the purposes of this section.
[S.C. 1993, c. 23, s. 4; S.C. 1997, c. 24, s. 45]

Effect of Fixing Royalties
68.2 (1) Without prejudice to any other remedies available to it, a collective society may, for the period specified in its approved tariff, collect the royalties specified in the tariff and, in default of their payment, recover them in a court of competent jurisdiction.
(2) *Proceedings barred if royalties tendered or paid.* — No proceedings may be brought for
(*a*) the infringement of the right to perform in public or the right to communicate to the public by telecommunication, referred to in section 3, or
(*b*) the recovery of royalties referred to in section 19 against a person who has paid or offered to pay the royalties specified in an approved tariff.
(3) *Continuation of rights.* — Where a collective society files a proposed tariff in accordance with subsection 67.1(1),
(*a*) any person entitled to perform in public or communicate to the public by telecommunication those works, performer's performances or sound recordings pursuant to the previous tariff may do so, even though the royalties set out therein have ceased to be in effect, and
(*b*) the collective society may collect the royalties in accordance with the previous tariff, until the proposed tariff is approved.
[R.S.C. 1985, c. 10 (4th Supp.), s. 12; S.C. 1993, c. 23, ss. 4-5; S.C. 1997, c. 24, s. 45]

PUBLIC PERFORMANCES IN PLACES OTHER THAN THEATRES
[S.C. 1997, c. 24, s. 45]

69. (1) [Repealed by R.S.C. 1985, c. 10 (4th Supp.), s. 14(1)]
(2) *Radio performances in places other than theatres.* — In respect of public performances by means of any radio receiving set in any place other than a theatre that is ordinarily and regularly used for entertainment to which an admission charge is made, no royalties shall be collectable from the owner or user of the radio receiving set, but the Board shall, in so far as possible, provide for the collection in advance from radio broadcasting stations of royalties appropriate to the condition produced by the provisions of this subsection and shall fix the amount of the same. [S.C. 1993, c. 44, s. 73(1)]
(3) *Expenses to be taken into account.* — In fixing royalties pursuant to subsection (2), the Board shall take into account all expenses of collection and other outlays, if any, saved or saveable by, for or on behalf of the owner of the copyright or performing right concerned or his agents, in consequence of subsection (2). [S.C. 1993, c. 44, s. 73(2)]
(4) [Repealed by R.S.C. 1985, c. 10 (4th Supp.), s. 14(3)]

70. [Repealed by R.S.C. 1985, c. 10 (4th Supp.), s. 15]

COLLECTIVE ADMINISTRATION IN RELATION TO RIGHTS UNDER SECTIONS 3, 15, 18 AND 21
[S.C. 1997, c. 24, s. 46]

Collective Societies

Collective Societies
70.1 Sections 70.11 to 70.6 apply in respect of a collective society that operates
(*a*) a licensing scheme, applicable in relation to a repertoire of works of more than one author, pursuant to which the society sets out the classes of uses for which and the royalties and terms and conditions on which it agrees to authorize the doing of an act mentioned in section 3 in respect of those works;
(*a.1*) a licensing scheme, applicable in relation to a repertoire of performer's performances of more than one performer, pursuant to which the society sets out the classes of uses for which and the royalties and terms and conditions on which it agrees to authorize the doing of an act mentioned in section 15 in respect of those performer's performances;
(*b*) a licensing scheme, applicable in relation to a repertoire of sound recordings of more than one maker, pursuant to which the society sets out the classes of uses for which and the royalties and terms and conditions on which it agrees to authorize the doing of an act mentioned in section 18 in respect of those sound recordings; or
(*c*) a licensing scheme, applicable in relation to a repertoire of communication signals of more than one broadcaster, pursuant to which the society sets out the classes of uses for which and the royalties and terms and conditions on which it agrees to authorize the doing of an act mentioned in section 21 in respect of those communication signals.
[R.S.C. 1985, c. 10 (4th Supp), s. 16; S.C. 1997, c. 24, s. 46]

Public Information
70.11 A collective society referred to in section 70.1 must answer within a reasonable time all reasonable requests from the public for information about its repertoire of works, performer's performances, sound recordings or communication signals. [S.C. 1997, c. 24, s. 46]

Tariff or Agreement
70.12 A collective society may, for the purpose of setting out by licence the royalties and terms and conditions relating to classes of uses,
(*a*) file a proposed tariff with the Board; or
(*b*) enter into agreements with users.
[S.C. 1997, c. 24, s. 46]

Tariffs

Filing of Proposed Tariffs
70.13 (1) Each collective society referred to in section 70.1 may, on or before the March 31 immediately before the date when its last tariff approved pursuant to subsection 70.15(1) expires, file with the Board a proposed tariff, in both official languages, of royalties to be collected by the collective society for issuing licences.
(2) *Where no previous tariff.* — A collective society referred to in subsection (1) in respect of which no tariff has been approved pursuant to subsection 70.15(1) shall file with the Board its proposed tariff, in both official languages, of all royalties to be collected by it for issuing licences, on or before the March 31 immediately before its proposed effective date.
[S.C. 1997, c. 24, s. 46]

Application of Certain Provisions
70.14 Where a proposed tariff is filed under section 70.13, subsections 67.1(3) and (5) and subsection 68(1) apply, with such modifications as the circumstances require. [S.C. 1997, c. 24, s. 46]

Certification
70.15 (1) The Board shall certify the tariffs as approved, with such alterations to the royalties and to the terms and conditions related thereto as the Board considers necessary, having regard to any objections to the tariffs.
(2) *Application of certain provisions.* — Where a tariff is approved under subsection (1), subsections 68(4) and 68.2(1) apply, with such modifications as the circumstances require.
[S.C. 1997, c. 24, s. 46]

Distribution, Publication of Notices
70.16 Independently of any other provision of this Act relating to the distribution or publication of information or documents by the Board, the Board shall notify persons affected by a proposed tariff, by
(*a*) distributing or publishing a notice, or
(*b*) directing another person or body to distribute or publish a notice,
in such manner and on such terms and conditions as the Board sees fit. [S.C. 1997, c. 24, s. 46]

Prohibition of Enforcement
70.17 Subject to section 70.19, no proceedings may be brought for the infringement of a right referred to in section 3, 15, 18 or 21 against a person who has paid or offered to pay the royalties specified in an approved tariff. [S.C. 1997, c. 24, s. 46]

Continuation of Rights
70.18 Subject to section 70.19, where a collective society files a proposed tariff in accordance with section 70.13,
(*a*) any person authorized by the collective society to do an act referred to in section 3, 15, 18 or 21, as the case may be, pursuant to the previous tariff may do so, even though the royalties set out therein have ceased to be in effect, and
(*b*) the collective society may collect the royalties in accordance with the previous tariff,
until the proposed tariff is approved. [S.C. 1997, c. 24, s. 46]

Where Agreement Exists
70.19 If there is an agreement mentioned in paragraph 70.12(*b*), sections 70.17 and 70.18 do not apply in respect of the matters covered by the agreement. [S.C. 1997, c. 24, s. 46]

Agreement
70.191 An approved tariff does not apply where there is an agreement between a collective society and a person authorized to do an act mentioned in section 3, 15, 18 or 21, as the case may be, if the agreement is in effect during the period covered by the approved tariff. [S.C. 1997, c. 24, s. 46]

Fixing of Royalties in Individual Cases

Application to Fix Amount of Royalty, etc.
70.2 (1) Where a collective society and any person not otherwise authorized to do an act mentioned in section 3, 15, 18 or 21, as the case may be, in respect of the works, sound recordings or communication signals included in the collective society's repertoire are unable to agree on the royalties to be paid for the right to do the act or on their related terms and conditions, either of them or a representative of either may, after giving notice to the other, apply to the Board to fix the royalties and their related terms and conditions.
(2) *Fixing royalties, etc.* — The Board may fix the royalties and their related terms and conditions in respect of a licence during such period of not less than one year as the Board may specify and, as soon as practicable after rendering its decision, the Board shall send a copy thereof, together with the reasons therefor, to the collective society and the person concerned or that person's representative. [R.S.C. 1985, c. 10 (4th Supp.), s. 16; S.C. 1997, c. 24, s. 46]

Agreement
70.3 (1) The Board shall not proceed with an application under section 70.2 where a notice is filed with the Board that an agreement touching the matters in issue has been reached.
(2) *Idem.* — An agreement referred to in subsection (1) is effective during the year following the expiration of the previous agreement, if any, or of the last period specified under subsection 70.2(2). [R.S.C. 1985, c. 10 (4th Supp.), s. 16]

Effect of Board Decision
70.4 Where any royalties are fixed for a period pursuant to subsection 70.2(2), the person concerned may, during the period, subject to the related terms and conditions fixed by the Board and to the terms and conditions set out in the scheme and on paying or offering to pay the royalties, do the act with respect to which the royalties and their related terms and conditions are fixed and the collective society may, without prejudice to any other remedies available to it, collect the royalties or, in default of their payment, recover them in a court of competent jurisdiction. [R.S.C. 1985, c. 10 (4th Supp.), s. 16; S.C. 1997, c. 24, s. 47]

Examination of Agreements
[S.C. 1997, c. 24, s. 47]

Definition of "Director"
70.5 (1) For the purposes of this section and section 70.6 "Director" means the Director of Investigation and Research appointed under the *Competition Act*.
(2) *Filing agreement with the Board.* — Where a collective society concludes an agreement to grant a licence authorizing a person to do an act mentioned in section 3, 15, 18 or 21, as the case may be, the collective society or the person may file a copy of the agreement with the Board within fifteen days after it is concluded. [S.C. 1997, c. 24, s. 48(1)]
(3) *Idem.* — Section 45 of the *Competition Act* does not apply in respect of any royalties or related terms and conditions arising under an agreement filed in accordance with subsection (2).
(4) *Access by Director.* — The Director may have access to the copy of an agreement filed in accordance with subsection (2).
(5) *Request for examination.* — Where the Director considers that an agreement filed in accordance with subsection (2) is contrary to the public interest, the Director may, after advising the parties concerned, request the Board to examine the agreement. [R.S.C. 1985, c. 10 (4th Supp.), s. 16]

Examination and Fixing of Royalty

70.6 (1) The Board shall, as soon as practicable, consider a request by the Director to examine an agreement and the Board may, after giving the Director and the parties concerned an opportunity to present their arguments, alter the royalties and any related terms and conditions arising under the agreement, in which case section 70.4 applies with such modifications as the circumstances require.

(2) *Idem.* — As soon as practicable after rendering its decision, the Board shall send a copy thereof, together with the reasons therefor, to the parties concerned and to the Director. [R.S.C. 1985, c. 10 (4th Supp.), s. 16]

ROYALTIES IN PARTICULAR CASES
[S.C. 1997, c. 24, s. 50]

70.61 - 70.67, 70.7, 70.8 [Repealed by S.C. 1997, c. 24, s. 50]

Filing of Proposed Tariffs

71. (1) Each collective society that carries on the business of collecting royalties referred to in subsection 29.6(2), 29.7(2) or (3) or paragraph 31(2)(*d*) shall file with the Board a proposed tariff, but no other person may file any such tariff.

(2) *Times for filing.* — A proposed tariff must be
(*a*) in both official languages; and
(*b*) filed on or before the March 31 immediately before the date that the approved tariff ceases to be effective.

(3) *Where no previous tariff.* — A collective society in respect of which no proposed tariff has been certified pursuant to paragraph 73(1)(*d*) shall file its proposed tariff on or before the March 31 immediately before its proposed effective date.

(4) *Effective period of tariffs.* — A proposed tariff must provide that the royalties are to be effective for periods of one or more calendar years.
 [S.C. 1988, c. 65, s. 65; S.C. 1997, c. 24, s. 50]

Publication of Proposed Tariffs

72. (1) As soon as practicable after the receipt of a proposed tariff filed pursuant to section 71, the Board shall publish it in the *Canada Gazette* and shall give notice that, within sixty days after the publication of the tariff, prospective retransmitters, educational institutions, persons with perceptual disabilities or their representatives may file written objections to the tariff with the Board.

(2) *Board to consider proposed tariffs and objections.* — The Board shall, as soon as practicable, consider a proposed tariff and any objections thereto referred to in subsection (1) or raised by the Board, and
(*a*) send to the collective society concerned a copy of the objections so as to permit it to reply; and
(*b*) send to the persons who filed the objections a copy of any reply thereto.
[S.c. 1988, c. 65, s. 65; S.C. 1997, c. 24, s. 50]

Certification

73. (1) On the conclusion of its consideration of proposed tariffs, the Board shall
(*a*) establish
(i) a manner of determining the royalties to be paid by retransmitters, educational institutions and any person making more than one copy or sound recording of a literary, musical or dramatic work in order to accommodate the needs of a person with a perceptual disability, and
(ii) such terms and conditions related to those royalties as the Board considers appropriate;
(*b*) determine the portion of the royalties referred to in paragraph (*a*) that is to be paid to each collective society;
(*c*) vary the tariffs accordingly; and
(*d*) certify the tariffs as the approved tariffs, whereupon the tariffs become for the purposes of this Act the approved tariffs.

(2) *No discrimination.* — For greater certainty, the Board, in establishing a manner of determining royalties under paragraph (1)(*a*) or in apportioning them under paragraph (1)(*b*), may not discriminate between owners of copyright on the ground of their nationality or residence.

(3) *Publication of approved tariffs.* — The Board shall publish the approved tariffs in the *Canada Gazette* as soon as practicable and send a copy of each approved tariff, together with the reasons for the Board's decision, to each collective society that filed a proposed tariff and to any person who filed an objection.
[S.C. 1988, c. 65, s. 65; S.C. 1997, c. 24, s. 50]

Special Case

74. (1) The Board shall, in establishing a manner of determining royalties under paragraph 73(1)(*a*), ensure that there is a preferential rate for small retransmission systems.

(2) *Regulations.* — The Governor in Council may make regulations defining "small retransmission systems" for the purpose of subsection (1).
[S.C. 1988, c. 65, s. 65; S.C. 1997, c. 24, s. 50]

Effect of Fixing Royalties

75. Without prejudice to any other remedies available to it, a collective society may, for the period specified in its approved tariff, collect the royalties specified in the tariff and, in default of their payment, recover them in a court of competent jurisdiction. [S.C. 1988, c. 65, s. 65; S.C. 1997, c. 24, s. 50]

Claims by Non-Members
76. (1) An owner of copyright who does not authorize a collective society to collect, for that person's benefit, royalties referred to in paragraph 31(2)(*d*) is, if the work is communicated to the public by telecommunication during a period when an approved tariff that is applicable to that kind of work is effective, entitled to be paid those royalties by the collective society that is designated by the Board, of its own motion or on application, subject to the same conditions as those to which a person who has so authorized that collective society is subject.
(2) *Royalties that may be recovered.* — An owner of copyright who does not authorize a collective society to collect, for that person's benefit, royalties referred to in subsection 29.6(2) or 29.7(2) or (3) is, if such royalties are payable during a period when an approved tariff that is applicable to that kind of work or other subject-matter is effective, entitled to be paid those royalties by the collective society that is designated by the Board, of its own motion or on application, subject to the same conditions as those to which a person who has so authorized that collective society is subject.
(3) *Exclusion of remedies.* — The entitlement referred to in subsections (1) and (2) is the only remedy of the owner of the copyright for the payment of royalties for the communication, making of the copy or sound recording or performance in public, as the case may be.
(4) *Regulations.* — The Board may, for the purposes of this section,
(*a*) require a collective society to file with the Board information relating to payments of royalties collected by it to the persons who have authorized it to collect those royalties; and
(*b*) by regulation, establish periods of not less than twelve months within which the entitlements referred to in subsections (1) and (2) must be exercised, in the case of royalties referred to in
(i) paragraph 29.6(2)(*a*), beginning on the expiration of the year during which no royalties are payable under that paragraph,
(ii) paragraph 29.6(2)(*b*), beginning on the performance in public,
(iii) subsection 29.7(2), beginning on the making of the copy,
(iv) subsection 29.7(3), beginning on the performance in public, or
(v) paragraph 31(2)(*d*), beginning on the communication to the public by telecommunication.
[S.C. 1988, c. 65, s. 65; S.C. 1997, c. 24, s. 50]

OWNERS WHO CANNOT BE LOCATED

Circumstances in which Licence May Be Issued by Board
77. (1) Where, on application to the Board by a person who wishes to obtain a licence to use
(*a*) a published work,
(*b*) a fixation of a performer's performance,
(*c*) a published sound recording, or
(*d*) a fixation of a communication signal
in which copyright subsists, the Board is satisfied that the applicant has made reasonable efforts to locate the owner of the copyright and that the owner cannot be located, the Board may issue to the applicant a licence to do an act mentioned in section 3, 15, 18 or 21, as the case may be.
(2) *Conditions of licence.* — A licence issued under subsection (1) is non-exclusive and is subject to such terms and conditions as the Board may establish.
(3) *Payment to owner.* — The owner of a copyright may, not later than five years after the expiration of a licence issued pursuant to subsection (1) in respect of the copyright, collect the royalties fixed in the licence or, in default of their payment, commence an action to recover them in a court of competent jurisdiction.
(4) *Regulations.* — The Copyright Board may make regulations governing the issuance of licences under subsection (1).
[R.S.C. 1985, c. 10 (4th Supp.), s. 16; S.C. 1997, c. 24, s. 50]

COMPENSATION FOR ACTS DONE BEFORE RECOGNITION OF COPYRIGHT OR MORAL RIGHTS

Board May Determine Compensation
78. (1) Subject to subsection (2), for the purposes of subsections 32.4(2), 32.5(2) and 33(2), the Board may, on application by any of the parties referred to in one of those provisions, determine the amount of the compensation referred to in that provision that the Board considers reasonable, having regard to all the circumstances, including any judgement of a court in an action between the parties for the enforcement of a right mentioned in subsection 32.4(3) or 32.5(3).
(2) *Limitation.* — The Board shall not
(*a*) proceed with an application under subsection (1) where a notice is filed with the Board that an agreement regarding the matters in issue has been reached; or
(*b*) where a court action between the parties for enforcement of a right referred to in subsection 32.4(3) or 32.5(3), as the case may be, has been commenced, continue with an application under subsection (1) until the court action is finally concluded.

(3) *Interim orders.* — Where the Board proceeds with an application under subsection (1), it may, for the purpose of avoiding serious prejudice to any party, make an interim order requiring a party to refrain from doing any act described in the order until the determination of compensation is made under subsection (1).
[S.C. 1994, c. 47, s. 68; S.C. 1997, c. 24, s. 50]

PART VIII
PRIVATE COPYING
[S.C. 1988, c. 65, s. 65]

Interpretation

Definitions
79. In this Part,
"audio recording medium" means a recording medium, regardless of its material form, onto which a sound recording may be reproduced and that is of a kind ordinarily used by individual consumers for that purpose, excluding any prescribed kind of recording medium;
"blank audio recording medium" means
(*a*) an audio recording medium onto which no sounds have ever been fixed, and
(*b*) any other prescribed audio recording medium;
"collecting body" means the collective society, or other society, association or corporation, that is designated as the collecting body under subsection 83(8);
"eligible author" means an author of a musical work, whether created before or after the coming into force of this Part, that is embodied in a sound recording, whether made before or after the coming into force of this Part, if copyright subsists in Canada in that musical work;
"eligible maker" means a maker of a sound recording that embodies a musical work, whether the first fixation of the sound recording occurred before or after the coming into force of this Part, if
(*a*) both the following two conditions are met:
(i) the maker, at the date of that first fixation, if a corporation, had its headquarters in Canada or, if a natural person, was a Canadian citizen or permanent resident of Canada within the meaning of the *Immigration Act*, and
(ii) copyright subsists in Canada in the sound recording, or
(*b*) the maker, at the date of that first fixation, if a corporation, had its headquarters in a country referred to in a statement published under section 85 or, if a natural person, was a citizen, subject or permanent resident of such a country;
"eligible performer" means the performer of a performer's performance of a musical work, whether it took place before or after the coming into force of this Part, if the performer's performance is embodied in a sound recording and
(*a*) both the following two conditions are met:
(i) the performer was, at the date of the first fixation of the sound recording, a Canadian citizen or permanent resident of Canada within the meaning of the *Immigration Act*, and
(ii) copyright subsists in Canada in the performer's performance, or
(*b*) the performer was, at the date of the first fixation of the sound recording, a citizen, subject or permanent resident of a country referred to in a statement published under section 85;
"prescribed" means prescribed by regulations made under this Part.
[S.C. 1997, c. 24, s. 50]

Copying for Private Use

Where No Infringement of Copyright
80. (1) Subject to subsection (2), the act of reproducing all or any substantial part of
(*a*) a musical work embodied in a sound recording,
(*b*) a performer's performance of a musical work embodied in a sound recording, or
(*c*) a sound recording in which a musical work, or a performer's performance of a musical work, is embodied onto an audio recording medium for the private use of the person who makes the copy does not constitute an infringement of the copyright in the musical work, the performer's performance or the sound recording.
(2) *Limitation.* — Subsection (1) does not apply if the act described in that subsection is done for the purpose of doing any of the following in relation to any of the things referred to in paragraphs (1)(*a*) to (*c*):
(*a*) selling or renting out, or by way of trade exposing or offering for sale or rental;
(*b*) distributing, whether or not for the purpose of trade;
(*c*) communicating to the public by telecommunication; or
(*d*) performing, or causing to be performed, in public.
[S.C. 1997, c. 24, s. 50]

Right of Remuneration

Right of Remuneration
81. (1) Subject to and in accordance with this Part, eligible authors, and eligible makers have a right to receive remuneration from manufacturers and importers of blank audio recording media in respect of the reproduction for private use of
(*a*) a musical work embodied in a sound recording;

(*b*) a performer's performance of a musical work embodied in a sound recording; or
(*c*) a sound recording in which a musical work, or a performer's performance of a musical work, is embodied.
(2) *Assignment of rights.* — Subsections 13(4) to (7) apply, with such modifications as the circumstances require, in respect of the rights conferred by subsection (1) on eligible authors, performers and makers.
[S.C. 1997, c. 24, s. 50]

Levy on Blank Audio Recording Media

Liability to Pay Levy
82. (1) Every person who, for the purpose of trade, manufactures a blank audio recording medium in Canada or imports a blank audio recording medium into Canada
(*a*) is liable, subject to subsection (2) and section 86, to pay a levy to the collecting body on selling or otherwise disposing of those blank audio recording media in Canada; and
(*b*) shall, in accordance with subsection 83(8), keep statements of account of the activities referred to in paragraph (*a*), as well as of exports of those blank audio recording media, and shall furnish those statements to the collecting body.
(2) *No levy for exports.* — No levy is payable where it is a term of the sale or other disposition of the blank audio recording medium that the medium is to be exported from Canada, and it is exported from Canada.
[S.C. 1997, c. 24, s. 50]

Filing of Proposed Tariffs
83. (1) Subject to subsection (14), each collective society may file with the Board a proposed tariff for the benefit of those eligible authors, eligible performers and eligible makers who, by assignment, grant of licence, appointment of the society as their agent or otherwise, authorize it to act on their behalf for that purpose, but no person other than a collective society may file any such tariff.
(2) *Collecting body.* — Without limiting the generality of what may be included in a proposed tariff, the tariff may include a suggestion as to whom the Board should designate under paragraph (8)(*d*) as the collecting body.
(3) *Times for filing.* — Proposed tariffs must be in both official languages and must be filed on or before the March 31 immediately before the date when the approved tariffs cease to be effective.
(4) *Where no previous tariff.* — A collective society in respect of which no proposed tariff has been certified pursuant to paragraph (8)(*c*) shall file its proposed tariff on or before the March 31 immediately before its proposed effective date.

(5) *Effective period of levies.* — A proposed tariff must provide that the levies are to be effective for periods of one or more calendar years.
(6) *Publication of proposed tariffs.* — As soon as practicable after the receipt of a proposed tariff filed pursuant to subsection (1), the Board shall publish it in the *Canada Gazette* and shall give notice that, within sixty days after the publication of the tariff, any person may file written objections to the tariff with the Board.
(7) *Board to consider proposed tariffs and objections.* — The Board shall, as soon as practicable, consider a proposed tariff and any objections thereto referred to in subsection (6) or raised by the Board, and
(*a*) send to the collective society concerned a copy of the objections so as to permit it to reply; and
(*b*) send to the persons who filed the objections a copy of any reply thereto.
(8) *Duties of Board.* — On the conclusion of its consideration of the proposed tariff, the Board shall
(*a*) establish, in accordance with subsection (9),
(i) the manner of determining the levies, and
(ii) such terms and conditions related to those levies as the Board considers appropriate, including, without limiting the generality of the foregoing, the form, content and frequency of the statements of account mentioned in subsection 82(1), measures for the protection of confidential information contained in those statements, and the times at which the levies are payable,
(*b*) vary the tariff accordingly,
(*c*) certify the tariff as the approved tariff, whereupon that tariff becomes for the purposes of this Part the approved tariff, and
(*d*) designate as the collecting body the collective society or other society, association or corporation that, in the Board's opinion, will best fulfil the objects of sections 82, 84 and 86,
but the Board is not obligated to exercise its power under paragraph (*d*) if it has previously done so, and a designation under that paragraph remains in effect until the Board makes another designation, which it may do at any time whatsoever, on application.
(9) *Factors Board to consider.* — In exercising its power under paragraph (8)(*a*), the Board shall satisfy itself that the levies are fair and equitable, having regard to any prescribed criteria.
(10) *Publication of approved tariffs.* — The Board shall publish the approved tariffs in the *Canada Gazette* as soon as practicable and shall send a copy of each approved tariff, together with the reasons for the Board's decision, to the collecting body, to each collective society that filed a proposed tariff, and to any person who filed an objection.

(11) *Authors, etc., not represented by collective society.* — An eligible author, eligible performer or eligible maker who does not authorize a collective society to file a proposed tariff under subsection (1) is entitled, in relation to

(*a*) a musical work,

(*b*) a performer's performance of a musical work, or

(*c*) a sound recording in which a musical work, or a performer's performance of a musical work, is embodied, as the case may be, to be paid by the collective society that is designated by the Board, of the Board's own motion or on application, the remuneration referred to in section 81 if such remuneration is payable during a period when an approved tariff that is applicable to that kind of work, performer's performance or sound recording is effective, subject to the same conditions as those to which a person who has so authorized that collective society is subject.

(12) *Exclusion of other remedies.* — The entitlement referred to in subsection (11) is the only remedy of the eligible author, eligible performer or eligible maker referred to in that subsection in respect of the reproducing of sound recordings for private use.

(13) *Powers of Board.* — The Board may, for the purposes of subsections (11) and (12),

(*a*) require a collective society to file with the Board information relating to payments of moneys received by the society pursuant to section 84 to the persons who have authorized it to file a tariff under subsection (1); and

(*b*) by regulation, establish the periods, which shall not be less than twelve months, beginning when the applicable approved tariff ceases to be effective, within which the entitlement referred to in subsection (11) must be exercised.

(14) *Single proposed tariff.* — Where all the collective societies that intend to file a proposed tariff authorize a particular person or body to file a single proposed tariff on their behalf, that person or body may do so, and in that case this section applies, with such modifications as the circumstances require, in respect of that proposed tariff.

[S.C. 1997, c. 24, s. 50]

Distribution of Levies Paid

Distribution by Collecting Body

84. As soon as practicable after receiving the levies paid to it, the collecting body shall distribute the levies to the collective societies representing eligible authors, eligible performers and eligible makers, in the proportions fixed by the Board.

[S.C. 1997, c. 24, s. 50]

Reciprocity

85. (1) Where the Minister is of the opinion that another country grants or has undertaken to grant to performers and makers of sound recordings that are Canadian citizens or permanent residents of Canada within the meaning of the *Immigration Act* or, if corporations, have their headquarters in Canada, as the case may be, whether by treaty, convention, agreement or law, benefits substantially equivalent to those conferred by this Part, the Minister may, by a statement published in the *Canada Gazette*,

(*a*) grant the benefits conferred by this Part to performers or makers of sound recordings that are citizens, subjects or permanent residents of or, if corporations, have their headquarters in that country; and

(*b*) declare that that country shall, as regards those benefits, be treated as if it were a country to which this Part extends.

(2) *Reciprocity.* — Where the Minister is of the opinion that another country neither grants nor has undertaken to grant to performers or makers of sound recordings that are Canadian citizens or permanent residents of Canada within the meaning of the *Immigration Act* or, if corporations, have their headquarters in Canada, as the case may be, whether by treaty, convention, agreement or law, benefits substantially equivalent to those conferred by this Part, the Minister may, by a statement published in the *Canada Gazette*,

(*a*) grant the benefits conferred by this Part to performers or makers of sound recordings that are citizens, subjects or permanent residents of or, if corporations, have their headquarters in that country, as the case may be, to the extent that that country grants those benefits to performers or makers of sound recordings that are Canadian citizens or permanent residents of Canada within the meaning of the *Immigration Act* or, if corporations, have their headquarters in Canada; and

(*b*) declare that that country shall, as regards those benefits, be treated as if it were a country to which this Part extends.

(3) *Application of Act.* — Any provision of this Act that the Minister specifies in a statement referred to in subsection (1) or (2)

(*a*) applies in respect of performers or makers of sound recordings covered by that statement, as if they were citizens of or, if corporations, had their headquarters in Canada; and

(*b*) applies in respect of a country covered by that statement, as if that country were Canada.

(4) *Application of Act.* — Subject to any exceptions that the Minister may specify in a statement referred to in subsection (1) or (2), the other provisions of this Act also apply in the way described in subsection (3).

[S.C. 1997, c. 24, s. 50]

Exemption from Levy

Where No Levy Payable
86. (1) No levy is payable under this Part where the manufacturer or importer of a blank audio recording medium sells or otherwise disposes of it to a society, association or corporation that represents persons with a perceptual disability.
(2) *Refunds.* — Where a society, association or corporation referred to in subsection (1)
(*a*) purchases a blank audio recording medium in Canada from a person other than the manufacturer or importer, and
(*b*) provides the collecting body with proof of that purchase, on or before June 30 in the calendar year following the calendar year in which the purchase was made,
the collecting body is liable to pay forthwith to the society, association or corporation an amount equal to the amount of the levy paid in respect of the blank audio recording medium purchased.
(3) *If registration system exists.* — If regulations made under paragraph 87(*a*) provide for the registration of societies, associations or corporations that represent persons with a /perceptual disability, subsections (1) and (2) shall be read as referring to societies, associations or corporations that are so registered.
[S.C. 1997, c. 24, s. 50]

Regulations

Regulations
87. The Governor in Council may make regulations
(*a*) respecting the exemptions and refunds provided for in section 86, including, without limiting the generality of the foregoing,
(i) regulations respecting procedures governing those exemptions and refunds,
(ii) regulations respecting applications for those exemptions and refunds, and
(iii) regulations for the registration of societies, associations or corporations that represent persons with a perceptual disability;
(*b*) prescribing anything that by this Part is to be prescribed; and
(*c*) generally for carrying out the purposes and provisions of this Part.
[S.C. 1997, c. 24, s. 50]

Civil Remedies

Right of Recovery
88. (1) Without prejudice to any other remedies available to it, the collecting body may, for the period specified in an approved tariff, collect the levies due to it under the tariff and, in default of their payment, recover them in a court of competent jurisdiction.
(2) *Failure to pay royalties.* — The court may order a person who fails to pay any levy due under this Part to pay an amount not exceeding five times the amount of the levy to the collecting body. The collecting body must distribute the payment in the manner set out in section 84.
(3) *Order directing compliance.* — Where any obligation imposed by this Part is not complied with, the collecting body may, in addition to any other remedy available, apply to a court of competent jurisdiction for an order directing compliance with that obligation.
(4) *Factors to consider.* — Before making an order under subsection (2), the court must take into account
(*a*) whether the person who failed to pay the levy acted in good faith or bad faith;
(*b*) the conduct of the parties before and during the proceedings; and
(*c*) the need to deter persons from failing to pay levies.
[S.C. 1997, c. 24, s. 50]

PART IX
GENERAL PROVISIONS

No Copyright, etc., Except by Statute
89. No person is entitled to copyright otherwise than under and in accordance with this Act or any other Act of Parliament, but nothing in this section shall be construed as abrogating any right or jurisdiction in respect of a breach of trust or confidence. [S.C. 1997, c. 24, s. 50]

Interpretation
90. No provision of this Act relating to
(*a*) copyright in performer's performances, sound recordings or communication signals, or
(*b*) the right of performers or makers to remuneration
shall be construed as prejudicing any rights conferred by Part I or, in and of itself, as prejudicing the amount of royalties that the Board may fix in respect of those rights.
[S.C. 1997, c. 24, s. 50]

Adherence to Berne and Rome Conventions
91. The Governor in Council shall take such measures as are necessary to secure the adherence of Canada to
(*a*) the Convention for the Protection of Literary and Artistic Works concluded at Berne on September 9, 1886, as revised by the Paris Act of 1971; and
(*b*) the International Convention for the Protection of Performers, Producers of Phonograms and Broadcasting Organisations, done at Rome on October 26, 1961.
[S.C. 1997, c. 24, s. 50]

Review of Act
92. (1) Within five years after the coming into force of this section, the Minister shall cause to be laid before both Houses of Parliament a report on the provisions and operation of this Act, including any recommendations for amendments to this Act.
(2) *Reference to parliamentary committee.* — The report stands referred to the committee of the House of Commons, or of both Houses of Parliament, that is designated or established for that purpose, which shall
(*a*) as soon as possible thereafter, review the report and undertake a comprehensive review of the provisions and operation of this Act; and
(*b*) report to the House of Commons, or to both Houses of Parliament, within one year after the laying of the report of the Minister or any further time that the House of Commons, or both Houses of Parliament, may authorize.
[S.C. 1997, c. 24, s. 50]

SCHEDULE I
(Section 60)

EXISTING RIGHTS

Column I Existing Rights	Column II Substituted Right
Works other than Dramatic and Musical Works	
Copyright	Copyright as defined by this Act**
Musical and Dramatic Works	
Both copyright and performing right	Copyright as defined by this Act
Copyright, but not performing right	Copyright as defined by this Act, except the sole right to perform the work or any substantial part thereof in public
Performing right, but not copyright	The sole right to perform the work in public, but none of the other rights comprised in copyright as defined by this Act

For the purposes of this Schedule the following expressions, where used in column I thereof, have the following meanings:
"Copyright" in the case of a work that according to the law in force immediately before January 1, 1924 has not been published before that date and statutory copyright wherein depends on publication, includes the right at common law, if any, to restrain publication or other dealing with the work;
"Performing right", in the case of a work that has not been performed in public before January 1, 1924, includes the right at common law, if any, to restrain the performance thereof in public.

** In the case of an essay, article or portion forming part of and first published in a review, magazine or other periodical or work of a like nature, the right shall be subject to any right of publishing the essay, article or portion in a separate form to which the author is entitled on January 1, 1924 or would if this Act had not been passed have become entitled under section 18 of An Act to amend the Law of Copyright, being chapter 45 of the Statutes of the United Kingdom, 1842.
[R.S., c. C-30, Sch. I; 1976-77, c. 28, s. 10.]

Registration
SOR/99-324   28 July, 1999

COPYRIGHT ACT

Book Importation Regulations

P.C. 1999-1350   28 July, 1999

His Excellency the Governor General in Council, on the recommendation of the Minister of Industry, pursuant to the definition "exclusive distributor"[a] in section on 2, section 2.6[b] subsections 27.1(5)[c] and (6)[c] and section 62[d] of the *Copyright Act*, hereby makes the annexed *Book Importation Regulations*.

BOOK IMPORTATION REGULATIONS

INTERPRETATION

1. The definitions in this section apply in these Regulations.

"Act" means the *Copyright Act*. (*Loi*)

"bookseller" means an individual, firm or corporation that is directly engaged in the sale of books in Canada for at least 30 consecutive days in a year and

(*a*) whose floor space is open to the public and is located on premises consisting of floor space, including book shelves and customer aisles, of an area of at least 183 m² (600 sq. ft.); or

(*b*) whose floor space is not open to the public and that derives 50% of his or her or its gross revenues from the sale of books. (*libraire*)

"Canadian edition" means an edition of a book that is published under an agreement conferring a separate right of reproduction for the Canadian market, and that is made available in Canada by a publisher in Canada. (*édition canadienne*)

"catalogue" means a publication in printed, electronic or microfiche form that

(*a*) is updated at least once a year;

(*b*) lists all book titles currently in print that are available from at least one exclusive distributor; and

(*c*) identifies the title, the International Standard Book Number, the exclusive distributor, the author and the list price in Canada for each book listed. (*catalogue*)

"current exchange rate" means the rate of exchange prevailing on the day on which a transaction takes place, as ascertained from a Canadian bank. (*taux de change courant*)

"format" in relation to a book, means

(*a*) the type or quality of binding;

(*b*) the typeface or size of print;

(*c*) the type or quality of paper; or

(*d*) the content, including whether the book is abridged or unabridged, or illustrated. (*format*)

"holiday" means a Saturday or a holiday as defined in subsection 35(1) of the *Interpretation Act*. (*jour férié*)

---

[a] S.C. 1997, c. 24, s. 1(5)
[b] S.C. 1997, c. 24, s. 2
[c] S.C. 1997, c. 24, s. 15
[d] S.C. 1997, c. 24, s. 37(2)

"list price" means the price for a book that is set out in a catalogue or printed on the cover or jacket of the book. (*prix de catalogue*)

"remaindered book" means a book

(*a*) that is sold by the publisher for less than the cost of paper, printing and binding; or

(*b*) that is sold at a reduced price by the publisher and for which the author or copyright owner receives no royalty. (*livre soldé*)

"retailer" means a person who sells books in the course of operating a business, but does not include an exclusive distributor or a book publisher. (*détaillant*)

"special order" means an order for a copy of a book that a bookseller or a retailer other than a bookseller does not have in stock and that the bookseller or retailer orders at the request of a customer. (*commande spéciale*)

APPLICATION

2. (1) These Regulations apply to

(*a*) English-language and French-language books that are imported into Canada and for which separate and distinct Canadian territorial rights have been created or contracted; and

(*b*) Canadian editions that are imported into Canada.

(2) For greater certainty, these Regulations apply to books referred to in subsection (1) that are added, after the coming into force of these Regulations, to an order placed before the coming into force of these Regulations.

(3) For greater certainty, these Regulations shall not be construed as authorizing anyone to do or to omit to do an act that would constitute an infringement of copyright under subsection 27(2) of the Act.

COMPUTATION OF TIME

3. (1) The computation of time under these Regulations is governed by sections 26 to 30 of the *Interpretation Act*.

(2) If a period of less than seven days is provided for in these Regulations, a day that is a holiday shall not be included in computing the period.

(3) If a period for the doing of a thing is provided for in these Regulations and is expressed to end on a specified day, the period ends at the close of business on the specified day.

NOTICE OF EXCLUSIVE DISTRIBUTOR

4. (1) An exclusive distributor, a copyright owner or an exclusive licensee shall give the notice referred to in subsection 27.1(5) of the Act to a person referred to in subsection 27.1(1) or (2) of the Act before the person places an order, in the following manner:

(*a*) in the case of a retailer other than a bookseller, in writing in accordance with subsection (2); and

(*b*) in the case of a bookseller, library or other institution established or conducted for profit that maintains a collection of documents, by setting out the fact that there is an exclusive distributor of the book in the latest edition of

(i) the *Canadian Telebook Agency Microfiche* and *Books in Print Plus — Canadian Edition*, published by R.R. Bowker,

a) soit dans des locaux accessibles au public dont la superficie, y compris les rayons de livres et les allées, est d'au moins 183 m^2 (600 pi^2);

b) soit dans des locaux non accessibles au public et dont au moins 50 % du revenu brut provient de la vente de livres. (*bookseller*)

« livre soldé » Livre :

a) soit qui est vendu par l'éditeur à un prix inférieur au coût du papier, de l'impression et de la reliure;

b) soit qui est vendu par l'éditeur à prix réduit et pour lequel l'auteur ou le titulaire du droit d'auteur ne reçoit aucune redevance. (*remaindered book*)

« Loi » La *Loi sur le droit d'auteur*. (*Act*)

« prix de catalogue » Le prix figurant dans un catalogue ou imprimé sur la couverture ou la jaquette d'un livre. (*list price*)

« taux de change courant » Le taux de change en vigueur le jour de la transaction, selon une banque canadienne. (*current exchange rate*)

APPLICATION

2. (1) Le présent règlement s'applique :

a) aux livres en anglais ou en français qui sont importés au Canada et pour lesquels des droits territoriaux canadiens distincts ont été créés ou accordés par contrat;

b) aux éditions canadiennes qui sont importées au Canada.

(2) Il est entendu que le présent règlement s'applique aux livres qui, après son entrée en vigueur, sont ajoutés à une commande passée avant celle-ci.

(3) Il est entendu que le présent règlement n'autorise pas l'accomplissement d'un acte ou une omission qui constituerait une violation du droit d'auteur aux termes du paragraphe 27(2) de la Loi.

CALCUL DES DÉLAIS

3. (1) Le calcul des délais prévus par le présent règlement est régi par les articles 26 à 30 de la *Loi d'interprétation*.

(2) Les jours fériés n'entrent pas dans le calcul d'un délai de moins de sept jours prévu par le présent règlement.

(3) Si le règlement prévoit qu'un délai se termine un jour donné, le délai expire à l'heure de fermeture des bureaux.

AVIS DE L'EXISTENCE D'UN DISTRIBUTEUR EXCLUSIF

4. (1) Avant que la personne visée aux paragraphes 27.1(1) ou (2) de la Loi passe sa commande, le distributeur exclusif, le titulaire du droit d'auteur ou le titulaire d'une licence exclusive lui donne l'avis mentionné au paragraphe 27.1(5) de la Loi, selon les modalités suivantes :

a) dans le cas d'un détaillant autre qu'un libraire, il lui envoie un avis écrit en conformité avec le paragraphe (2);

b) dans le cas d'un libraire, d'une bibliothèque ou d'un autre établissement constitué ou administré pour réaliser des profits qui gère des collections de documents, il mentionne le fait qu'il existe un distributeur exclusif du livre en cause :

(i) soit dans la dernière édition du *Canadian Telebook Agency Microfiche* et celle de *Books in Print Plus — Canadian*

if the book is an English-language book, and the *Banque de titres de langue française*, if the book is a French-language book, or

(ii) a catalogue supplied by the exclusive distributor, copyright owner or exclusive licensee to the bookseller, library or other institution, at the request of, and in the form requested by, the bookseller, library or other institution.

(2) The notice referred to in paragraph (1)(*a*) shall be sent to the retailer at the retailer's last known address by personal delivery, by mail, or by facsimile or other electronic means.

(3) Instead of the notice referred to in subsection (1), an exclusive distributor that represents all of the titles published by a particular publisher may send a notice to that effect to a person referred to in subsection 27(1) or (2) of the Act, at that person's last known address, by personal delivery, by mail, or by facsimile or other electronic means, before the person places an order.

(4) A notice given in accordance with subsection (1) or (3) is valid and subsisting in respect of any title covered by the notice until the notice is revoked or amended by the exclusive distributor, copyright owner or exclusive licensee, as the case may be.

(5) The notice referred to in subsection (2) or (3) is deemed to have been received by the retailer, if it is

(*a*) delivered personally, on the day of delivery;

(*b*) sent by mail, on the tenth day after the day on which the notice was mailed; or

(*c*) sent by facsimile or other electronic means, on the date and at the time indicated by the sending apparatus.

IMPORTED BOOKS

5. (1) For the purpose of section 2.6 of the Act, where an order for imported books is placed, the following distribution criteria are established:

(*a*) an exclusive distributor shall

(i) ship the order to the person who placed the order

(A) for books imported into Canada and in stock in Canada,

(I) within 12 months after the coming into force of these Regulations, no later than five days after the day on which the order is received from the person who placed the order,

(II) after the end of the 12-month period referred to in subclause (I), no later than three days after the day on which the order is received from the person who placed the order, in the case of English-language books, and

(III) after the end of the 12-month period referred to in subclause (I), no later than five days after the day on which the order is received from the person who placed the order, in the case of French-language books,

(B) for books imported from the United States and not in stock in Canada,

(I) within 12 months after the coming into force of these Regulations, no later than 15 days after the day on which the order is received from the person who placed the order, and

(II) after the end of the 12-month period referred to in subclause (I), no later than 12 days after the day on which the order is received from the person who placed the order,

Edition, publiées par R.R. Bowker, si le livre est en anglais, et dans la dernière édition de la *Banque de titres de langue française*, si le livre est en français,

(ii) soit dans la dernière édition du catalogue qu'il leur a fournie sur demande et sous la forme demandée.

(2) L'avis prévu à l'alinéa (1)*a*) est envoyé au détaillant à sa dernière adresse connue par messager, par la poste ou par télécopieur ou autre moyen électronique.

(3) S'il est distributeur exclusif pour tous les titres d'un éditeur donné, le distributeur peut, au lieu d'envoyer l'avis prévu au paragraphe (1), envoyer un avis à cet effet à la personne visée aux paragraphes 27(1) ou (2) de la Loi à sa dernière adresse connue par messager, par la poste ou par télécopieur ou autre moyen électronique, et ce avant que celle-ci passe sa commande.

(4) L'avis envoyé conformément aux paragraphes (1) ou (3) produit ses effets à l'égard des titres en question tant qu'il n'a pas été révoqué ou modifié par le distributeur exclusif, le titulaire du droit d'auteur ou le titulaire d'une licence exclusive, selon le cas.

(5) L'avis mentionné aux paragraphes (2) ou (3) est réputé reçu par le détaillant :

a) s'il est envoyé par messager, le jour de sa livraison;

b) s'il est envoyé par la poste, le dixième jour suivant sa mise à la poste;

c) s'il est envoyé par télécopieur ou autre moyen électronique, aux date et heure indiquées par l'appareil de transmission.

LIVRES IMPORTÉS

5. (1) Pour l'application de l'article 2.6 de la Loi, les critères de distribution régissant les commandes de livres importés sont les suivants :

a) le distributeur exclusif doit :

(i) expédier les livres commandés au destinataire dans le délai suivant :

(A) dans le cas des livres importés et en stock au Canada :

(I) au cours des 12 mois suivant l'entrée en vigueur du présent règlement, dans les cinq jours suivant la date de réception de la commande,

(II) après l'expiration de cette période de 12 mois, dans les trois jours suivant la date de réception de la commande visant des livres en anglais,

(III) après l'expiration de cette période de 12 mois, dans les cinq jours suivant la date de réception de la commande visant des livres en français,

(B) dans le cas des livres importés des États-Unis mais non en stock au Canada :

(I) au cours des 12 mois suivant l'entrée en vigueur du présent règlement, dans les 15 jours suivant la date de réception de la commande,

(II) après l'expiration de cette période de 12 mois, dans les 12 jours suivant la date de réception de la commande,

(C) dans le cas des livres importés d'Europe mais non en stock au Canada :

(I) au cours des 12 mois suivant l'entrée en vigueur du présent règlement, dans les 35 jours suivant la date de réception de la commande visant des livres en anglais,

(C) for books imported from Europe and not in stock in Canada,

(I) within 12 months after the coming into force of these Regulations, no later than 35 days after the day on which the order is received from the person who placed the order, in the case of English-language books,

(II) after the end of the 12-month period referred to in subclause (I), no later than 30 days after the day on which the order is received from the person who placed the order, in the case of English-language books, and

(III) no later than 60 days after the day on which the order is received from the person who placed the order, in the case of French-language books, and

(D) for books imported from any other country and not in stock in Canada,

(I) within 12 months after the coming into force of these Regulations, no later than 60 days after the day on which the order is received from the person who placed the order, and

(II) after the end of the 12-month period referred to in subclause (I), no later than 50 days after the day on which the order is received from the person who placed the order,

(ii) provide the book in the format requested by the person who placed the order, if the format exists, and

(iii) subject to any law of any province with respect to prices concerning the distribution of books, provide the book at a price no greater than

(A) if the book is imported from the United States, the list price in the United States, plus the current exchange rate, plus 10% of the price after conversion, minus any applicable discounts, or

(B) if the book is imported from a country in Europe or any other country, the list price in the country from which the book is imported, plus the current exchange rate, plus 15% of the price after conversion, minus any applicable discounts; and

(b) if the person who placed the order so requests, an exclusive distributor shall confirm to that person whether the order can be filled

(i) if the confirmation is made by telephone, no later than two days after the day on which the order is placed,

(ii) if the confirmation is sent by mail or facsimile, no later than five days after the day on which the order is placed, and

(iii) if the confirmation is sent by electronic means other than facsimile,

(A) where the order is placed within 12 months after the coming into force of these Regulations, no later than two days after the day on which the order is placed, and

(B) where the order is placed after the end of the 12-month period referred to in clause (A), no later than the day after the day on which the order is placed.

(2) In the case of books provided to libraries, the applicable discounts referred to in clause (1)(a)(iii)(A) shall be based on generally prevailing market conditions in North America.

(3) Subsections (1) and (2) apply to an exclusive distributor of a book in paperbound format only after the end of 12 months after the book first becomes available in that format in North America. If the exclusive distributor provides the book in that

(II) après l'expiration de cette période de 12 mois, dans les 30 jours suivant la date de réception de la commande visant des livres en anglais,

(III) dans les 60 jours suivant la date de réception de la commande visant des livres en français,

(D) dans le cas des livres importés d'autres pays mais non en stock au Canada :

(I) au cours des 12 mois suivant l'entrée en vigueur du présent règlement, dans les 60 jours suivant la date de réception de la commande,

(II) après l'expiration de cette période de 12 mois, dans les 50 jours suivant la date de réception de la commande,

(ii) fournir les livres dans le format demandé, si celui-ci existe,

(iii) sous réserve des lois provinciales régissant les prix en matière de distribution de livres, fournir les livres à un prix ne dépassant pas :

(A) dans le cas des livres importés des États-Unis, le prix de catalogue aux États-Unis converti selon le taux de change courant, plus 10 % du prix ainsi converti, les remises applicables étant soustraites du total,

(B) dans le cas des livres importés d'un pays d'Europe ou d'un autre pays, le prix de catalogue dans le pays d'importation converti selon le taux de change courant, plus 15 % du prix ainsi converti, les remises applicables étant soustraites du total;

b) à la demande de la personne qui a passé la commande, le distributeur exclusif doit lui faire savoir, dans le délai suivant, s'il peut ou non exécuter la commande :

(i) si la confirmation se fait par téléphone, dans les deux jours suivant la date de la commande,

(ii) si la confirmation se fait par la poste ou par télécopieur, dans les cinq jours suivant la date de la commande,

(iii) si la confirmation se fait par un moyen électronique autre que le télécopieur :

(A) dans le cas d'une commande passée au cours des 12 mois suivant l'entrée en vigueur du présent règlement, dans les deux jours suivant la date de la commande,

(B) dans le cas d'une commande passée après l'expiration de la période visée à la division (A), le jour suivant la date de la commande.

(2) Si les livres sont fournis à une bibliothèque, les remises visées à la division (1)a)(iii)(A) sont établies d'après les conditions générales du marché en Amérique du Nord.

(3) Les paragraphes (1) et (2) ne s'appliquent au distributeur exclusif de livres de format de poche qu'à l'expiration de la période de 12 mois débutant le jour où ils ont été disponibles dans ce format pour la première fois en Amérique du Nord. Si le

format before the end of that period, subsections (1) and (2) shall apply.

(4) If an exclusive distributor is unable to meet the criteria for an order set out in subsections (1) and (2), the person who placed the order may import the book through a person other than the exclusive distributor.

CANADIAN EDITIONS

6. (1) For the purpose of section 2.6 of the Act, the following distribution criteria are established for Canadian editions:

(*a*) the exclusive distributor shall make sufficient copies of the Canadian edition available in Canada; and

(*b*) before an order is placed, the Canadian edition must be

(i) identified as a Canadian edition

(A) on the cover or jacket of the book,

(B) in the latest edition of the *Canadian Telebook Agency Microfiche* and of *Books in Print Plus — Canadian Edition*, published by R.R. Bowker, if the edition is an English-language edition, and in the latest edition of the *Banque de titres de langue française*, if the edition is a French-language edition, or

(C) in the latest edition of a catalogue supplied by the exclusive distributor, copyright owner or exclusive licensee to the bookseller, library or other institution, at the request of, and in the form requested by, the bookseller, library or other institution, and

(ii) listed

(A) in the latest edition of the *Canadian Telebook Agency Microfiche* and of *Books in Print Plus — Canadian Edition*, published by R.R. Bowker, if the edition is a English-language edition, and in the latest edition of the *Banque de titres de langue française*, if the edition is a French-language edition, or

(B) in the latest edition of a catalogue supplied by the exclusive distributor, copyright owner or exclusive licensee to the bookseller, library or other institution, at the request of, and in the form requested by, the bookseller, library or other institution.

(2) If an exclusive distributor is unable to meet the criteria for an order set out in subsection (1) the person who placed the order may import the book through a person other than the exclusive distributor.

REMAINDERED AND OTHER BOOKS

7. For the purpose of subsection 27.1(6) of the Act, a book may be imported if

(*a*) the book is marked as a remaindered book or the original foreign publisher has given notice to the exclusive distributor, if any, that the book has been remaindered, and the book is not sold in Canada before the end of 60 days after the day on which it was first offered for sale as a remaindered book by the original foreign publisher in the country from which the book is imported;

(*b*) the book is marked as a damaged book by the importer or the retailer; or

(*c*) the book is imported solely for the purpose of re-export, and the importer is able to provide evidence, on request, that an order for re-export has been made for the book before its importation.

distributeur fournit les livres dans ce format avant l'expiration de la période, ces paragraphes lui sont alors applicables.

(4) Si le distributeur exclusif n'est pas en mesure de satisfaire aux critères énoncés aux paragraphes (1) et (2) pour une commande donnée, la personne qui l'a passée peut importer les livres en cause par un autre intermédiaire.

ÉDITIONS CANADIENNES

6. (1) Pour l'application de l'article 2.6 de la Loi, les critères de distribution régissant les éditions canadiennes sont les suivants :

a) le distributeur exclusif doit mettre sur le marché canadien un nombre suffisant d'exemplaires de l'édition canadienne en cause;

b) avant que la commande soit passée :

(i) le fait qu'il s'agit d'une édition canadienne doit :

(A) soit être mentionné sur la couverture ou la jaquette du livre,

(B) soit figurer, si l'édition est en anglais, dans la dernière édition du *Canadian Telebook Agency Microfiche* et celle de *Books in Print Plus — Canadian Edition*, publiées par R.R. Bowker, et, si l'édition est en français, dans la dernière édition de la *Banque de titres de langue française*,

(C) soit figurer dans la dernière édition du catalogue que le distributeur exclusif, le titulaire du droit d'auteur ou le titulaire d'une licence exclusive a fournie sur demande et sous la forme demandée au libraire, à la bibliothèque ou à un autre établissement,

(ii) l'édition canadienne doit par ailleurs :

(A) soit figurer, si l'édition est en anglais, dans la dernière édition du *Canadian Telebook Agency Microfiche* et celle de *Books in Print Plus — Canadian Edition*, publiées par R.R. Bowker, et, si l'édition est français, dans la dernière édition de la *Banque de titres de langue française*,

(B) soit figurer dans la dernière édition du catalogue que le distributeur exclusif, le titulaire du droit d'auteur ou le titulaire d'une licence exclusive a fournie sur demande et sous la forme demandée au libraire, à la bibliothèque ou à un autre établissement.

(2) Si le distributeur exclusif n'est pas en mesure de satisfaire aux critères énoncés au paragraphe (1) pour une commande donnée, la personne qui l'a passée peut importer le livre en cause par un autre intermédiaire.

LIVRES SOLDÉS ET AUTRES

7. Pour l'application du paragraphe 27.1(6) de la Loi, peuvent être importés :

a) les livres qui sont marqués comme étant des livres soldés ou à l'égard desquels l'éditeur original étranger a envoyé au distributeur exclusif, s'il existe, un avis annonçant leur mise en solde, d'une part, et qui ne sont pas vendus au Canada avant l'expiration du délai de 60 jours suivant la date à laquelle ils ont été mis en vente comme livres soldés pour la première fois par l'éditeur dans le pays d'où ils sont importés, d'autre part;

b) les livres que l'importateur ou le détaillant a marqués comme étant des livres endommagés;

c) les livres importés exclusivement en vue de leur réexportation et à l'égard desquels le distributeur exclusif peut, sur demande, prouver qu'une commande en vue de leur réexportation a été passée avant leur importation.

TEXTBOOKS

8. For the purpose of subsection 27.1(6) of the Act, a textbook may be imported if

(*a*) at the time of importation, the importer provides documentation such as a certificate or an invoice establishing that the textbook is a used textbook;

(*b*) the textbook is to be offered for sale or distribution in Canada as a used textbook; and

(*c*) the textbook is of a scientific, technical or scholarly nature and is for use within an educational institution or an educational body established or conducted for profit.

SPECIAL ORDERS

9. (1) For the purpose of subsection 27.1(6) of the Act, a book that is the subject of a special order may be imported through a person other than the exclusive distributor if the exclusive distributor is unable to fill the order within the time specified by the person who placed the order.

(2) The exclusive distributor shall confirm within 24 hours after the special order is received whether or not the order can be filled within the time specified by the person who placed the order.

LEASED BOOKS

10. A library may import leased books through a person other than an exclusive distributor.

COMING INTO FORCE

11. These Regulations come into force on September 1, 1999.

REGULATORY IMPACT ANALYSIS STATEMENT

(*This statement is not part of the Regulations.*)

Description

Bill C-32, *An Act to amend the Copyright Act*, received Royal Assent on April 25, 1997. This bill introduced additional restrictions on the parallel importation of printed books. Parallel importation refers to books which were legitimately produced in their country of origin but which have been imported into Canada without the consent of the rights owner in Canada. Bill C-32 contains provisions which greatly increase the ability of rights holders in Canada to protect their exclusive distribution rights in the Canadian market. Previously, the Act allowed only copyright owners and exclusive licensees to limit the parallel importation of printed books. Bill C-32 extends this right to exclusive distributors. Exclusive distributors are those who have received acquired rights of exclusive distribution in Canada but who do not have property right in the book, e.g. they do not have a right to authorize the reproduction of the book.

As a result of the amendments made in Bill C-32, there are two new provisions in the *Copyright Act* which allow rights holders in Canada to protect their exclusive distribution rights in the Canadian market. One gives the rights holder certain abilities to sue persons after a book has been imported without authorization.

The other allows the rights holder and the exclusive distributor to obtain a court order requiring the detention of particular shipments of parallel imports by customs officials.

In order to protect booksellers, libraries and consumers against the possibility that increased market exclusivity will result in excessive book prices or lower standards of service, the *Copyright Act* confers specific regulatory power to the Governor in Council to establish the criteria or standards exclusive distributors are required to adhere to in order to benefit from the additional protection they have under the regime. The Regulations set out these standards which include: the form of the notice stating that there is an exclusive distributor for a particular book, confirmation time for orders, delivery time which the exclusive distributor must meet, and price differential. In addition, there are rules for remaindered books, damaged books, books intended for re-export, special orders and leased books. It was decided that these criteria and standards could be best dealt with through regulations so that they can be easily modified and also, because they necessarily contain extensive details.

The Regulations specify the categories of books to be partially or wholly excluded from the parallel importation provisions. The Regulations allow for the importation of used textbooks. If restrictions on the importation of used textbooks are ever warranted, the government will consult with all interested parties before amending the Regulations to implement any such restrictions.

These Regulations have been developed to reflect, as closely as possible, competitive market conditions for the distribution of imported books, consistent with voluntary industry guidelines that were negotiated by industry stakeholders. Recourse to the provisions in the *Copyright Act* against parallel importations of books will only be made available to exclusive distributors in those circumstances where mark-up beyond the list price of a book is no greater than a prescribed percentage, which varies according to whether the books are imported from one of three areas: the U.S., Europe or the rest of the world. These percentages correspond to the average actual costs currently paid by book importers for transportation and related expenses — including shipping, handling and receiving, inventory, financial reporting, general overhead and sales and marketing — for imports from each of the three areas. These simple percentage marks-ups ensure that importers, libraries and book retailers will have a straightforward mechanism with which to evaluate costs and that they will thereby be protected against unfair pricing practices.

Alternatives

The Act requires Regulations in order to extend parallel importation provisions to exclusive distributors. Without these Regulations, no person could qualify as an "exclusive distributor", and exclusive distributors would not be entitled to the new protection against parallel imports provided in the amendments made by Bill C-32.

Benefits and Costs

Exclusive distributors pay for the right to distribute books in Canada, and the amount of the payment may be based on an

poursuivre une personne pour importation non autorisée d'un livre. L'autre confère au titulaire des droits et au distributeur exclusif le droit d'obtenir une ordonnance du tribunal pour la saisie, par les douaniers, de convois particuliers de livres faisant l'objet d'une importation parallèle.

Dans le but de protéger les libraires, les bibliothèques et les consommateurs contre la possibilité que l'exclusivité grandissante sur le marché ne fasse grimper le prix des livres ou ne nuise aux normes de service, la *Loi sur le droit d'auteur* accorde des pouvoirs de réglementation particuliers au gouverneur en conseil afin que celui-ci puisse établir des critères ou des normes que les distributeurs exclusifs devront respecter s'ils veulent profiter de la protection supplémentaire que leur accorde le régime. Le règlement établit ces critères, qui comprennent les modalités de présentation de l'avis d'existence d'un distributeur exclusif, les délais de livraison et de confirmation, ainsi que les écarts de prix. En outre, l'importation de livres soldés, de livres endommagés et de livres destinés à la réexportation, les commandes spéciales et les livres loués sont régis par des règles. Il a été décidé qu'il serait préférable d'adopter ces normes par voie de règlement parce qu'elles peuvent ainsi être facilement modifiées et parce que les règlements contiennent nécessairement une abondance de détails.

Le règlement précise les catégories de livres qui sont partiellement ou complètement exclues des mesures relatives à l'importation parallèle. Le règlement autorise l'importation de manuels scolaires d'occasion. S'il s'avérait nécessaire d'apporter des limitations à l'importation de manuels scolaires d'occasion, le gouvernement consulterait toutes les parties intéressées avant d'adopter tout règlement.

Ce règlement a été élaboré de manière à refléter, le plus fidèlement possible, les conditions compétitives du marché relatives à l'importation de livres, telles qu'elles ont été négociées par les intervenants concernés. Les distributeurs exclusifs ne pourront recourir aux dispositions de la *Loi sur le droit d'auteur*, sur les importations parallèles de livres, que dans les cas où la majoration des prix, au-delà du prix du catalogue, ne sera pas plus élevée que les pourcentages indiqués. Ces derniers varient selon que les livres proviennent de l'un des trois territoires suivants : les États-Unis, l'Europe ou le reste du monde. Ces pourcentages correspondent à la moyenne des frais que doivent payer les importateurs de livres pour le transport et les dépenses reliées, incluant : l'expédition, la manutention et la réception, le stockage, les rapports financiers, les frais généraux, les ventes et les coûts de marketing, pour des importations provenant des trois territoires mentionnés précédemment. Ces pourcentages garantissent aux importateurs, bibliothèques et détaillants un mécanisme permettant de déterminer les frais reliés au transport ce qui, en conséquence, les protège contre une pratique inéquitable de fixation des prix.

Solutions envisagées

La Loi doit être accompagnée d'un règlement pour que les dispositions sur l'importation parallèle s'appliquent aux distributeurs exclusifs. Sans ce règlement, personne ne pourrait être désigné « distributeur exclusif » et les distributeurs exclusifs n'auraient pas droit à la nouvelle protection contre l'importation parallèle qu'accordent les modifications apportées au projet de loi C-32.

Avantages et coûts

Les distributeurs exclusifs paient pour obtenir le droit de distribuer des livres au Canada, et ce montant peut être fondé sur un

expectation of a certain volume of sales. The provisions in the Act limiting parallel importation give exclusive distributors greater commercial certainty with respect to the rights they have purchased. Without these Regulations, the parallel importation provisions of the Act would be ineffective, and those with exclusive distribution contracts would not in all cases derive the full benefits of their distribution contracts. This would be detrimental to the Canadian publishing sector, as a whole.

As a result of the Regulations, there may be additional costs to retailers and institutional buyers. To protect against excessive prices, the regulation requires that exclusive distributors meet certain standards with regard to pricing, and these are based on mark-ups reflecting prevailing market conditions.

There will be no additional costs to the government due to the implementation of these Regulations.

Consultation

Consultations with the major interested parties (The Association of Canadian Publishers, The Canadian Publishers' Council, Canadian Booksellers Association, Canadian Library Association, Book and Periodical Council, Wholesalers, Canadian Telebook Agency, Association Nationale des Éditeurs de Livres, Association des Libraires du Québec) have taken place over the last two years. These parties met on a number of occasions to negotiate the terms of the Regulations and were provided with different drafts of these Regulations.

In addition, there were consultations with Western Canadian College Stores Association, Eastern Campus Booksellers, Canadian Federation of Students, Canadian Alliance of Student Associations and Follett Campus Resources on the issue of used textbooks.

These Regulations and accompanying Regulatory Impact Analysis Statement (RIAS) were prepublished in the January 30, 1999 issue of the *Canada Gazette*, Part I. Interested parties were invited to make any representations concerning these Regulations within 45 days of the date of prepublication.

Comments were received from The Canadian Publishers' Council, the Association of Canadian Publishers, l'Association des distributeurs exclusifs de livres en langue française, The Writers' Union of Canada, Canadian Library Association, Book Depot, The Ontario Library Association, McNally Robinson, and Lang Michener (for Follett Campus Resources).

While views remained divergent on certain issues, the resulting Regulations represent a reasonable compromise.

Minor modifications (drafting issues) were made to the Regulations in order to better reflect the agreement reached by the parties during the consultations or to clarify the intention of the Government:

Notice of exclusive distributor: section 27.1(5) states that no exclusive distributor is entitled to a remedy unless, before the infringement occurred, notice has been given within the prescribed time and in the prescribed manner described in the Regulations. Section 4 of the Regulations states that the exclusive distributor shall give this notice (in the case of a bookseller, library or other institution) by setting out the fact that there is an exclusive distributor of the book in the publications mentioned in

certain volume de ventes prévu. Les dispositions de la Loi limitant l'importation parallèle donnent aux distributeurs exclusifs une plus grande certitude commerciale quant aux droits qu'ils ont achetés. Sans l'application des dispositions réglementaires, les mesures relatives à l'importation parallèle seraient sans effet et les distributeurs exclusifs ne tireraient aucun avantage du nouveau régime, ce qui nuirait au secteur de l'édition canadienne dans son ensemble.

Les détaillants et les acheteurs institutionnels pourraient devoir payer des frais supplémentaires par suite de l'application du règlement. Pour éviter les prix exorbitants, le règlement exige des distributeurs exclusifs qu'ils respectent certaines normes relatives à l'établissement de prix. Ces normes sont fondées sur la majoration des prix reflétant la conjoncture du marché.

Le gouvernement n'aura à payer aucun coût supplémentaire par suite de l'application de ce règlement.

Consultations

Des consultations se sont déroulées auprès des principales parties intéressées (Association des éditeurs canadiens, Canadian Publishers' Council, Canadian Booksellers Association, Canadian Library Association, Book and Periodical Council, les grossistes, Canadian Telebook Agency, Association nationale des éditeurs de livres et Association des libraires du Québec) au cours des deux dernières années. Ces parties se sont réunies à plusieurs occasions pour négocier les modalités du règlement et ont reçu les différents projets de règlement.

Des consultations sur les manuels scolaires d'occasion ont également eu lieu avec les organismes suivants : Western Canadian College Stores Association, Eastern Campus Booksellers, Canadian Federation of Students, Canadian Alliance of Student Associations et Follet Campus Resources.

Ce règlement ainsi que le Résumé de l'étude d'impact de la réglementation ont fait l'objet d'une publication préalable dans la *Gazette du Canada,* Partie I, le 30 janvier 1999. Les personnes intéressées étaient invitées à présenter leurs observations au sujet du règlement dans les 45 jours suivant la date de publication au préalable.

The Canadian Publishers' Council, l'Association des éditeurs canadiens, l'Association des distributeurs exclusifs de livres en langue française, The Writers' Union of Canada, la Canadian Library Association, Book Depot, l'Association des bibliothèques de l'Ontario, McNally Robinson ainsi que Lang Michener (au nom de Follett Campus Resources) ont présenté leurs observations.

Même si les opinions demeuraient divergentes sur certaines questions, le règlement qui en a résulté constitue un compromis raisonnable.

Des modifications mineures (relatives à la rédaction) ont été apportées au règlement afin de mieux refléter l'entente à laquelle sont parvenues les parties lors des consultations ou pour préciser l'intention du gouvernement.

Avis de l'existence d'un distributeur exclusif : selon le paragraphe 27.1(5), un distributeur exclusif ne peut exercer les recours prévus que si, avant les faits qui donnent lieu au litige, les personnes intéressées ont été avisées selon les modalités réglementaires. Aux termes de l'article 4 du règlement, le distributeur exclusif doit, dans le cas d'un libraire, d'une bibliothèque ou d'une autre institution, publier une mention du fait qu'il existe un distributeur exclusif du livre en cause dans les publications

paragraph (i), a catalogue (paragraph (ii)) or the *Banque de titres de langue française* (paragraph (iii)). In response to concerns expressed by publishers and libraries, section 4 was modified to clarify that the catalogue mentioned in paragraph (ii) will be supplied at the request of a bookseller, library or other institution.

Notice of exclusive distributor: the title "Canadian Telebook Agency Microfiche and Ordering System" and "Books in Print Plus on Disc- Canadian Edition" were changed to their official titles "Canadian Telebook Agency Microfiche" and "Books in Print Plus - Canadian Edition".

Application: section 5(5) and 6(3) stated: "for greater certainty, this section shall not be constructed as authorizing anyone to do or to omit to do an act that would constitute an infringement of copyright under subsection 27(2) of the Act". As this statement applies to the regulation in its entirety, it was moved to the "application" section.

Imported books: in section 5(1)(iii) the words "minus any applicable discounts" should have appeared in paragraph (B) as it does in paragraph (A), and was therefore added to paragraph (B).

Imported books: section 5(1)(iii) was also modified in order to better reflect the intention of the government not to interfere with laws of any province with respect to prices concerning the distribution of books.

Canadian edition: in section 6(1)(*b*) the phrase "before an order can be placed" is replaced by "before an order is placed" to reflect the intention of the parties.

Remaindered and other books: in response to concerns expressed by Book Depot to the effect that there is no incentive for a foreign publisher to respect the conditions set in the Regulations, the word "or" was added in section 7(*a*) between "...marked as a remaindered book" and "the original foreign publisher has given notice...". For the same reason, it is specified in paragraph (*b*) that the book is marked as damaged book "by the importer or the retailer".

Special orders: in section 9(2), the calculation of the 24 hours is from the receipt of the special order rather than from the time the special order is placed as previously stated. This is to conform to the intention of the parties and to other calculations of time stated in the Regulations.

These modifications do not in any way change the policy formulated by Industry Canada and Canadian Heritage.

Other comments were received from stakeholders; however, after careful consideration, they did not result in any changes in the Regulations for the following reasons:

- they were drafting issues not required for better understanding of the Regulations;

- they exceeded the regulatory power stated in *Copyright Act*; and,

- they were contrary to the policy developed by Industry Canada and Canadian Heritage, in consultation with the stakeholders.

mentionnées au paragraphe (i), un catalogue (paragraphe (ii)) ou la *Banque de titres de langue française* (paragraphe (iii)). En réponse aux préoccupations exprimées par les éditeurs et les bibliothèques, le paragraphe 4 a été modifié en apportant la précision suivante : le catalogue mentionné au paragraphe (ii) sera fourni à la demande d'un libraire, d'une bibliothèque ou d'une autre institution.

Avis de l'existence d'un distributeur exclusif : les titres « Canadian Telebook Agency Microfiche and Ordering System » et « Books in Print Plus on Disc- Canadian Edition » ont été remplacés par leur version officielle, soit « Canadian Telebook Agency Microfiche » et « Books in Print Plus - Canadian Edition ».

Application : en vertu des paragraphes 5(5) et 6(3), « Il est entendu que le présent article n'autorise pas l'accomplissement d'un acte ou une omission qui constituerait une violation du droit d'auteur aux termes du paragraphe 27(2) de la Loi ». Étant donné que cet énoncé s'applique à l'ensemble du règlement, il fait maintenant partie de la section portant sur l'« application ».

Livres importés : les mots « les remises applicables étant soustraites du total », qui font partie de l'alinéa 5(1)(iii), auraient dû faire partie du paragraphe (B), comme c'est le cas pour le paragraphe (A). Ils ont donc été ajoutés au paragraphe (B).

Livres importés : l'alinéa 5(1)(iii) a également été modifié afin de mieux refléter l'intention du gouvernement de ne pas intervenir dans l'établissement de prix pour la distribution de livres régi par les lois provinciales.

Édition canadienne : dans l'alinéa 6(1)(*b*), les termes « avant que des commandes puissent être passées » est replacé par « avant que des commandes ne soient passées » afin de respecter l'intention des parties.

Livres soldés et autres : en réponse aux préoccupations exprimées par Book Depot du fait qu'il n'existe aucune mesure incitant les éditeurs étrangers à respecter les conditions établies dans le règlement, le terme « ou » a été ajouté dans le paragraphe 7(*a*) entre «...sont marqués comme étant des livres soldés » et « l'éditeur original étranger a envoyé au distributeur exclusif, s'il existe, un avis... ». Pour la même raison, le paragraphe (*b*) précise que les livres sont marqués comme étant des livres endommagés par « l'importateur ou le détaillant ».

Commandes spéciales : dans le paragraphe 9(2), les 24 heures prescrites sont calculées à partir de la réception de la commande spéciale, plutôt qu'à partir du moment où la commande est passée, comme il était précédemment énoncé. Cette modification a été apportée afin de respecter l'intention des parties ainsi que les calculs mentionnés dans le règlement.

Ces modifications ne changent en aucune façon la politique formulée par Industrie Canada et Patrimoine Canada.

D'autres commentaires ont été reçus des intervenants. Cependant, après une étude minutieuse, ils n'ont pas été retenus aux fins de la modification du règlement pour les raisons suivantes :

- ils portaient sur des questions relatives à la rédaction n'étant pas nécessaires pour clarifier le règlement;

- ils outrepassaient le pouvoir de réglementation conféré par la *Loi sur le droit d'auteur*;

- ils ne respectaient pas la politique élaborée par Industrie Canada et Patrimoine Canada en consultation avec les intervenants.

Compliance and Enforcement

Compliance and enforcement mechanisms are not required. The exclusive distributor who does not respect the standards prescribed in these Regulations will not benefit from the additional protection offered by the parallel importation regime. On the other hand, it is an infringement of copyright in a book for any person to import a book in a manner contrary to what is stipulated in the *Copyright Act* and these Regulations.

Respect et exécution

Il n'y a pas lieu de mettre en place des mécanismes de surveillance du respect et de l'exécution. D'un côté, le distributeur exclusif qui ne respecte pas les normes prescrites par ce règlement ne profitera pas de la protection supplémentaire que lui accorde le régime réglementant l'importation de livres. D'un autre côté, l'importation, par quiconque, d'un livre d'une manière contraire aux dispositions de la *Loi sur le droit d'auteur* et du règlement constitue une violation du droit d'auteur qui protège le livre en question.

Contacts

Bruce Couchman
Senior Legal Analyst
Intellectual Property Policy Directorate
Industry Canada
5th Floor West, Room 521-F
235 Queen Street
Ottawa, Ontario
K1A 0H5
Tel.: (613) 952-2621
FAX: (613) 952-1980
E-mail: couchman.bruce@ic.gc.ca

Edith St-Hilaire
Senior Policy Analyst
Copyright Policy
Department of Canadian Heritage
4th Floor, Room 135
15 Eddy Street
Hull, Quebec
K1A 0M5
Tel.: (819) 997-5998
FAX: (819) 997-5685
E-mail: edith_st-hilaire@pch.gc.ca

Personnes-ressources

Bruce Couchman
Analyste juridique principal
Direction de la politique de la propriété intellectuelle
Industrie Canada
5ᵉ étage ouest, pièce 521-F
235, rue Queen
Ottawa (Ontario)
K1A 0H5
Tél. : (613) 952-2621
TÉLÉCOPIEUR : (613) 952-1980
Courriel : couchman.bruce@ic.gc.ca

Édith St-Hilaire
Analyste politique principale
Politique du droit d'auteur
Ministère du Patrimoine canadien
4ᵉ étage, pièce 135
15, rue Eddy
Hull (Québec)
K1A 0M5
Tél. : (819) 997-5998
TÉLÉCOPIEUR : (819) 997-5685
Courriel : edith_st-hilaire@pch.gc.ca

Published by the Queen's Printer for Canada, 1999

Publié par l'Imprimeur de la Reine pour le Canada, 1999

Registration
SOR/99-325   28 July, 1999

COPYRIGHT ACT

Exception for Educational Institutions, Libraries, Archives and Museums Regulations

P.C. 1999-1351   28 July, 1999

His Excellency the Governor General in Council, on the recommendation of the Minister of Industry, pursuant to subsections 30.2(6)[a], 30.21(4)[a] and (6)[a] and 30.3(5)[a] of the *Copyright Act*, hereby makes the annexed *Exceptions for Educational Institutions, Libraries, Archives and Museums Regulations*.

EXCEPTIONS FOR EDUCATIONAL INSTITUTIONS, LIBRARIES, ARCHIVES AND MUSEUMS REGULATIONS

INTERPRETATION

1. (1) In these Regulations, "Act" means the *Copyright Act*.

(2) In these Regulations, a reference to a copy of a work is a reference to a copy of all or any substantial part of a work.

NEWSPAPER OR PERIODICAL

2. For the purpose of subsection 30.2(6) of the Act, "newspaper or periodical" means a newspaper or a periodical, other than a scholarly, scientific or technical periodical, that was published more than one year before the copy is made.

RECORDS KEPT UNDER SECTION 30.2 OF THE ACT

3. In respect of activities undertaken by a library, an archive or a museum under subsection 30.2(1) of the Act, section 4 applies only to the reproduction of works.

4. (1) Subject to subsection (2), a library, an archive or a museum, or a person acting under the authority of one, shall record the following information with respect to a copy of a work that is made under section 30.2 of the Act:

(*a*) the name of the library, archive or museum making the copy;

(*b*) if the request for a copy is made by a library, archive or museum on behalf of a person who is a patron of the library, archive or museum, the name of the library, archive or museum making the request;

(*c*) the date of the request; and

(*d*) information that is sufficient to identify the work, such as
  (i) the title,
  (ii) the International Standard Book Number,
  (iii) the International Standard Serial Number,

---
[a] S.C. 1997, c. 24, s. 18(1)

Enregistrement
DORS/99-325   28 juillet 1999

LOI SUR LE DROIT D'AUTEUR

Règlement sur les cas d'exception à l'égard des établissements d'enseignement, des bibliothèques, des musées et des services d'archives

C.P. 1999-1351   28 juillet 1999

Sur recommandation du ministre de l'Industrie et en vertu des paragraphes 30.2(6)[a], 30.21(4)[a] et (6)[a] et 30.3(5)[a] de la *Loi sur le droit d'auteur*, Son Excellence le Gouverneur général en conseil prend le *Règlement sur les cas d'exception à l'égard des établissements d'enseignement, des bibliothèques, des musées et des services d'archives*, ci-après.

RÈGLEMENT SUR LES CAS D'EXCEPTION À L'ÉGARD DES ÉTABLISSEMENTS D'ENSEIGNEMENT, DES BIBLIOTHÈQUES, DES MUSÉES ET DES SERVICES D'ARCHIVES

DÉFINITION ET INTERPRÉTATION

1. (1) Dans le présent règlement, « Loi » s'entend de la *Loi sur le droit d'auteur*.

(2) Dans le présent règlement, la mention de la reproduction d'une oeuvre vaut mention de la reproduction de l'intégralité ou de toute partie importante de celle-ci.

JOURNAL ET PÉRIODIQUE

2. Pour l'application du paragraphe 30.2(6) de la Loi, « journal ou périodique » s'entend, selon le cas, d'un journal ou d'un périodique qui a paru plus d'un an avant sa reproduction. Sont exclus de la présente définition les revues savantes et les périodiques de nature scientifique ou technique.

REGISTRE TENU EN VERTU DE L'ARTICLE 30.2 DE LA LOI

3. En ce qui a trait aux actes accomplis par une bibliothèque, un musée ou un service d'archives en vertu du paragraphe 30.2(1) de la Loi, seule la reproduction d'oeuvres est visée par l'article 4.

4. (1) Sous réserve du paragraphe (2), la bibliothèque, le musée ou le service d'archives, ou la personne agissant sous son autorité, obtient les renseignements suivants relativement à la reproduction d'une oeuvre en vertu de l'article 30.2 de la Loi :

a) le nom de la bibliothèque, du musée ou du service d'archives reproduisant l'oeuvre;

b) si la demande de reproduction est faite par une bibliothèque, un musée ou un service d'archives pour le compte d'un de ses usagers, le nom de la bibliothèque, du musée ou du service d'archives;

c) la date de la demande;

d) tout renseignement permettant d'identifier l'oeuvre, notamment :
  (i) le titre de l'oeuvre,
  (ii) le Numéro international normalisé du livre,

---
[a] L.C. 1997, ch. 24, par. 18(1)

(iv) the name of the newspaper, the periodical or the scholarly, scientific or technical periodical in which the work is found, if the work was published in a newspaper, a periodical or a scholarly, scientific or technical periodical,

(v) the date or volume and number of the newspaper or periodical, if the work was published in a newspaper or periodical,

(vi) the date or volume and number of the scholarly, scientific or technical periodical, if the work was published in a scholarly, scientific or technical periodical, and

(vii) the numbers of the copied pages.

(2) A library, an archive or a museum, or a person acting under the authority of one, does not have to record the information referred to in subsection (1) if the copy of the work is made under subsection 30.2(1) of the Act after December 31, 2003.

(3) A library, an archive or a museum, or a person acting under the authority of one, shall keep the information referred to in subsection (1)

(a) by retaining the copy request form; or

(b) in any other manner that is capable of reproducing the information in intelligible written form within a reasonable time.

(4) A library, an archive or a museum, or a person acting under the authority of one, shall keep the information referred to in subsection (1) with respect to copies made of a work for at least three years.

(5) A library, an archive or a museum, or a person acting under the authority of one, shall make the information referred to in subsection (1), with respect to copies made of a work, available once a year to one of the following persons, on request made by the person in accordance with subsection (7):

(a) the owner of copyright in the work;

(b) the representative of the owner of copyright in the work; or

(c) a collective society that is authorized by the owner of copyright in the work to grant licences on their behalf.

(6) A library, an archive or a museum, or a person acting under the authority of one, shall make the information referred to in subsection (1) available to the person making the request, within 28 days after the receipt of the request or any longer period that may be agreed to by both of them.

(7) A request referred to in subsection (5) must be made in writing, indicate the name of the author of the work and the title of the work, and be signed by the person making the request and include a statement by that person indicating that the request is made under paragraph (5)(a), (b) or (c).

RECORDS KEPT UNDER SUBSECTION 30.21(6) OF THE ACT

5. (1) An archive, or a person acting under the authority of one, shall record the following information with respect to a copy of a work that is made under subsection 30.21(5) of the Act:

(a) the name of the archive making the copy;

(b) the name of the person requesting the copy or, if the request for a copy is made by another archive on behalf of a person who is a patron of the other archive, the name of the patron and the archive making the request;

(c) the date of the request; and

(d) information that is sufficient to identify the work copied.

(2) An archive, or a person acting under the authority of one, shall keep the information referred to in subsection (1)

(a) in a record maintained by the archive of the names of all individuals who have had access to the work in question;

(b) by retaining the copy request form; or

(c) in any other manner that is capable of reproducing the information in intelligible written form within a reasonable time.

(3) An archive, or a person acting under the authority of one, shall keep the information referred to in subsection (1) with respect to copies made of a work for at least three years.

(4) An archive, or a person acting under the authority of one, shall make the information referred to in subsection (1), with respect to copies made of a work, available, on request in writing, to

(a) the author of the work;

(b) the owner of copyright in the work; or

(c) the representative of the author or owner of copyright.

(5) An archive, or a person acting under the authority of one, shall inform a person requesting a copy of a work under subsection 30.21(5) of the Act, in writing, at the time of the request, or if the person has registered as a patron of the archive, at the time of registration, of the fact that the archive will make the information referred to in subsection (1) available, on request, to the persons referred to in paragraphs (4)(a) to (c).

PATRONS OF ARCHIVES

6. (1) If a person requests a copy of a work from an archive under section 30.21 of the Act and the person has registered as a patron of the archive, the archive shall inform the patron in writing at the time of registration

(a) that any copy is to be used solely for the purpose of research or private study; and

(b) that any use of a copy for a purpose other than research or private study may require the authorization of the copyright owner of the work in question.

(2) If a person requests a copy of a work from an archive under section 30.21 of the Act and the person has not registered as a patron of the archive, the archive shall inform the person in writing at the time of the request

(a) that any copy is to be used solely for the purpose of research or private study; and

(b) that any use of a copy for a purpose other than research or private study may require the authorization of the copyright owner of the work in question.

STAMPING OF COPIED WORKS

7. A library, archive or museum, or a person acting under the authority of one, that makes a copy of a work under section 30.2 or 30.21 of the Act shall inform the person requesting the copy, by means of text printed on the copy or a stamp applied to the copy, if the copy is in printed format, or by other appropriate means, if the copy is made in another format,

(a) that the copy is to be used solely for the purpose of research or private study; and

c) la date de la demande;

d) tout renseignement permettant d'identifier l'oeuvre reproduite.

(2) Le service d'archives ou la personne agissant sous son autorité conserve les renseignements visés au paragraphe (1) :

a) soit dans un registre qu'il tient des noms de ceux qui ont eu accès à l'oeuvre en cause;

b) soit en gardant le formulaire de demande de la reproduction;

c) soit de toute autre façon pouvant donner, dans un délai raisonnable, les renseignements sous une forme écrite compréhensible.

(3) Le service d'archives ou la personne agissant sous son autorité conserve les renseignements visés au paragraphe (1) pendant au moins trois ans.

(4) Le service d'archives ou la personne agissant sous son autorité met les renseignements visés au paragraphe (1) relatifs aux reproductions d'une oeuvre à la disposition des personnes suivantes qui en font la demande par écrit :

a) l'auteur de l'oeuvre;

b) le titulaire du droit d'auteur sur l'oeuvre;

c) le représentant de l'auteur ou du titulaire du droit d'auteur.

(5) Le service d'archives ou la personne agissant sous son autorité informe par écrit la personne qui demande la reproduction d'une oeuvre dans le cadre du paragraphe 30.21(5) de la Loi que les renseignements visés au paragraphe (1) seront mis à la disposition des personnes visées aux alinéas (4)a) à c) qui en font la demande. Cette information est donnée au moment de la présentation de la demande ou, si la personne est un usager inscrit du service d'archives, au moment de son inscription.

USAGERS DES SERVICES D'ARCHIVES

6. (1) Si la personne qui demande la reproduction d'une oeuvre à un service d'archives dans le cadre de l'article 30.21 de la Loi est un usager inscrit du service d'archives, celui-ci doit l'informer par écrit au moment de son inscription :

a) que la reproduction ne doit servir qu'à des fins d'études privées ou de recherche;

b) que tout usage de la reproduction à d'autres fins peut exiger l'autorisation du titulaire du droit d'auteur sur l'oeuvre en cause.

(2) Si la personne qui demande la reproduction d'une oeuvre à un service d'archives dans le cadre de l'article 30.21 de la Loi n'est pas un usager inscrit du service d'archives, celui-ci doit l'informer par écrit au moment de la demande :

a) que la reproduction ne doit servir qu'à des fins d'études privées ou de recherche;

b) que tout usage de la reproduction à d'autres fins peut exiger l'autorisation du titulaire du droit d'auteur sur l'oeuvre en cause.

ESTAMPILLAGE DES OEUVRES REPRODUITES

7. La bibliothèque, le musée ou le service d'archives, ou la personne agissant sous son autorité, qui reproduit une oeuvre en vertu des articles 30.2 ou 30.21 de la Loi informe la personne qui a demandé la reproduction, par impression d'un texte ou apposition d'une estampille sur la reproduction, si celle-ci est sous une forme imprimée, ou selon tout autre moyen indiqué, si elle est sur un autre support :

a) que la reproduction ne doit servir qu'à des fins d'études privées ou de recherche;

(*b*) that any use of the copy for a purpose other than research or private study may require the authorization of the copyright owner of the work in question.

NOTICE

8. An educational institution, a library, an archive or a museum in respect of which subsection 30.3(2), (3) or (4) of the Act applies shall ensure that a notice that contains at least the following information is affixed to, or within the immediate vicinity of, every photocopier in a place and manner that is readily visible and legible to persons using the photocopier:

"WARNING!

Works protected by copyright may be copied on
this photocopier only if authorized by

(*a*) the *Copyright Act* for the purpose of fair dealing or under specific exceptions set out in that Act;
(*b*) the copyright owner; or
(*c*) a licence agreement between this institution and a collective society or a tariff, if any.

For details of authorized copying, please consult the licence agreement or the applicable tariff, if any, and other relevant information available from a staff member.

The Copyright Act provides for civil and criminal remedies for infringement of copyright."

COMING INTO FORCE

9. These Regulations come into force on September 1, 1999.

REGULATORY IMPACT
ANALYSIS STATEMENT

(*This statement is not part of the Regulations.*)

Description

Bill C-32, *An Act to amend the Copyright Act*, received Royal Assent on April 25, 1997. Among the measures introduced in this bill were exceptions to allow the copying of material by non-profit educational institutions, libraries, archives, and museums.

Under the Act a person may engage in "fair dealing" (normally copying) for purposes of research, private study, criticism or review of copyrighted material without infringing copyright. The *Copyright Act* allows non-profit libraries, archives, and museums, or persons acting under their authority to do these same things on behalf of a person engaged in such activities. In addition, non-profit libraries, archives and museums, or persons acting under their authority, may make a single copy of certain articles appearing in a newspaper or periodical, if they are satisfied that the copy is to be used by the person for purposes of research or private study. The Act provides that the above exceptions also apply to interlibrary loans. However, where the requested copy is transmitted electronically between two institutions, the Act

b) que tout usage de la reproduction à d'autres fins peut exiger l'autorisation du titulaire du droit d'auteur sur l'oeuvre en cause.

AVERTISSEMENT

8. L'établissement d'enseignement, la bibliothèque, le musée ou le service d'archives qui sont visés par les paragraphes 30.3(2), (3) ou (4) de la Loi veillent à ce qu'un avertissement contenant au moins les renseignements suivants soit apposé sur chaque photocopieuse, ou placé à proximité de celle-ci, de façon à être bien visible et lisible pour les utilisateurs :

« AVERTISSEMENT!

Les oeuvres protégées par un droit d'auteur peuvent être
reproduites avec cette photocopieuse seulement si la
reproduction est autorisée :

a) soit par la *Loi sur le droit d'auteur* à des fins équitables ou s'il s'agit de cas d'exception prévues par elle;
b) soit par le titulaire du droit d'auteur;
c) soit par une entente visant une licence entre cet établissement et une société de gestion ou par un tarif, le cas échéant.

Pour plus de renseignements sur la reproduction autorisée, veuillez consulter l'entente visant la licence, le tarif applicable et tout autre renseignement pertinent qui sont disponibles auprès d'un membre du personnel.

La Loi sur le droit d'auteur prévoit des recours civils et criminels en cas de violation du droit d'auteur. »

ENTRÉE EN VIGUEUR

9. Le présent règlement entre en vigueur le 1er septembre 1999.

RÉSUMÉ DE L'ÉTUDE D'IMPACT
DE LA RÉGLEMENTATION

(*Ce résumé ne fait pas partie du règlement.*)

Description

Le projet de Loi C-32, *Loi modifiant la Loi sur le droit d'auteur*, a reçu la sanction royale le 25 avril 1997. Parmi les mesures énoncées dans le projet de loi, on comptait des exceptions visant à permettre aux établissements d'enseignement, aux bibliothèques, aux archives et aux musées à but non lucratif de faire des copies de certains ouvrages.

En vertu de la Loi, une personne peut exercer une activité qualifiée d' « utilisation équitable » (normalement la copie de documents) en vue d'effectuer des recherches ou une étude particulière, de préparer une critique ou d'examiner des documents protégés par le droit d'auteur sans porter atteinte à ce droit. Aux termes de la *Loi sur le droit d'auteur*, les bibliothèques, archives et musées à but non lucratif, ou les personnes agissant sous leur autorité, peuvent faire, au nom d'une personne, tout ce que cette personne peut faire lorsqu'elle effectue de tels travaux. En outre les bibliothèques, archives et musées à but non lucratif, ou les personnes agissant sous leur autorité, peuvent faire une copie unique de certains articles parus dans un journal ou un périodique, s'ils sont convaincus que la personne se servira de la copie

specifies that the copy given to the patron must not be in digital form.

The Regulations prescribe the information to be recorded by such institutions concerning copies of copyrighted material they have made for patrons under the exceptions. The Regulations further provide that the information must be retained by the institutions for three years, and set conditions for access to the records. However, where copying is done by an institution at its premises for patrons engaged in "fair dealing", records need to be kept only for copies made prior to January 1, 2004. This "sunset" clause will provide libraries, archives, museums and copyright owners the opportunity to assess, over a set period of time, the costs and benefits of this particular record keeping requirement. Prior to the "sunset" date, the Departments of Industry and Canadian Heritage will review the operation of this provision with affected stakeholders.

The Regulations give effect to provisions in the Act which allow a non-profit archive to make a copy of an unpublished work deposited in the archive after these provisions come into effect, provided that the copyright owner has not prohibited copying and the archive is satisfied that the copy will be used for purposes of research or private study. In the event that a copyright owner cannot be located, and the work was deposited in the archive prior to the coming into force of the exception, the Regulations set out what records must be kept by the archive. These records are open to inspection by the author of the work, the copyright owner of the work, or the representative of the author or copyright owner.

Under the Act, non-profit educational institutions, libraries, archives and museums are not liable with respect to independent uses of photocopiers on their premises if they have an agreement with a copyright collective or if a copyright collective has filed a tariff with the Copyright Board or the Copyright Board has approved such a tariff, provided that a sign containing information set out in the Regulations has been posted in the immediate vicinity of the machine. The notice is to warn against copyright infringement. (Copyright collectives are organizations which collect royalties on behalf of copyright owners.)

Alternatives

Three alternatives were considered with respect to the scope of record keeping: record keeping Regulations only where required under the Act, recording keeping for all types of uses allowed for under the exceptions, and record keeping for selected uses permitted under the exceptions. The third option was chosen. It was felt that only in the case of certain uses would record keeping assist copyright owners in detecting possible infringements.

Record keeping was not required under the section of the Act dealing with the "Management and maintenance of collections" because it was felt that these activities were of a routine nature and the possibility of infringement was minimal. Record keeping

aux fins de recherches ou d'étude particulière. En vertu de la Loi, ces exceptions s'appliquent également aux prêts entre bibliothèques. Toutefois, lorsque la copie demandée est transmise électroniquement entre les deux établissements, la Loi précise qu'on ne peut envoyer à l'usager une copie numérique.

Le règlement dicte quelle information les établissements doivent enregistrer concernant des copies de documents protégés par le droit d'auteur qu'ils ont faites pour des usagers en vertu des exceptions. Le règlement prévoit en outre que les établissements doivent conserver l'information pendant trois ans, et il fixe les conditions d'accès aux registres. Toutefois, lorsque des copies sont faites par un établissement dans ses locaux pour des usagers exerçant une activité qualifiée d' « utilisation équitable », il faut conserver des dossiers uniquement dans le cas de copies faites avant le 1er janvier 2004. Ce régime de temporisation donnera aux bibliothèques, aux archives, aux musées et aux détenteurs d'un droit d'auteur l'occasion d'évaluer, au cours d'une période précise, les coûts et les avantages de cette exigence particulière en matière de tenue de registres. Avant la date limitative, le ministère de l'Industrie et celui du Patrimoine canadien examineront le fonctionnement de cette disposition de concert avec les groupes d'intérêt touchés.

Le règlement donne effet aux dispositions de la Loi qui permettent aux archives à but non lucratif de faire une copie d'une oeuvre non publiée déposée aux archives après l'entrée en vigueur de l'exception lorsque le détenteur du droit d'auteur n'a pas prohibé la copie et que les archives à but non lucratif sont convaincues que la copie servira aux fins de recherche ou d'étude particulière. Lorsqu'on n'arrive pas à retracer le détenteur du droit d'auteur et que l'oeuvre a été déposée aux archives avant l'entrée en vigueur de l'exception, le règlement précise quels registres doivent être tenus par les archives. Ces registres sont ouverts à l'inspection par l'auteur de l'oeuvre, le détenteur du droit d'auteur ou leur représentant.

En vertu de la Loi, les établissements d'enseignement, les bibliothèques, les archives et les musées à but non lucratif ne sont pas responsables en ce qui concerne l'utilisation indépendante de photocopieurs dans leurs locaux s'ils ont conclu des accords avec des sociétés de gestion collective du droit d'auteur, si une telle société de droit d'auteur a déposé un tarif devant la Commission du droit d'auteur ou si la Commission du droit d'auteur a approuvé un tel tarif et si une affiche renfermant l'information précisée dans le règlement a été placée à proximité de la machine. L'avis sert à mettre les usagers en garde contre la violation du droit d'auteur. (Les sociétés de gestion collective du droit d'auteur sont des organismes qui recueillent les redevances au nom des titulaires d'un droit d'auteur.)

Solutions envisagées

Trois possibilités ont été examinées concernant l'étendue de la tenue de registres : règlement sur la tenue de registres seulement dans les cas où la Loi l'exige, tenue de registres pour tous les types d'utilisation permis à titre d'exceptions, et tenue de registres dans le cas de certains types d'utilisation permis à titre d'exceptions. La troisième option a été choisie. On estime que, seul dans le cas de certains types d'utilisation, la tenue de registres aiderait les titulaires d'un droit d'auteur à détecter des atteintes possibles à ce droit.

La tenue de registres n'était pas exigée en vertu de l'article de la Loi portant sur la gestion et l'entretien des collections, car on jugeait de telles activités routinières et les violations peu probables. La tenue de registres était exigée en vertu d'autres articles,

was required elsewhere because it was felt that this could deter or provide evidence of possibly infringing activities. The Regulation prescribes the nature of the notice to be displayed near photocopy machines because this would provide certainty and avoid disputes over the nature or adequacy of the notice.

There is no overlap or duplication. The federal government has exclusive jurisdiction in this matter.

Benefits and Costs

These Regulations may help copyright owners detect infringement, i.e., copying which exceeds or is outside of the statutory exception, and will protect the institutions against liability for unauthorized copying done on photocopying machines on their premises.

The Regulations will impose an administrative burden on the institutions. However, the cost to institutions will depend upon how many copies are made under the exceptions, the number of requests from copyright owners for access to the records, and the nature of the institutions' record keeping processes.

There will be no additional costs to the government due to these Regulations.

Consultation

As a result of consultations undertaken by the Departments of Industry and Canadian Heritage, the following were provided with informal drafts of these Regulations:

The Writers' Union of Canada (TWUC), Periodical Writers Association of Canada (PWAC), Playwrights Union of Canada, League of Canadian Poets, CANCOPY, COPIBEQ, Association nationale des éditeurs de livres (ANEL), Canadian Publishers' Council, Association of Canadian Publishers, Canadian Association of University Teachers (CAUT), National Library of Canada (NLC), Canadian Library Association (CLA), Canadian Association of Research Libraries (CARL), Association of Universities and Colleges of Canada (AUCC), Association pour l'avancement des sciences et des techniques de la documentation (ASTED), Archival Community Copyright Committee (ACCC), National Archives of Canada (NAC), Canadian Museums Association (CMA), Canadian Newspaper Association.

Groups representing creators and copyright owners supported record keeping for all types of copying done on behalf of patrons of libraries, archives and museums. Representatives of libraries felt that records should be kept only with respect to interlibrary loans. In particular, representatives of libraries were opposed to keeping records with respect to copies made for fair dealing purposes on behalf of patrons on the same premises.

While views remained divergent on certain issues, attempts were made to address in the Regulations many of the concerns raised in comments received by the two departments.

The Regulations and accompanying Regulatory Impact Analysis Statement were prepublished in the January 30, 1999, issue of the *Canada Gazette*, Part I. Interested parties were invited to make any representations concerning the Regulations within 45 days of the date of prepublication.

car on jugeait que cela pourrait prévenir les violations ou fournir des preuves de violations possibles. Le règlement prescrit la nature de l'avis qui doit être affiché à proximité des photocopieurs afin de donner une certitude et d'éviter les différends sur la nature ou la suffisance de l'avis.

Il n'y a pas de chevauchement. Cette question est du ressort exclusif du gouvernement fédéral.

Avantages et coûts

Ce règlement peut aider les détenteurs d'un droit d'auteur à détecter une atteinte à ce droit, c.-à-d., la copie qui va au-delà ou est en dehors de l'exception statutaire, et il protégera les établissements contre la responsabilité de copies non autorisées au moyen de photocopieurs dans leurs locaux.

Le règlement imposera une charge administrative aux établissements. Cependant, le coût à assumer par les établissements dépendra du nombre des copies faites à titre d'exceptions, du nombre de demandes présentées par des titulaires d'un droit d'auteur pour avoir accès aux registres et de la nature des méthodes de tenue de registres des établissements.

Ce règlement n'entraînera pas de coûts supplémentaires pour le gouvernement.

Consultations

Suite à des consultations entreprises par le ministère de l'Industrie et celui du Patrimoine canadien, les organismes suivants ont reçu une ébauche non officielle du règlement :

The Writers' Union of Canada (WUC), Periodical Writers Association of Canada (PWAC), Playwrights Union of Canada, League of Canadian Poets, CANCOPY, COPIBEQ, Association nationale des éditeurs de livres (ANEL), Canadian Publishers' Council, Association of Canadian Publishers, Association canadienne des professeurs d'université (ACPU), Bibliothèque nationale du Canada (BNC), Canadian Library Association (CLA), Association des bibliothèques de recherche du Canada (ACBRC), Association des universités et collèges du Canada (AUCC), Association pour l'avancement des sciences et des techniques de la documentation (ASTED), Comité du droit d'auteur de la communauté archivistique (CDACA), Archives nationales du Canada (ANC), Association des musées canadiens (AMC) et Association canadienne des éditeurs de journaux.

Les groupes représentant les créateurs et les titulaires d'un droit d'auteur ont appuyé la tenue de registres pour tous les types de copies faites au nom des usagers de bibliothèques, d'archives et de musées. Les représentants des bibliothèques étaient d'avis qu'il fallait tenir des registres uniquement dans le cas des prêts entre bibliothèques. En particulier, les représentants des bibliothèques s'opposent à l'obligation de tenir des registres dans le cas de copies qui seront utilisées de façon équitable et qui sont faites sur les lieux au nom d'usagers.

Les avis demeurent partagés sur certains sujets, mais on s'est efforcé de tenir compte, dans le règlement, d'un grand nombre des préoccupations soulevées dans les commentaires reçus par les deux ministères.

Ce règlement ainsi que le Résumé de l'étude d'impact de la réglementation ont fait l'objet d'une publication préalable dans la *Gazette du Canada*, Partie I, le 30 janvier 1999. Les personnes intéressées étaient invitées à présenter leurs observations au sujet du règlement dans les 45 jours suivant la date de publication préalable.

Comments were received from the Canadian Library Association, Canadian Association of University Teachers, Canadian Association of Research Libraries, Association pour l'avancement des sciences et des techniques de la documentation, Association of Universities and Colleges of Canada, Association of Canadian Community Colleges, The Writers' Union of Canada, Periodical Writers Association of Canada, Playwrights Union of Canada, League of Canadian Poets, Canadian Copyright Licensing Agency, The Law Society of British Columbia, Law Society of Upper Canada, Canadian Association of Law Libraries, The Law Society of Saskatchewan, British Columbia Courthouse Library Society, Association of Canadian Publishers, Canadian Publishers' Council, Ontario Library Association, Forum of Public Libraries of Ottawa-Carleton, Ottawa Public Library, McGill Medical and Health Libraries Association, Royal Columbian Hospital Library Simon Fraser Health Region.

Minor changes were made to the Regulations in order to clarify the intention of the Government or to ensure consistency in language.

Records kept under section 30.2 of the Act: in response to concerns, subsection 4(5) was redrafted to clarify the Government's intention to prevent the making of multiple requests to the same institution in the course of a calendar year, in respect to a particular work. This means that a right holder may not make more than one request with respect to the copying of a work in a single calendar year.

In this same subsection, paragraphs (*b*) and (*c*) were reworded to ensure consistency with the language contained in paragraph (*a*).

These modifications do not in any way change the policy formulated by Industry Canada and Canadian Heritage.

Notice: Comments were also received regarding section 8, seeking clarification that staff members would not be required to give an interpretation of the law as to what constitutes authorized copying. No modifications were made to the Regulations as it is not expected that this section of the Regulations would result in staff members having to provide interpretations of the law.

Other comments were received from stakeholders, but after careful consideration, they did not result in changes to the Regulations, for the following reasons:
— they exceeded the regulatory power provided for in the *Copyright Act*;
— they were contrary to the policy developed by Industry Canada and Canadian Heritage, in consultation with stakeholders; and,
— they were issues of terminology not required for a better understanding of the Regulations.

Compliance and Enforcement

Compliance and enforcement mechanisms are not required. Failure to keep the records required by the Regulations would constitute copyright infringement.

La Canadian Library Association, l'Association canadienne des professeurs d'université, l'Association des bibliothèques de recherche du Canada, l'Association pour l'avancement des sciences et des techniques de la documentation, l'Association des universités et collèges du Canada, l'Association des collèges communautaires du Canada, la Writers' Union of Canada, la Periodical Writers Association of Canada, la Playwrights Union of Canada, la League of Canadian Poets, la Canadian Copyright Licensing Agency, la Law Society of British Columbia, le Barreau du Haut-Canada, l'Association canadienne des bibliothèques de droit, la Law Society of Saskatchewan, la British Columbia Courthouse Library Society, l'Association of Canadian Publishers, le Canadian Publishers' Council, l'Ontario Library Association, le forum des bibliothèques publiques d'Ottawa-Carleton, la bibliothèque publique d'Ottawa, la McGill Medical and Health Libraries Association ainsi que la Royal Columbian Hospital Library Simon Fraser Health Region ont présenté leurs observations.

Des modifications mineures ont été apportées au règlement afin de préciser l'intention du gouvernement ou d'assurer l'uniformité de la terminologie.

Registre tenu en vertu de l'article 30.2 de la Loi : en réponse aux préoccupations exprimées, le paragraphe 4(5) a été réécrit de façon à préciser l'intention du gouvernement d'éviter que le même document ne fasse l'objet de plusieurs demandes auprès d'un établissement donné au cours d'une même année civile. Cela signifie que le détenteur d'un droit ne peut présenter plus d'une demande concernant la reproduction d'une oeuvre au cours d'une même année civile.

Dans le même paragraphe, la formulation des alinéas *b*) et *c*) a été modifiée pour assurer l'uniformité avec l'alinéa *a*).

Ces modifications ne changent en aucune façon la politique formulée par Industrie Canada et Patrimoine Canada.

Avis : Des commentaires ont également été reçus concernant l'article 8. Les auteurs de ces commentaires désiraient qu'il soit précisé que le personnel ne sera pas tenu d'interpréter la loi quant à la définition de « reproduction autorisée ». Aucune modification n'a été apportée au règlement, puisqu'on ne s'attend pas à ce que le personnel se voit obligé d'interpréter la loi en raison de l'article 8.

D'autres commentaires ont été reçus des intervenants. Cependant, après une étude minutieuse, ils n'ont pas été retenus aux fins de la modification du règlement pour les raisons suivantes.
— ils outrepassaient le pouvoir de réglementation conféré par la *Loi sur le droit d'auteur*;
— ils ne respectaient pas la politique élaborée par Industrie Canada et Patrimoine canadien en consultation avec les groupes d'intérêt;
— ils portaient sur des questions de terminologie n'étant pas nécessaires pour clarifier le règlement.

Respect et exécution

Il n'y a pas lieu de mettre en place des mécanismes de surveillance du respect et de l'exécution. Ne pas tenir les registres prescrits par le règlement peut constituer une violation du droit d'auteur.

Contacts

Bruce Couchman
Senior Legal Analyst
Intellectual Property Policy Directorate
Industry Canada
5th Floor West, Room 521-F
235 Queen Street
Ottawa, Ontario
K1A 0H5
Tel.: (613) 952-2621
FAX: (613) 952-1980
E-mail: couchman.bruce@ic.gc.ca

Édith St-Hilaire
Senior Policy Analyst
Copyright Policy
Department of Canadian Heritage
4th Floor, Room 135
15 Eddy Street
Hull, Quebec
K1A 0M5
Tel.: (819) 997-5998
FAX: (819) 997-5685
E-mail: edith_st-hilaire@pch.gc.ca

Personnes-ressources

Bruce Couchman
Analyste juridique principal
Direction de la politique de la propriété intellectuelle
Industrie Canada
5e étage ouest, pièce 521-F
235, rue Queen
Ottawa (Ontario)
K1A 0H5
Tél. : (613) 952-2621
TÉLÉCOPIEUR : (613) 952-1980
Courriel : couchman.bruce@ic.gc.ca

Édith St-Hilaire
Analyste politique principale
Politique du droit d'auteur
Ministère du Patrimoine canadien
4e étage, pièce 135
15, rue Eddy
Hull (Québec)
K1A 0M5
Tél. : (819) 997-5998
TÉLÉCOPIEUR : (819) 997-5685
Courriel : edith_st-hilaire@pch.gc.ca

Online Research (Library)
Ministry of Education & Training
13th Floor, Mowat Block, Queen's Park
Toronto, Ontario M7A 1L2